WOOD
MAGAZINE®
ARTS AND CRAFTS FURNITURE

Sterling Publishing Co., Inc.
New York

Library of Congress Cataloging-in-Publication Data

Wood magazine: Arts and crafts furniture / editors of Wood magazine

p. cm.

Includes index.

ISBN 1-4027-1174-3

1. Furniture making. 2. Interior decoration. 3. Arts and craft movement—Influence. I.

Title: Arts and crafts furniture. II. Better homes and gardens wood.

TT194.W65 2006

684.1'04—dc22

2005018822

Edited by Peter J. Stephano

10 9 8 7 6 5 4 3 2 1

Published by Sterling Publishing Co., Inc.

387 Park Avenue South, New York, NY 10016

© 2006 by WOOD® magazine editors

Distributed in Canada by Sterling Publishing

℅ Canadian Manda Group, 165 Dufferin Street

Toronto, Ontario, Canada M6K 3H6

Distributed in Great Britain by GMC Distribution Services

Castle Place, 166 High Street, Lewes, East Sussex, England BN791XU

Distributed in Australia by Capricorn Link (Australia) Pty. Ltd.

P.O. Box 704, Windsor, NSW 2756, Australia

Sterling ISBN-13: 978-1-4027-1174-9

ISBN-10: 1-4027-1174-3

For information about custom editions, special sales, or premium and

corporate purchases, please contact Sterling Special Sales

Department at 800-805-5489 or special sales@sterlingpub.com.

CONTENTS

CHAPTER 1

A Brief History of the Arts and Crafts Movement

ARTS AND CRAFTS IS THE *featured design for the projects in this book. The Arts and Crafts Movement, as it was called, emerged in mid-19th-century Great Britain partly as a revolt against the overly elaborate, mass-produced furniture spawned in the Victorian age.*

However, it also was a reaction to the social consequences of the Industrial Revolution, especially the declining public interest in handcraftsmanship.

William Morris, an English architect and artist, was the leading proponent and evangelist of the Arts and Crafts movement. He and his followers shunned the practice of employing technology to produce inexpensive furniture that copied historical pieces. Furniture and other household items of Morris' design were simple, handcrafted adaptations of

1–1. In this book, we'll show you how to build all the furniture pieces in this room, plus add the wood paneling and built-in bookcases.

medieval pieces. An underlying theme of the Arts and Crafts movement was Morris' vision of a world where artists and craftsmen worked in harmony, creating "simple and beautiful" items for everyone. But in actuality, the hand-built pieces he called for proved so expensive that only the wealthy could afford them.

THE ARTS AND CRAFTS MOVEMENT CROSSES THE ATLANTIC

Morris' movement eventually found its way across the Atlantic and began to flourish in the United States about 1876. It lasted into the early 1920s. Although the philosophy behind the movement covered all the decorative arts—from electrical lighting (electricity was just coming into its own in the home) to pottery—the furniture style it spawned became popularly known as "Craftsman." This was primarily due to the promotion of Arts and Crafts, and his Craftsman line of furniture, by American designer and manufacturer Gustav Stickley, who had studied the writings and designs of Morris extensively while on a visit to England.

Despite the fact that furniture of this style was at times, and even today, called "mission," that's really a misnomer. It

1–2.

Look for this Morris chair design on page 38. *There's an Ottoman and coffee table to match.*

seems that a furniture dealer began romanticizing Arts and Crafts style in advertising that associated it with the heavy furniture found in California missions. But the term struck a chord with the public and is still widely used today.

American Arts and Crafts furniture, with the Morris chair (first designed by William Morris) as its signature piece, was intended to be of honest design, simple, and durable. Structural lines and joinery were obvious, not obscured. (See **1–2** and *pages 38–47* for an example of a Morris chair design.)

Any ornamentation usually was the result of construction, thus it appeared as a natural part of the object. Although individual craftsmanship was central to the Arts and Crafts movement, Stickley's successful furniture—and that of others that soon copied the style—was factory-built. Its angular lines enabled machines to be both efficient and vehicles for the expression of beauty, according to him. Machinery also made well-designed and constructed furniture more affordable for many people.

Intricately crafted lamps were a definite aspect of Arts and Crafts. See how to make this one on page 140.

Not all American (and much of England's) Arts and Crafts furniture was as elegantly simple as Stickley's. The pieces made in smaller shops or by individual woodworkers had many decorative details, such as inlays of ceramic tile, pearl, pewter, and exotic woods. In the case of Californians Greene and Greene, their furniture reflected an Oriental influence. Yet, it is primarily Stickley's interpretations that have resurrected Arts and Crafts furniture for renewed popularity today.

With corbels on its frame and quartersawn white oak in its construction, this sofa becomes an Arts and Crafts classic. Turn to page 59 *to learn how to make it.*

AN EMPHASIS ON NATIVE AND NATURAL WOOD

Quartersawn white oak was the chosen wood for most American Arts and Crafts furniture. (Some historians point out that sawmills already were set up for quartersawing due to the wood's use in the "ice boxes" of the time.) It definitely was the staple for the furniture line produced by Gustav Stickley.

The quartersawn wood was both strong and durable. As a bonus, the stock displayed a ray figure that enhanced otherwise straightforward design lines. Other native American woods, such as ash, chestnut, and even

1-5.

This classic bookcase features glass-framed doors, reproduction hardware, and side-panel cutouts that capture the characteristics of the arts and crafts movement.

mahogany (Stickley offered it), also were used to some extent. English furnituremakers leaned toward darker flatsawn oak and mahogany. Illus. **1–4** shows a sofa made of quartersawn oak.

In Great Britain, as well as the United States, clear finishes were used to enhance the wood. In the Stickley factory, and in those of other American furnituremakers, workers "fumed" the white oak to enhance its natural color and grain without muddying it. Fuming was done by placing the pieces inside a chamber with ammonia and leaving them there until sufficiently darkened. Aniline dyes then were employed to match sapwood to heartwood. Preferred shades were medium to dark brown, a stark contrast to the popular "golden oak" of the time. Even black and dark-greenish shades appeared. On *page 29*, we'll describe a modern, less-toxic, method to achieve the original look and bring out the grain figure.

Satin, not gloss, clear finishes were the choice for Arts and Crafts furniture. Stickley relied on quick-drying shellac mixed with German lacquer. A protective coat of wax usually was added.

JOINERY AS DECORATION

Woodworkers for centuries had employed the mortise-and-tenon joint, but it became a visual element of Arts and Crafts furniture. Extending the tenon through the furniture's surface—a tabletop,

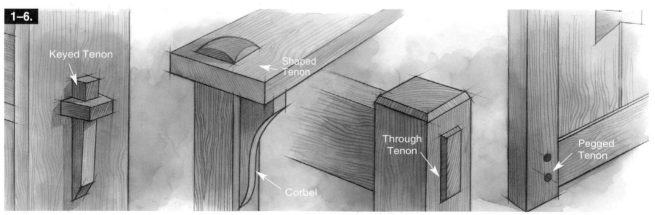

1-6.

Keyed Tenon

Shaped Tenon

Corbel

Through Tenon

Pegged Tenon

Mortise-and-tenon joinery are common elements of Arts and Craft construction.

1–7.

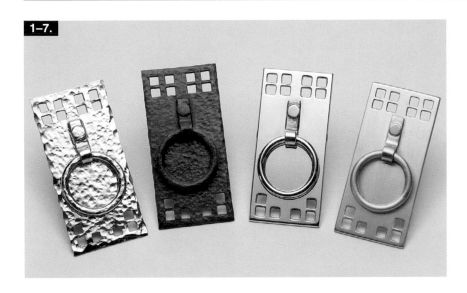

Arts and Crafts hardware was a distinct and elegant element. And you can make it!

a chair leg   turned a structural element into a subtle, ornamental one.

Stickley's Craftsman furniture first featured keyed tenons, as shown in **1–6**. But during the years of production, they were replaced by less labor-intensive, non-keyed, through tenons (**1–8**), and then blind tenons. Shop-built Arts and Crafts furniture usually used the visual tenons, frequently shaped for interest. (Although we've opted for more simple tenons in our projects, you may want to try shaping the tenon ends where applicable.)

Dowels, too, were visible when used for joining. They served to peg mortise-and-tenon joints.

ACCENTS ADD SIMPLE LINES

Wooden brackets, called corbels (refer to **1–6**), supported the wide arms of parlor chairs and other furniture, as well as wall-mounted shelves. However, these were purely

accents, as the sturdy joinery did not require them.

Copper hardware, artificially aged and frequently hammered, served to enhance the dark oak prominent in the Arts and Crafts style (**1–7**). Turn to *page 32* to find out how to make your own. In England, German silver was popular. On the West Coast of the United Sates, Greene and Greene's work often included knobs and pulls of wood.

Upholstery materials for chair seats ranged from leather to rush.

Featuring through tenons, this coffee table is an Arts and Crafts standout, but it even fits in a contemporary setting, as shown here.

1–8.

And leather occasionally was chosen to cover tabletops and desk surfaces, but frequently was the upholstery of choice on sofas and settees also. In this book, you'll learn a no-sew technique for upholstering.

Well, now that you know about Arts and Crafts design, it's time to start building some pieces. We hope you enjoy reading this book as much as we did assembling it.

SHOP SAFETY CHECKLIST

No matter your level of woodworking and furnituremaking expertise, you can never take safety for granted. Here are eleven things to ponder before you begin any woodworking project. Just check them off one by one.

Is your work area clean? Keep your work area uncluttered, swept, and well lighted. The work space around equipment must be adequate to safely perform the job you're going to do.

What are you wearing? Don't wear loose clothing, work gloves, neckties, rings, bracelets, or wristwatches. They can become entangled with moving parts. Tie back long hair or wear a cap.

Do you have the right blade or cutter for the job? Be sure that any blade or cutter you're going to use is clean and sharp so it will cut freely without being forced.

Are all power tool guards in place? Guards—and anti-kickback devices—also must work. Check to see that they're in good condition and in position before operating the equipment.

Where are the start/stop switches? Ensure that all the woodworking machines you'll use have working start/stop buttons or switches within your easy reach.

Are the power cords in shape? Don't use tools with signs of power-cord damage; replace them. Only work with an extension cord that's the proper size for the job (see chart), and route it so it won't be underfoot.

Minimum Extension Cord Wire Gauge Size				
Nameplate Amps	Wire Gauge Size by Cord Length			
	25'	50'	100'	150'
0-6	18	16	16	14
6-10	18	16	14	12
10-12	16	16	14	12
12-16	14	12	(not recommended)	

From the Power Tool Institute, Inc.

Do you have your power tools properly grounded? Tools other than double-insulated ones come with three-wire grounding systems that must be plugged into three-hole, grounded receptacles. Never remove the grounding prong from the plug.

Do you know what safety equipment you'll need for the job? Around cutting tools, always wear safety glasses, goggles, or a face shield. Add a dust mask when sanding. Wear hearing protection when required. (If you can't hear someone from 3' away, the machine is too loud and hearing damage may occur.)

Where are the chuck keys and wrenches? Check that all chuck keys, adjusting wrenches, and other small tools have been removed from the machine so they won't interfere with the operation.

Have you checked your stock? Inspect the wood you're going to use for nails, loose knots, and other materials. They can be hidden "bombs" that possibly may injure you or damage your equipment.

Where's your pushstick? Keep a pushstick or push-block within reach before beginning any cut or machining operation. And avoid getting into awkward stances where a sudden slip could cause a hand to move into the blade or cutter.

CHAPTER 2

Joinery for Generations

IN THE OPENING CHAPTER, YOU LEARNED *that the joinery employed in building Arts and Crafts furniture is one of its most distinctive aspects. And although the step-by-step instructions for making each of the projects in this book tell you how to cut the joints necessary to* assemble them, what you'll learn how to do in this chapter will make the crafting much easier.

Begin with the not-always-so-simple technique of edge-joining a few narrow boards to make up a panel that's wide enough for a tabletop or side piece. Do you know how to avoid gaps? Arrange the grain for eye appeal? Avoid a wavy surface? You'll see how to glue up the perfect panel on the pages immediately following.

Then, because mortise-and-tenon joinery is a trademark of Arts and Crafts furniture, you'll read about a technique for making these joints that you'll want to master. To help simplify the task, first check out page 16, *where we describe how to make a nifty jig that is a must for every shop. It'll come in handy for many of the projects presented in this book.*

Of course, many craftsman prefer to hand-cut joinery. That's why we've included the information on page 25. *You'll learn the skill of cutting neat mortises without the help of jigs or machines.*

GLUE UP THE PERFECT PANEL

Even if you've edge-joined boards before to "make up width," don't skip reading about this basic technique (**2–1**). By doing it right, you'll start with a few boards and end up with a panel that's worthy of a show-piece tabletop.

All Boards are Not Created Equal

Some boards follow the rules and stay straight and flat. Others rebel. If you take time to find cooperative ones when you set out to make a panel, the task will be much easier.

Here's what you need to consider when you visit the lumber rack at the home center or wood supplier: straightness, color, and grain figure.

Checking Boards for Color, Grain Pattern, Etc.

Once you've found some boards that you might like to take home, stand them up side by side to make sure they get along with each other visually. We used red oak for the example here, and found significant color variations. Some boards showed a pink tinge, others looked brown, and a couple were almost white. Stick with boards of the same color.

Grain matching isn't as straightforward as color matching, but think ahead. Can you see similar patterns on all the boards? If so, you'll have an easy time making joints that seem to disappear instead of standing out.

Cutting Boards to Size

If you buy lumber that has been stored inside a store, you can start to work it as soon as you get it into your shop. Lumber that's been stored outdoors or in an unheated, uncooled warehouse will need a few days to adjust to your shop's humidity.

Before making any cuts, double-check your tablesaw and jointer to make sure they're set at exactly 90°. You might have been told that a slightly rough surface glues better. Not so. Smoother is better. Still, if you use a high-quality ripping blade on your saw, you can produce edges suitable for gluing without even going to the jointer.

You'll probably buy stock that's surfaced on both sides and one or both edges. If it has one rough edge, rip that away on the tablesaw. Then crosscut the boards to length plus a few extra inches. That allows for planer snipe and also comes in handy when you're searching for the best grain match.

Spread glue on only one board when gluing up a panel.

2–1.

SHOP TIP

Reading the Grain

It's not a jigsaw puzzle, it's a lumber puzzle. Here's an example of nice matching grain and an example of a match that would annoy you for years to come (2–2).

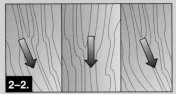

GO WITH THIS ONE   LET THIS ONE GO

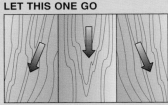

2–2.

These boards feature grain lines of similar direction and width, so they blend well. Different grain directions and shapes doom the other boards to a jarring visual effect.

Now take those wide boards and rip them into pieces no wider than 4". It seems like a shame, but doing this virtually eliminates a wider board's natural tendency to cup. Even if you rip a board in half and wind up gluing those two halves right back together again, you have relieved tension within the stock. That will help keep your panel flat.

Glue the Board

Now comes your chance to imitate nature. Lay the boards on your workbench, as you see in **2–3**. Look for an arrangement in which the grain on each piece seems to flow visually into the adjacent piece. (See *Reading the Grain*.)

Again, consider color. For example, you'll get a better-looking result by placing a couple of light boards at the sides of the panel, rather than alternating them with darker pieces.

Some woodworkers swear by flipping every other board to alternate the growth rings that you see on the end grain. However, you can ignore that factor once you've ripped the boards to 4" wide for stability.

After you've decided how the boards will go together, mark them in alphabetical order with chalk, as shown in **2–4**. The chalk rubs off easily after glue-up.

Check the fit one last time. If any gaps show, go back to the tablesaw or to the jointer, or get

After cutting your stock to size, lay the boards on your workbench and begin looking for the perfect match, as shown here.

When you've figured out the best arrangement, mark the boards with chalk. It's easily removed later when finish sanding.

2–3.

2–4.

Here's another marking method: Pencil in Xs and Os. Write them on masking tape and you won't have to sand them off.

out a long, sharp jointer plane. Make the edges as straight as you can along the length of the board and keep them square with the face, too.

When the boards fit tight, place waxed paper on your workbench to catch any stray glue drips. Set bar clamps or pipe clamps on the paper, spaced about 12" apart. It wouldn't hurt to put waxed paper directly on the clamps, too. The waxed paper will keep the clamps clean and won't stick to your glued-up boards.

We used four square-jaw bar clamps underneath our 36 x 24" assembly. The jaws stay parallel to the workpiece and keep the boards flat. Other kinds of clamps might need alignment help from two more clamps placed on the top side of the assembly.

Our finished panel ended up six boards wide. But we glued up just half of the panel—three boards— at a time. Otherwise, it takes some scrambling to keep all of the joints in perfect alignment. This method also allows you to run each three-board assembly through a 12" planer after the glue dries.

SHOP TIP

Four Other Ways to Align Edges in a Glued-Up Panel

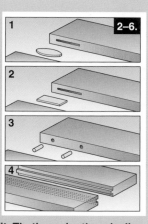

All you need is glue to make super-strong edge joints. However, long stock can be tricky to keep lined up while clamping. You can reduce your stress level with one of these methods (2–6).

BISCUITS (1)
A plate, or biscuit joiner, rates as the easiest and quickest way to line up the panel's mating pieces.

SPLINES (2)
Equip your router with a slot cutter to make short grooves along both mating edges, then use your tablesaw to rip wood splines to fit. That's easier than dealing with one long slot.

DOWELS (3)
Oh-so-convenient biscuits are pushing dowels out of the picture. If you still prefer dowels, make sure they're straight and fit the holes perfectly.

ROUTED PROFILES (4)
You can rout a tongue on one piece and a matching groove on its mate. Two drawbacks: the cost of a special bit and the challenge of keeping long stock perfectly flat as you run it across your router table.

Lay the three sequentially marked boards on the clamps between the jaws and reach for the glue bottle. We recommend yellow woodworker's glue. It does set up quickly, though, so be prepared to work fast.

You don't need special tools to spread the glue. Simply lay down a bead from your glue

Spread a moderate amount of glue with your finger to set an even coat. Apply glue on only one mating edge.

2–8.

2–9.

Working quickly, jockey the boards up and down as necessary to get them flat all along each joint. You can clamp a troublesome joint to the bar clamp sitting underneath.

Rather than make a mess trying to wipe up wet glue, let it set up for a while; then scrape it off.

Start at one end, make sure the joints are flat on top, and tighten that clamp. Overtightening will just force glue out of the joint, so take it easy. You're making a panel, not arm-wrestling.

Work toward the other end of the assembly, checking the joints and tightening the clamps as you go, as shown in **2–8**. If you applied the perfect amount of glue, it will show up as tiny beads along each joint.

Clean Up the Board, Repeat the Gluing, and Square the Ends

Let the glue set up until it's rubbery. Then skim it off the wood with a putty knife or a scraper, as shown in **2–9**. Leave the clamps in place for an hour or so.

For a panel 24" wide, we glued up another three board piece, then ran both pieces through our 12" planer to take down any high spots. Then we joined the two halves with the same gluing and clamping procedures as before.

The final panel won't fit through the planer, but that's not a problem. You can clean up that single, middle joint easily with a scraper or a random-orbit sander.

Trim the ends square on the tablesaw, if your panel isn't too wide for comfort. A crosscut sled makes that job easier and safer. Otherwise, clamp a straight-edge across the panel and use it as a guide for your circular saw or router.

bottle, then spread it into an even coat with a finger, as shown in **2–7**—you'll develop a feel for the right amount. And you only need to apply glue to one of two mating edges. If you put glue on both boards, you're certain to overdo it.

Rub the glue joints together and line up the boards for the grain effect you planned. Don't worry about getting the ends exactly even; that's one reason you cut them a little long. Snug up all of your clamps, but don't apply much pressure yet.

TENONING JIG FOR MORTISES AND TENONS

You can build this easy-to-make tablesaw jig (**2–10**) in just an evening or two. It makes creating mortises and tenons a simpler job, and you can rely on it for a lifetime of accuracy.

Start with the Base and Sliding Table

1 Cut two pieces of ¾" plywood for the base (A) and two pieces for the sliding table (B) to the sizes given in the Materials List, plus ½" in length and width. (Due to its stability and strength, we used ¾" [actual size 18mm] Baltic-birch plywood.)

2 With the edges and ends flush, glue and clamp the two base pieces together face-to-face. Repeat with the two remaining pieces to form the sliding table. Later, remove the clamps and cut the base (A) and sliding table (B) to the finished sizes given in the Materials List.

3 Measure the exact width of the miter-gauge groove in your tablesaw. Cut the base guide bar (C), using solid maple or birch, or ultra-high molecular weight (UHMW) polyethylene, to size. (We found polyethylene slides easier in the groove than wood. Plus, polyethylene will not change in size with seasonal changes in humidity.) The guide should slide in the groove without slop. Set it aside; you'll add it later.

4 Using a dado head in your tablesaw, cut a dado the width of your guide bar (C) and ⅛" deep on the bottom side of the base (A), where

MATERIALS LIST FOR JIG

PART	FINISHED SIZE			Mat.	Qty.
	T	W	L		
A* base	1½"	10"	10"	LBP	1
B* sliding table	1½"	9"	10"	LBP	1
C guide bar	⁷⁄₁₆"	¾"	11"	M	1
D guide bar	⁵⁄₁₆"	¾"	10"	M	1
E* horz. support	¾"	3¾"	8¼"	BP	1
F fence	¾"	6"	9¼"	BP	1
G radiused end	¾"	3"	3¾"	BP	1
H dadoed end	¾"	4½"	10"	BP	1

*Initially cut parts oversized. Trim to finished sizes according to the how-to instruction.

Materials Key: LBP = laminated Baltic birch plywood; BP = Baltic birch plywood; M = maple.
Supplies: Seven # 8 x ¾" flathead wood screws; fifteen #8 x 1½" flathead wood screws; four ½" magnets ¼" thick; 6" metal rule; ⅜" carriage bolt 3" long with mating washer and plastic knob; ⅛ x 4 x 4" acrylic for cursor; UHMW polyethylene for the guide bar (C); epoxy; clear finish.

dimensioned on **2–11** and **2–12**. The guide bar (C) will fit into this dado later.

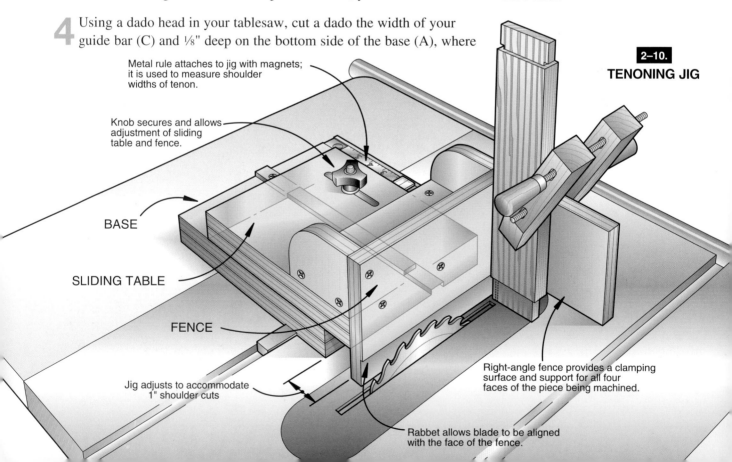

Metal rule attaches to jig with magnets; it is used to measure shoulder widths of tenon.

Knob secures and allows adjustment of sliding table and fence.

BASE

SLIDING TABLE

FENCE

Jig adjusts to accommodate 1" shoulder cuts

2–10.
TENONING JIG

Right-angle fence provides a clamping surface and support for all four faces of the piece being machined.

Rabbet allows blade to be aligned with the face of the fence.

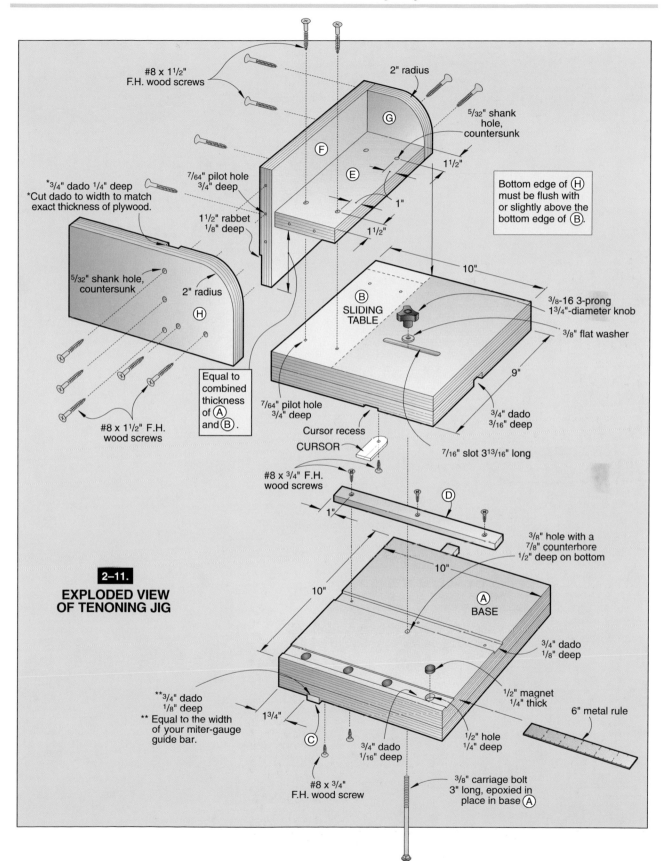

#8 x 1¹⁄₂"
F.H. wood screws

2" radius

⁵⁄₃₂" shank
hole,
countersunk

G

F

E

7/64" pilot hole
3/4" deep

1¹⁄₂"

1"

1¹⁄₂"

Bottom edge of (H)
must be flush with
or slightly above the
bottom edge of (B).

*³⁄₄" dado ¹⁄₄" deep
*Cut dado to width to match
exact thickness of plywood.

1¹⁄₂" rabbet
¹⁄₈" deep

⁵⁄₃₂" shank hole,
countersunk

2" radius

H

Equal to
combined
thickness
of (A)
and (B).

B
SLIDING
TABLE

10"

³⁄₈-16 3-prong
1³⁄₄"-diameter knob

³⁄₈" flat washer

9"

³⁄₄" dado
³⁄₁₆" deep

7/64" pilot hole
3/4" deep

Cursor recess
CURSOR

⁷⁄₁₆" slot 3¹³⁄₁₆" long

#8 x 1¹⁄₂" F.H.
wood screws

#8 x ³⁄₄" F.H.
wood screws

1"

D

³⁄₈" hole with a
⁷⁄₈" counterbore
¹⁄₂" deep on bottom

10"

2–11.

**EXPLODED VIEW
OF TENONING JIG**

10"

A
BASE

³⁄₄" dado
¹⁄₈" deep

¹⁄₂" magnet
¹⁄₄" thick

6" metal rule

**³⁄₄" dado
¹⁄₈" deep
** Equal to the width
of your miter-gauge
guide bar.

1³⁄₄"

C

³⁄₄" dado
¹⁄₁₆" deep

¹⁄₂" hole
¹⁄₄" deep

#8 x ³⁄₄"
F.H. wood screw

³⁄₈" carriage bolt
3" long, epoxied in
place in base (A)

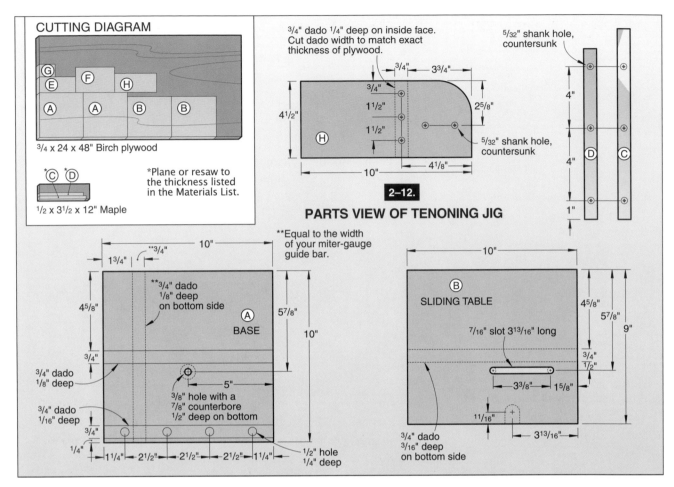

CUTTING DIAGRAM

3/4 x 24 x 48" Birch plywood

*Plane or resaw to the thickness listed in the Materials List.

1/2 x 3 1/2 x 12" Maple

3/4" dado 1/4" deep on inside face. Cut dado width to match exact thickness of plywood.

5/32" shank hole, countersunk

5/32" shank hole, countersunk

2–12.

PARTS VIEW OF TENONING JIG

**Equal to the width of your miter-gauge guide bar.

**3/4" dado 1/8" deep on bottom side

BASE

3/4" dado 1/8" deep

3/4" dado 1/16" deep

3/8" hole with a 7/8" counterbore 1/2" deep on bottom

1/2" hole 1/4" deep

SLIDING TABLE

7/16" slot 3 13/16" long

3/4" dado 3/16" deep on bottom side

---

5 Cut a ¾" dado ⅛" deep on the top side of the base (A) and a mating ¾" dado 3⁄16" deep on the bottom side of the sliding table (B), where shown in **2–12**. Later, you'll screw the guide bar (D) into the dado in the top of the base. And when assembled, the sliding table (B) will slide on the top, exposed portion of this guide bar.

6 Cut a ¾" dado 1⁄16" deep in the top of the base (A) to house the 6" metal rule.

7 Cut the second guide bar (D) so it fits snugly in the top dado in the base, and slides smoothly in the ¾" dado on the bottom of the sliding table. Set this guide aside also.

8 Mark the centerpoints, where dimensioned in **2–12**, and drill the holes for the magnets in the dado in the top of the base (A). Measure your magnets before drilling; they may vary in size. You

want the magnets to sit just a hair below the surface of the dado.

9 Mark the centerpoint, and drill a ⅞" hole ½" deep on the bottom side of the base (A). Then, drill a ⅜" hole centered in the ⅞" hole and through the base for the ⅜" carriage bolt. Check the fit to make sure the bottom of the carriage bolt doesn't protrude.

10 Mark a pair of centerpoints, drill a 7⁄16" hole at each point, and cut between the holes with a scrollsaw or jigsaw to form the 7⁄16"-wide slot in the sliding table (B), where dimensioned in **2–12**.

11 Drill countersunk mounting holes in the guides (C, D), where dimensioned in **2–12**. Screw the guides in place, making sure the screw heads are set below the surface.

2–13. **FORMING THE CURSOR**

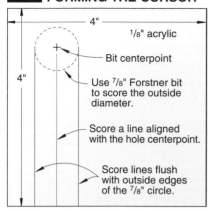

- 4"
- 1/8" acrylic
- Bit centerpoint
- 4"
- Use 7/8" Forstner bit to score the outside diameter.
- Score a line aligned with the hole centerpoint.
- Score lines flush with outside edges of the 7/8" circle.

Form the Cursor Next

1 Cut a piece of 1/8" clear acrylic to 4 × 4". Chuck a 7/8" Forstner bit into your drill press, and position the bit over the acrylic, roughly where shown in **2–13**. Clamp the acrylic securely to your drill-press table.

2 Start the drill press, and slowly lower the bit until the outside edge and centerpoint of the bit just barely scores the acrylic surface.

3 Using a small square and a craft knife held sideways (it scores better this way), score the three lines on the bottom side of the acrylic where shown on **2–13** and in **2–14**.

4 To make the centerline on the cursor more visible, use a felt-tipped marker to highlight the middle scribed line. Wipe any excess marker off the surface of the cursor.

5 Using your bandsaw fitted with a 1/8" blade or a scrollsaw with a #10 blade, cut the cursor to shape. Sand the edges smooth.

6 Working from the bottom side of the cursor, drill a 5/16" countersunk shank hole centered over the bit centerpoint where shown on the Cursor Full-Size Pattern (**2–15**).

7 Using the Cursor Location drawing (**2–16**) for reference, form the cursor recess on the bottom side of the sliding table (B).

Add the Workpiece Support

*Note: Plywoods vary in thickness. All dimensions are based on plywood measuring exactly 3/4" thick. See the tinted boxes in **2–11,** on page 17, before locating the horizontal support (E) against the fence (F).*

1 Cut the horizontal support (E) to size plus 1/2" in length. Then, cut the fence (F), radiused end (G), and dadoed end (H) to the size in the Materials List.

2 Cut the rabbet along the outside face of the fence (F), where shown on the Exploded View drawing.

3 Cut a 1/4"-deep dado in the inside face of H to the same exact thickness as your plywood.

4 Mark the centerpoints, and drill holes in H, where dimensioned in **2–12,** on *page 18*. Clamp the end (H) to the fence (F) and drive the screws. Drill the

2–14.

Drag the blade of a craft knife sideways to scribe the centerline and cutlines on the acrylic cursor blank.

2–15.

CURSOR FULL-SIZE PATTERN

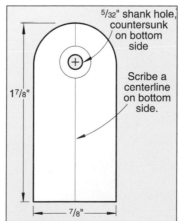

5/32" shank hole, countersunk on bottom side

1⁷⁄₈"

Scribe a centerline on bottom side.

7/8"

2–16.

CURSOR LOCATION

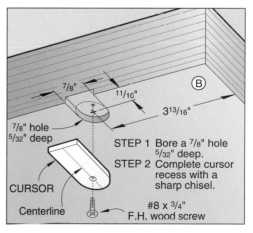

7/8"
11/16"
B
3¹³⁄₁₆"
7/8" hole 5/32" deep
CURSOR
Centerline
STEP 1 Bore a 7/8" hole 5/32" deep.
STEP 2 Complete cursor recess with a sharp chisel.
#8 × 3/4" F.H. wood screw

2–17.

Use a strip of wood, a pair of clamps, and waxed paper to hold the magnets in place until the epoxy cures.

holes, and screw the opposite end (G) to the fence. Measure the distance between the ends (G, H), and cut the horizontal support (E) to final length and screw it in place, making sure parts G and H meet at right angles to part E.

5 Clamp the support (E, F, G, H) to the sliding table (B), and screw the two assemblies together, keeping the outside face of F square to the sliding table.

Finishing and Final Assembly

1 Finish-sand all the pieces and seal with polyurethane.

2 Cut a piece of wood to ¾ × 1¹⁄₁₆ × 12". Then, put a drop of epoxy in each magnet hole, fit the magnets into the holes, and wipe off any excess epoxy. As shown in **2–17**, position a strip of wood over the magnets, and use it as a clamping bar to hold the magnets in place until the epoxy cures. Later, remove the clamping block and clamps.

3 Screw the acrylic cursor in place in the recess on the bottom of the sliding table (B).

4 Position the sliding table (B) on the base (A). Slide a ⅜" carriage bolt through the ⅜" hole in the base (A) and through the ⁷⁄₁₆" slot in the sliding table (B). Slide the two assemblies back and forth to check the fit; then epoxy the carriage bolt in place. Attach a washer and plastic knob onto the bolt, where shown in **2–11**. To prevent the jig from possibly rocking on the saw table, make sure that the bottom edge of the fence (F) is flush with the bottom surface of the base (A). If F is higher, you may encounter a bit of rocking when the sliding table/fence is away from the base when cutting tenons. This can result in poorly cut tenons.

5 Lay the metal 6" rule in place on the magnets in the shallow dado. See the following pages about cutting mortise-and-tenons for information on positioning the rule in relation to the fence.

2–18. ## ANATOMY OF A MORTISE-AND-TENON JOINT

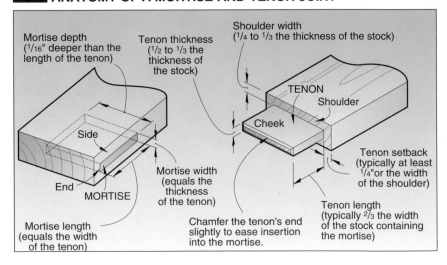

Mortise depth (¹⁄₁₆" deeper than the length of the tenon)

Tenon thickness (½ to ⅓ the thickness of the stock)

Shoulder width (¼ to ⅓ the thickness of the stock)

TENON
Shoulder

Cheek

Side

End

MORTISE

Mortise width (equals the thickness of the tenon)

Tenon setback (typically at least ¼"or the width of the shoulder)

Mortise length (equals the width of the tenon)

Chamfer the tenon's end slightly to ease insertion into the mortise.

Tenon length (typically ⅔ the width of the stock containing the mortise)

Professional quality mortise-and-tenon joints can be made with the help of the tenoning jig. Few woodworking joints match the mortise-and-tenon joint. That's why this old standby shows up so often in leg-and-rail construction and other adaptations that subject a joint to stress.

Adjust the Tenoning Jig

Now that you've built the tenoning jig, it's time to learn how to adjust it. To adjust your jig for precision cuts, start by placing the tenoning jig on your tablesaw, with the bar in the miter-gauge slot. Loosen the knob on the sliding table and position it so the fence clears the saw blade (**2–20**). Raise the blade to 1"; then move the sliding table so the face of the fence aligns flush with the outside edge of the blade, as shown in **2–21**. Tighten the knob to hold the sliding table in place.

With the blade properly aligned with the fence, slide the jig's built-in steel rule until the cursor lines up directly over the 1" mark, as shown in Step 2 in **2–21**. (Using the 1" mark provides more accuracy than trying to align the mark on the "zero" end of the rule.)

Now, loosen the knob on the sliding table, and adjust the cursor along the rule to make the desired shoulder width, as shown in **2–21**. Our example shows the setting for a ¼" cut, but for other widths, adjust the cursor the appropriate distance from the 1" mark on the scale.

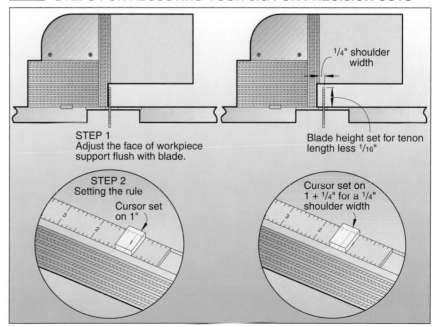

Adjusting the tenoning jig.

2–21. **STEPS FOR ADJUSTING YOUR JIG FOR PRECISION CUTS**

STEP 1
Adjust the face of workpiece support flush with blade.

STEP 2
Setting the rule
Cursor set on 1"

¼" shoulder width

Blade height set for tenon length less ¹/₁₆"

Cursor set on 1 + ¼" for a ¼" shoulder width

HOW TO MAKE FLUSH MORTISE-AND-TENON JOINTS

When we developed the tenoning jig just described, we also were looking for a simpler way to create tight-fitting mortise-and-tenon joints. Rather than the traditional method of cutting the mortise first and fitting the tenon to it, we decided to use the precision-cut tenons produced with the tenoning jig to accurately lay out the matching mortises.

Our technique, described here, uses a guide block to aid in both the mortise layout and cutting processes. Cut using the same jig settings as the tenon, the guide-block ensures accurate placement of the mortise. It also keeps your chisel aligned vertically when you square up the mortise. (See *page 25* for how to accurately cut mortises with a chisel.)

Note: Before you start cutting, choose and mark the best side of your workpieces. Use these reference marks when laying out your mortises and tenons so the best sides get the exposure.

Make the Tenon

1 Lay out the tenon as shown in **2–22**. A combination square and a sharp pencil or scratch awl work great for transferring marks to all four sides. For our sample project, we made the tenon 1" long, with ½" setbacks and ¼" shoulders.

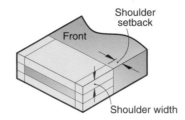

2–22. LAYING OUT THE TENON

Shoulder setback

Front

Shoulder width

2 Next, cut the shoulders. Using a miter gauge with an auxiliary fence, align the shoulder of the tenon with the saw blade. Attach a stopblock to the auxiliary fence to duplicate the cuts.

Lay the workpiece flat on the saw table, and adjust the height of the blade so it just touches the marked edge of the tenon cheek. Cut the shoulders on both sides of the tenon, as shown in **2–23**. Using a 12"-long piece of scrapwood the same thickness and width as your workpiece, make a shoulder cut in one side only (see **2–27**). Set this piece aside for the guide block. Align the tenon end with the stop-block, and cut the two setback shoulders as shown in **2–24**.

3 Cut the tenon cheeks. With the tenoning jig set for a ¼"-wide cut, raise the blade to $^{15}/_{16}$". Secure the workpiece, as shown in **2–25**; turn on the tablesaw, and push the workpiece through the blade. Rotate the workpiece 180°, clamp it down, and cut the second cheek. Without changing the jig setup, make one cheek cut in the guide block piece, and then set it aside.

2–23.

Adjust the saw blade depth, and use a miter gauge with an auxiliary fence and a stop-block to cut the tenon shoulders in the workpiece and one side of the guide block.

2–24.

Turn the workpiece on edge, butt it against the stop-block, and cut the tenon setback shoulder. Rotate the piece 180°, and cut the other setback shoulder.

4 Finish up with the tenon setbacks. Set the jig to make a ½"-wide cut, clamp the workpiece in the jig, as shown in **2–26**, and cut the setback. Rotate the workpiece 180°, and cut the second tenon setback.

5 Finally, crosscut the scrapwood guide block to finished length, making it 2" longer than the length of the tenon cut (**2–27**).

Make the Matching Mortise

To lay out the mortise, position the guide block on the piece to be mortised; then mark the side of the mortise, as shown in **2–28**. Then, place the guide block on the other side of the workpiece and mark the opposite mortise side. Using the tenon as a guide, mark the proper length of the mortise, as shown in **2–29**. Be sure to keep the edge of the tenoned board flush with the end of the mortise piece.

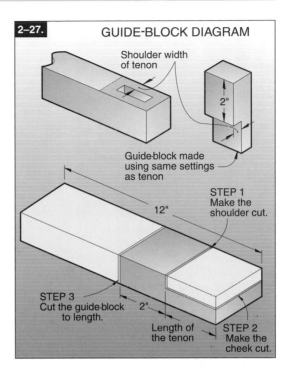

2–27. GUIDE-BLOCK DIAGRAM

2–25.

With the jig cursor set at 1¼" (for a ¼" cut), clamp the board against the jig fence, and cut the tenon cheeks in your workpiece and in the one side of the guide block.

Adjust the jig to the proper setback, clamp the workpiece against the jig's dadoed end, and cut the tenon setbacks.

2–26.

2–28.

Hold the guide block firmly on the piece to be mortised, and mark the location of the mortise sides with a sharp pencil or scratch awl.

2–29.

Position the tenon atop the piece to be mortised, and mark the mortise ends. Be sure to keep the two workpieces flush and square.

2-30.

Using a bit ¹⁄₁₆" smaller than the mortise width, drill a series of holes the length of the mortise. Drill the end holes first and make all holes ¹⁄₁₆" deeper than the length of the tenon.

2-31.

Clamp the guide block to the workpiece. Keep the flat side of a wide chisel held firmly against the block, and shear the excess wood from the sides of the mortise.

2-32.

Sand slight chamfers on the end of the tenon to make it easier to insert the tenon in the mortise. Dry-fit the mating joint pieces and sand the tenon faces or chisel the mortise as necessary.

2-33. JOINT VARIATIONS

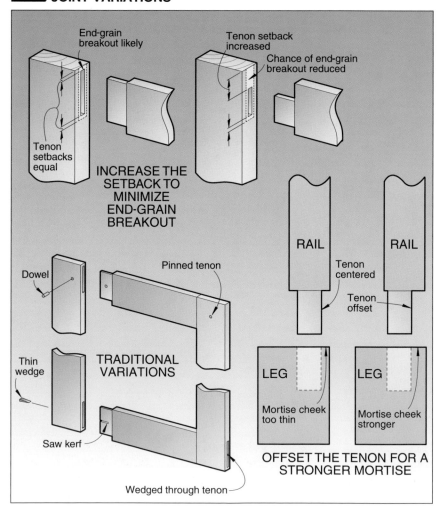

To rough out the mortise, clamp the workpiece in a drill press, and using a brad-point bit ¹⁄₁₆" smaller in diameter than the width of the mortise, drill a series holes the length of the mortise, as shown in **2–30**. The holes should just touch or have a small gap between them to avoid drill bit deflection and poor alignment. The holes should be 1¹⁄₁₆" deep, or ¹⁄₁₆" deeper than the length of the tenon.

To square-up the mortise, clamp the guide block in position on the mortised piece, and hold your chisel flat against the block, as shown in **2–31**. The guide block keeps the chisel vertical as you shear away the waste from the sides of the mortise. Use a chisel the same width as the mortise to square up the ends.

Final Fitting, Gluing, and Cleanup

Before you try fitting the joint together, sand slight chamfers on the end of the tenon, as shown in **2–32**. This lets you fit the tenon into the mortise more easily.

Test-fit the mating workpieces before applying glue, and sand the tenon or chisel the mortise as necessary. Apply glue to all faces of both sides of the joint as well as the tenon shoulders, then clamp the workpieces together. Use a putty knife or chisel to scrape off any glue squeeze-out after a tough skin forms.

Despite the jig's accuracy, the faces of the mating pieces may not always align perfectly flush. To get them flush, we prefer to use a random-orbit sander to avoid cross-grain scratches.

JOINT VARIATIONS FOR ADDED STRENGTH

The flush joint we just showed you works well in many applications, but you can make the joint even stronger. By adjusting the tenon's placement, you can strengthen the corresponding mortise. These adaptations work well in leg-rail construction.

By shifting the tenon setback (see **2–33**), you cut the mortise farther away from the end of the leg, reducing the chance for endgrain breakout.

In some situations, the rail fits flush with the front face of the leg. If the tenon were centered, the outside mortise wall would be thin and weak. But by offsetting the tenon, you can keep the rail

flush with the leg without weakening the tenon or the mortise wall (see **2–33**).

Early craftsmen used a variety of methods to reinforce mortise-and-tenon joints. While today's glues will hold joints tight, using pins or wedges, as illustrated in **2–33**, still bolsters strength while lending an old-world touch to your project.

To pin a tenon, first assemble the mortise-and-tenon joint. When the glue dries, drill a centered hole completely through the joint. Apply glue to the dowel and tap it into place, saw off the excess, and sand it flush. In a through-tenon joint, the tenon extends completely through the mortised workpiece. A wedge driven into the end of the tenon effectively locks it in place. To wedge a through tenon, cut a saw kerf into the end of the tenon, about three-quarters of its length. Glue and assemble the joint; then apply glue to a thin wedge, and drive the wedge into the saw kerf. When the glue dries, saw off the excess tenon and sand it flush.

MORTISING WITH CHISELS

You need to cut a mortise; so which power tool will you switch on: the router, the drill press, maybe a mortising machine? Before you start setting up a power tool and searching for jigs and fixtures, consider this: You can make a fine mortise in a

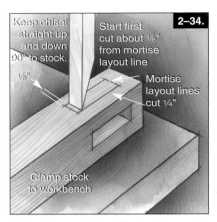

Strike the mortising chisel with a mallet or dead-blow hammer, and drive the blade ¼" into the wood.

couple of minutes with a hammer (a deadblow type works best) and sharp chisel.

You'll need the right kind of chisel, of course. Thick, sturdy mortising chisels are designed specifically to do this job. Mortising chisels come in sets of various widths, or you can buy just one and try it. For this project, we used a quality ⅜", heavy-duty mortising chisel.

1 Carefully lay out the dimensions of your mortise, choosing a width that matches one of your chisels. Clamp the workpiece securely to a solid surface. Then set the cutting edge squarely within the lines and ⅛" from the far end, as shown in **2–34**. Strike the chisel with a mallet or dead-blow hammer, and drive it ¼" into the wood.

2 Keep the bevel down, incline the chisel handle toward yourself, and begin to chop out material to a depth of ¼", as shown in **2–35**. Pull the chisel

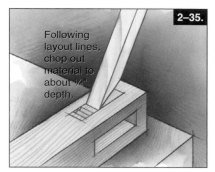

Following layout lines, chop out material to about ¼" depth.

2–35.

Keep the chisel bevel down.

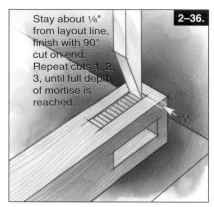

Stay about ⅛" from layout line, finish with 90° cut on end. Repeat cuts 1, 2, 3, until full depth of mortise is reached.

2–36.

⅛"

Turn the bevel edge away, and set the chisel vertically ⅛" from the end line.

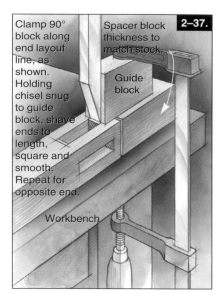

Clamp 90° block along end layout line, as shown. Holding chisel snug to guide block, shave ends to length, square and smooth. Repeat for opposite end.

Spacer block thickness to match stock.

Guide block

2–37.

Workbench

Use a spacer block to cut perfectly smooth, straight ends in a mortise.

edge back ⅛" for each new cut. Be careful not to angle the chisel left or right.

3 When you reach the near end of the mortise, turn the bevel edge away and set the chisel vertically ⅛" from the end line, as shown **2–36**. Make a 90° cut. Then go back to the other end and repeat step one. Continue in this way, checking the depth with a ruler or combination square, until you've reached the desired mortise depth.

4 Here's the key to cutting perfectly smooth, straight ends in a mortise—the kind of accuracy that results in a strong, tight fit for the tenon. If your mortise is close to the end of the workpiece, find or cut a spacer block of the same thickness as your workpiece, and place it at the end, as shown in **2–37**. Clamp a 90° guide block on the layout

line that marks the mortise end. Hold the flat side of the chisel firmly against this guide with one hand, and drive the chisel straight down to the bottom of the mortise.

CHAPTER 3

Finishing and Hardware Considerations

T HE JOINERY USED IN THE MAKING *of Arts and Crafts furniture is but one of the style's distinctive features. The finish is another.*

Because most furniture in this style is made from quartersawn white oak—not only for durability but visual appeal—you're immediately faced with a finishing problem.

How do you get the rays and flecks exposed by this method of sawing to really jump out and catch the eye? Pigmented stains won't do a satisfactory job because they cloud the grain as they color it. The same thing applies to toned topcoat finishes.

The only way to get the look you want with this costly wood is to use aniline dyes. If they're new to you, experiment with the simple technique explained on page 28. *You'll get satisfactory results using this technique on small projects.*

But beginning on page 29, *you'll discover a far more advanced (yet not difficult) technique employed by a small commercial maker of Arts and Crafts furniture. We were highly impressed with the results they obtain. Try it, and you will be, too.*

Finishing large expanses of oak—such as a paneled wall—is quite a different story from the the technique used on furniture. That's why we've included the information that begins on *page 31*. And to add the finishing touch, see how to create your own Arts and Crafts hardware on *page 32*. Ready to read on?

MAKE QUARTER-SAWN FIGURE POP

We developed this method for quatersawn white oak. But, you can use it on any highly figured wood, such as curly maple or flame birch. Try it on small projects, like the table lamp on *page 140*.

1 Set the Tone with Aniline Dye

Begin the process by applying aniline dye (**3–1**). These dyes are available in dry-powder or liquid-concentrate form. Choose a water-soluble aniline dye, and apply it with a disposable foam brush. Work from top to bottom, applying dye to one part at a time. As the dye in the brush is depleted, go back over each part to blend lap marks or areas where dye has pooled. You can blend areas even after the dye dries by brushing with a clean foam brush dampened with water.

Note: We choose water-soluble aniline dye because of its fade resistance, lack of fumes, and ease of application. Alcohol-soluble dyes don't raise the grain. However, we don't suggest brushing alcohol-soluble dyes because they dry so quickly that you'll find it difficult to brush them on without leaving lap marks.

2 Sand to Bring Out the Figure

With the dye dry (allow 12 hours), lightly sand the surfaces with 220-grit sandpaper (**3–2**). Sand just enough to remove the dyed surface of the quartersawn wood's dense rays, while leaving the dye in the more porous parts of the grain, as shown. Sanding this way removes any raised grain, as well. Back your sandpaper with a firm sanding block to avoid sanding through the dye on corners and edges. Remove the dust using a shop vacuum or compressed air.

3 Add the Topcoat Finish

You'll notice that the dyed surface that looked so rich when wet now looks dull and unappealing. Don't worry, applying a clear finish brings it back to life.

For easy coverage of a project's nooks and crannies, we turned to an aerosol shellac, as shown in **3–3**. Shellac, readily available at hardware stores and home centers, has several advan-

Apply aniline dye with a foam brush.

Lightly sand the surfaces with 220-grit sandpaper.

Apply a topcoat of shellac.

tages over other aerosol clear finishes. First, it thoroughly dries in less than one hour, so you can apply three light coats in an afternoon. Second, although you'll need to smooth rough areas, successive coats of shellac adhere by slightly dissolving the previous coat, so you don't need to sand between coats. And finally, shellac has low odor, so you can use it in your shop with moderate ventilation. Avoid water-based finishes because they will reactivate the dye and may cause it to run.

THE PERFECT ARTS AND CRAFTS FINISH: ANILINE DYE AND LACQUER

The popular Arts and Crafts furniture produced by Gustav Stickley in the early 20th century was mostly of quartersawn white oak fumed to a dark brown. That's a process that involves ammonia fumes reacting with the wood's high tannic acid content in a sealed chamber. "This process is the only one known that acts upon the glassy pith rays as well as the softer parts of the wood, coloring all together in an even tone so that the figure is marked only by its difference in texture," Stickley wrote.

The fuming process, however, proves extremely dangerous—ammonia is harmful if its fumes are inhaled or it comes in contact with the skin. And the shellac used as a final finish on Stickley's

mission furniture (as it came to be called), while it added warmth to the wood's tone, won't hold up like today's finishes.

To capture the dark look of Gustav Stickley's furniture without the danger, Michael Schmitt and his family at Arkansas-based Mountain Springs Woodcraft turn to water-soluble aniline dyes (**3–4** and **3–5**). And the mission pieces they create on their mountaintop would turn Stickley's head—each with a deep, warm clarity of color that highlights the rays and flecks of the wood. Careful applications of

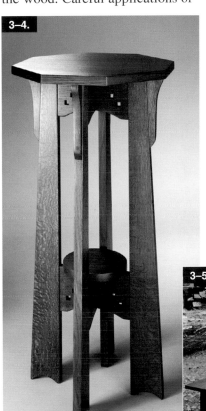

3–4.

This taboret table made at Mountain Springs Woodcraft really shows off the rays and flecks of its quartersawn oak.

toned lacquer contribute protection and smoothness. But the Schmitts' success also comes from dedication in preparation and an in-depth knowledge of the materials.

How to Dye to Perfection

Because the wood has been thoroughly smoothed before glue-up, the water-based aniline dye solution (five parts hot water to one part dye, with the dye first predissolved in a bit of denatured alcohol) raises the grain little after it's applied. And the staining with the first base coat, such as the "light fumed" aniline noted on *page 30*, goes quickly.

Armed with sponges and often hand sprayers, Michael's wife and their son and daughters (all employees) carefully apply dye to every inch of wood, as shown in **3–6**. Then, they allow the dyed

Water-soluble aniline dyes give the white oak in these Arts and Crafts pieces a deep, rich color and clarity to highlight the grain.

3–5.

3–6.

The Schmitt family teams up to apply the first toning coat of a water-soluble dye solution to an oak baby crib built in the Arts and Crafts style. Masks are always worn because the first coat contains a bit of denatured alcohol.

Lacquer Locks in the Dye

"Before I start spraying lacquer," explains Michael, "we make sure the dye has completely dried. If it hasn't, moisture collects under the surface film and the finish deteriorates in just a few months. My helpers also lightly sand the dry, dyed wood with 400 grit to eliminate any final grain fuzzies."

To lock the dye in, he begins spraying with two quick sealer coats of lacquer cut 50 percent with thinner. When the sealer has dried, his helpers again sand with 320-grit silicon carbide paper. This sanding makes the sealer coat absolutely smooth.

"Before the final lacquer, I spray on a toned glaze (clear lacquer tinted with black, umber, and raw sienna glazing stain).

assembly to soak several minutes before drying it off with cloths and using compressed air to blow excess from seams and corners.

After the dyed pieces have dried for 12 to 24 hours, the crew lightly hand-sands them with gray nylon abrasive pads or quarter sheets of 320 grit. "The dye is very forgiving at this stage," notes Michael, "and they can work over any mistakes or missed glue spots and reapply the stain. It blends right back into itself."

Next come two coats of the final aniline, a slightly different color to give the piece depth and enhance the grain (see notes at right). "The only limit to how much aniline we can put on from here is the saturation point of the wood fibers," he adds. "Once they have absorbed all the dye they can take, it begins to build on the surface and looks muddy. When

we add more dye coats, we always let the wood dry thoroughly. Wet wood won't absorb dye."

Favorite Aniline Dye Colors at Mountain Springs Woodcraft

Water-soluble anilines are easy to work with, and their light-fastness (resistance to fading) rates higher than other types. They are many brands available (from finish suppliers or woodworking supply dealers). In powder form, they cost about $4 per ounce, which makes more than a quart of stain (with Michael's ratio). Listed below are the aniline colors that give the perfect shades for their furniture, along with some of Michael's comments.

Light fumed. *"For an even tone under the final color."*

Medium fumed. *"Used as above, but has a greenish cast to create richer browns."*

Dark fumed. *"As a final color over either of the above."*

English brown. *"Similar to, but richer in red and deeper in color, than dark fumed."*

Flemish brown. *"A final color that duplicates Stickley's deepest tone, which he called dark fumed. It grabs onto the quartersawn oak's rays for breathtaking effects."*

Flemish black. *"A final-coat black with brown overtones. Not for the timid, so try it on scrap first."*

After it has dried for a few hours, I follow with from three semi-gloss lacquer coats on the surfaces of least wear to eight coats on tabletops," says Michael. Between each, the wood is sanded with 400-grit paper.

"Finally, after the sprayed pieces have dried for a day or so, we rub them out with a rubbing lubricant and water," he concludes. "The overall effect is a piece that looks mellow, old, and comfortable anywhere it's placed. Old Gustav would have been just as proud to put his name on it as we are."

FINISHING RED OAK PANELS

If you're into the wood paneling look to go with your Arts and Crafts furniture, as we were when we did the family-room redo on *page 167* in Chapter 8, you'll appreciate this technique!

1 Great Finishes Begin with Good Surface Preparation

It makes a lot of sense to sand all of the workpieces through a full succession of grits before installing them. This gives better results with much less effort compared to installing workpieces, and then sanding. And, it's a lot easier to deal with sanding dust in your shop.

Begin by sanding all of the solid stock with a random-orbit sander, using a succession of

120-, 150-, and 180-grit discs. Follow by a final hand-sanding with a hardwood block and 180-grit sandpaper. Sand the plywood panels with just the 180-grit hardwood block, to eliminate any risk of sanding through the panels.

After final sanding, remove any traces of sanding dust by blowing it with compressed air. For your health, wear a dust mask, ventilate the shop with fresh air, and always direct the compressed air away from yourself.

2 To Prevent Bleed-Back, Choose a Gel Stain

After installing all of the woodwork, apply a number of stains to red-oak scraps. Look for a stain that gives exactly the coloring you desire, with no bleed-back. An "aged oak" gel stain generally will fill the bill.

Because gel stains sit on top of a wood surface, rather than soaking into them, there's no chance of bleed-back. However,

gel stains create a new set of challenges to deal with.

Even after you apply them with a brush and wipe them off with a rag, the thick viscosity of gel stains makes them collect excessively in corners. You can get that extra stain out of tight spots with a dry brush, and then go over the surface again with a clean rag to even out the coloration. Stop from time to time to clean the dry brush with mineral spirits to maintain its effectiveness.

3 Top Off the Stain with a Durable Clear Coat

Because of its durability and short time span between applications, use a fast-drying polyurethane to protect the stained surfaces. After brushing on a first coat of the gloss version of this finish, wait 24 hours for it to dry. This time period may be longer depending on temperature and humidity—just be sure the finish cures enough to sand it off as a dry powder.

3–7.

When reapplying polyurethane to the red oak surface, use tape to mask off the adjoining pieces.

During application, position a strong light to the side of the finished surface so it casts a reflection. Use this glare to help spot runs, sags, or missed areas. A halogen work light on a stand is helpful. Repeat this inspection a half-hour after application; at that point, with the finish still workable, you can still brush out noticeable imperfections.

To remove any dust nibs in the finish, and give it "bite" for holding the next coat, lightly sand the surface with a hardwood block and 180-grit abrasive. Be careful not to sand into the stain. Remove the dust with a vacuum cleaner and round-brush attachment. Follow that with a tack cloth.

Apply a final coat of satin polyurethane in the same way as the first coat. If, despite your best efforts, you wind up with runs or sags in the dried finish, sand them off carefully with a hardwood block and 220-grit sandpaper. Then, lightly sand the panel or rail that had the imperfection, and reapply polyurethane to the entire surface, being careful to mask off adjoining pieces, as shown in **3–7**.

For small imperfections, you don't have to reapply finish. Just sand off the run or sag as described earlier, but don't sand the entire panel or rail. Buff the sanded area with an ultra-fine woven-plastic-pad abrasive (gray-colored works well). Then, go over the same area with an even finer pad, such as a white, to match the sheen of the rest of the satin surface.

4 Fill the Nail Holes, and You're Done

Now's the best time to fill nail holes with a flexible (non-hardening) putty that matches the color of the stained wood.

MAKE ARTS AND CRAFTS HARDWARE

Do you realize that you can make unique, eye-popping hardware using basic skills, a few simple tools, and common materials from the hardware store? It just takes some imagination and a little elbow grease.

Make a Pull

You can make the classic beauty shown in **3–8** with just the materials shown beside it. You'll need $\frac{1}{16}$"-thick brass in $\frac{1}{4}$" and $1\frac{1}{2}$" widths, a 1" inside-diameter brass harness ring, #8-32 × 2" brass roundhead screw, #8-32 hex nut, and #18 × $\frac{1}{2}$" brass escutcheon pin. Your total cost: under $3.

Many hardware stores carry all of these supplies, although you may have to go to a hobby store to find the brass plate.

To make this pull, first cut a $1\frac{1}{2}$ × $3\frac{1}{4}$" backplate from a piece of $\frac{1}{16}$"-thick brass. (You can use a tablesaw outfitted with a blade designed for nonferrous metals. A hacksaw, bandsaw, or scrollsaw with 3/0 jewelers' blade also would work.) Straighten and smooth the edges with a flat file.

Apply a copy of the pattern

With just a few basic tools, you can make custom hardware like this Craftsman-style pull.

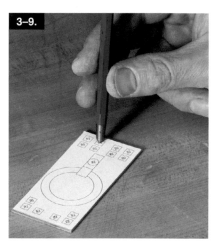

Punch the centerpoint of each hole location before drilling.

from *page 35* to the plate using a spray adhesive. Strike each of the hole centerpoints with a metal punch, as shown in **3–9**. Drill the holes noted on the pattern.

Secure the backplate in a vise mounted to a solid workbench, and use a square file to shape the square holes, as shown in **3–10**. Squaring all 14 holes took us about 30 minutes, so find a comfortable sitting position.

If you would like a hammered surface like the one on our pull, use a permanent pen to mark the approximate location of the strap that holds the ring (**3–11**). Strike the entire surface, except for the marked area, with a ball peen hammer. You'll have good success with a 12-ounce model. Then, strike all along the edges to give them a scalloped look. In place of an anvil, we secured a

Use a small square file to shape each of the square holes.

Hammer all of the backplate surface except where the ring strap will be soldered in place.

heavy piece of angle iron in our woodworker's vise.

To shape the ring strap, clamp a ¼"-diameter steel rod atop a strip of ¹⁄₁₆" brass, as shown in **3–12**. Heat the brass strip with a propane torch until it glows red, grip its far end with a pliers, and bend the strip completely over the rod. Reheat the brass if necessary, and use an angle iron and hammer to pound a sharp bend into the strap, as shown in **3–13**. Cut off the excess length of brass strip with a hacksaw, and file the ends smooth.

To complete the hammered look, slip the harness ring over a length of steel rod secured in a vise, as shown in **3–14**. Peen the outside surface of the ring; then move the ring to a flat iron surface and hammer as much of its inside surface as possible.

Pry open the brass strap enough to slip the ring into place, and squeeze the strap shut with a pliers. Secure the strap in a hand-screw clamp and drill a centered ⁵⁄₁₆" hole.

Attach the strap/ring assembly to the backplate with the brass screw and nut. Tighten the nut so the strap compresses completely. Secure the threaded end of the screw in a vise and apply silver solder flux to the joints between the backplate, strap, and screw head. Heat these joints with a propane torch until silver solder melts when you touch it to the brass, as shown in **3–15**. Do not overheat the joint or apply too much solder—if you do, some

Brass bends easily once you apply some heat to it.

A short length of angle iron helps you pound a crisp bend into the ring strap.

Hammer the outside of the ring as you rotate it on a steel rod secured in a vise.

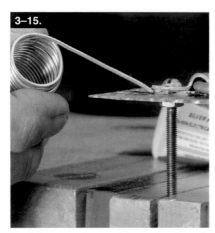

3–15.

Touch some silver solder to the fluxed and heated joints to secure them.

3–16.

An abrasive disc mounted on a motorized rotary tool helps you quickly remove excess solder.

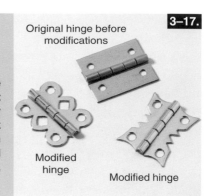

Turn Ordinary Hinges Into Sparkling Beauties

Ordinary 1½ x 1¼" brass hinges like the ones shown at right cost about $2 for a pair. You can easily modify such a nondescript hinges to look like the other two shown here with just a little sawing, filing, and polishing. Use the patterns opposite, or design some to your own liking.

3–17.

Original hinge before modifications

Modified hinge

Modified hinge

solder may seep behind the back-plate and lock the nut to the back of the plate.

Back off the nut and clamp the screw threads in a vise. (If the nut is stuck, heat it with the torch.) Remove the excess solder with a sanding disc attached to a motorized rotary tool, as shown in **3–16**.

File down the screw head until you remove its slot. Do not hammer this surface or the ring strap—doing so may break the soldered joints. For help in deciding what finish to put on the pull, see the following section on finish choices.

Apply a Finish to the Hardware

The pulls in **3–18** show four different ways to give your hardware a distinctive finish. The polished pulls were buffed to a high luster using a buffing wheel mounted on a bench grinder, as shown in **3–20**. We first charged the buffing wheel with a Tripoli compound (available in sticks from hardware

Pulls with four different finishes.

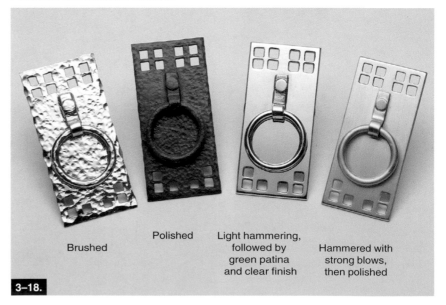

Brushed

Polished

Light hammering, followed by green patina and clear finish

Hammered with strong blows, then polished

3–18.

3–19.
FULL-SIZE PULL PATTERNS

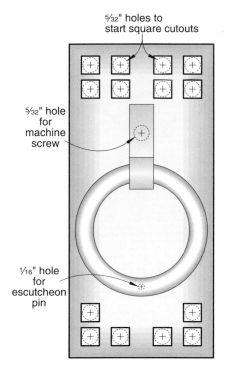

⁵⁄₃₂" holes to start square cutouts

⁵⁄₃₂" hole for machine screw

¹⁄₁₆" hole for escutcheon pin

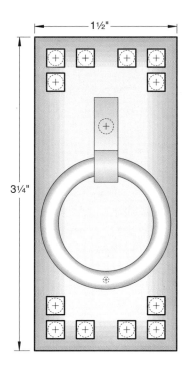

1½"

3¼"

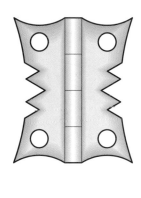

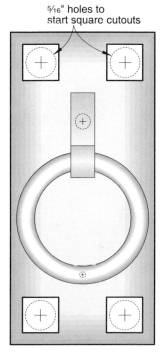

⁵⁄₁₆" holes to start square cutouts

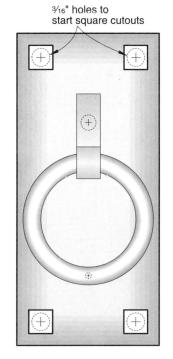

³⁄₁₆" holes to start square cutouts

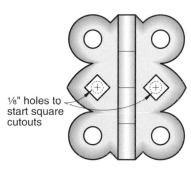

⅛" holes to start square cutouts

Wear light gloves and eye protection to guard you from the debris that flies off a buffing wheel.

Sources of Low-Cost Brass and Aluminum

You'll find a bounty of dirt-cheap brass and aluminum at salvage yards and shops that repair truck and car transmissions, rear differentials, and brakes. Once these parts have outlived their original purpose, their scrap value is minimal; we got most of the brake and transmission parts shown in *3–21* for free simply by asking to look through scrap bins (don't forget to wear gloves).

stores) by holding the wax-like compound against the spinning wheel. We then buffed the entire surface. (To reach tight spots we used a buffing wheel attachment on a motorized rotary tool.) Next, we cleaned the wheel by holding a piece of scrap wood against the spinning wheel. We buffed the pull to its final luster with jewelers' rouge compound.

We treated the green pull with an ammonium chloride/copper sulphate solution (from finishing and/or jewelry supply houses) formulated for brass.

To achieve the brushed look we sanded the surface with 400-grit wet/dry silicon carbide abrasive paper. Sand with straight back-and-forth strokes in one direction only.

These pulls will scratch or tarnish if left unprotected, so we coated them with a clear spray lacquer. You can use any clear finish over a patinaed brass surface, but keep in mind that the finish will darken the patina as it did on our sample. We suggest experimenting on scrap brass before deciding to coat a patina.

CHAPTER 4

Furniture Favorites for the Den or Living Room

BY NOW YOU KNOW WHAT MAKES ART AND *Crafts furniture distinctive. From here on, you'll learn how to build some. The designs chosen are visibly inspired by the style, yet serve well in almost any setting.*

Back at the height of Arts and Crafts popularity, the hallmark piece was the Morris chair. With an adjustable back, it was the precursor of today's recliner. You can build one with the instructions that begin on the next page. *Then, you'll want to add the coffee table and Ottoman that accompany this classic. See how on* page 48.

To fill out a living room or den, look to page 59 *for the step-by-step technique to create a matching sofa, often called a settee. By shortening the dimensions, you can use the same construction steps to build a stylish Arts and Crafts chair to go with it. As a bonus, we'll show you how to upholster the pair—without sewing a stitch!*

An Arts and Crafts room wouldn't be complete without a rocking chair. Pages 75 to 86 contain instructions for building one to go with the pieces mentioned above. You also have the option of building it as a simple occasional chair.

To top off the furniture in this chapter, plans are included for a stunningly elegant bookcase in the Arts and Crafts style. Refer to pages 87 to 98.

MORRIS CHAIR

Believed to have originated with William Morris, father of the English Arts and Crafts movement, the so-called Morris chair combines comfort with simply stated good looks. True to form, this version features loose cushions, curved arms, and an adjustable back.

MORRIS CHAIR CUTTING DIAGRAM
*Plain or resaw to thickness listed in the Materials List.

¾ x 9¼ x 96" Oak (6.7 bd. ft.)

1¹⁄₁₆ x 9¼ x 96" Oak (8.3 bd.ft.)

½ x 5½ x 96" Oak (2 bd. ft.)

½ x 7¼ x 96" Oak (3 pieces needed) (2.7 bd.ft.)

1¹⁄₁₆ x 7¼ x 96" Oak (6.7 bd. ft.)

½ x 5½ x 96" Oak (2. bd.ft.)

½ x 7¼ x 48" Oak (1.3 bd.ft.)   ⅝" Oak dowel 16" long

Morris chair

MATERIALS LIST FOR MORRIS CHAIR

PART	FINISHED SIZE T	W	L	Mtl.	QTY.
SIDE FRAMES					
A* front legs	2¼"	2¼"	21¾"	LO	2
B* rear legs	2¼"	2¼"	21¾"	LO	2
C lower side rails	1¹⁄₁₆"	3¾"	30"	O	2
D upper side rails	1¹⁄₁₆"	3¾"	27"	O	2
E center side slats	⅜"	4¼"	13"	O	2
F side slats	⅜"	1¼"	13"	O	12
G* spacers	⅜"	⅝"	1¼"	O	24
H* spacers	⅜"	⅝"	2⅞"	O	8
I* armrests	1⅛"	5½"	36"	LO	2
J corbels	1¹⁄₁₆"	1⅜"	8¾"	O	4
STRETCHERS AND CLEATS					
K stretchers	1¹⁄₁₆"	4½"	28¼"	O	2
L cleats	1¹⁄₁₆"	1¹⁄₁₆"	23¼"	O	2
SEAT FRAME					
M ends	1¹⁄₁₆"	1¾"	23"	O	2
N slats	1¹⁄₁₆"	1¾"	23¾"	O	2
O slats	⅜"	1¾"	23¾"	O	7
P* spacers	⅜"	⅝"	²⁹⁄₃₂"	O	16
BACKREST					
Q stiles	1¹⁄₁₆"	1⅝"	29"	O	2
R rails	1¹⁄₁₆"	3½"	22"	O	2
S splats	⅜"	3¼"	20"	O	4
T* spacers	⅜"	⅝"	1½ "	O	10
U back pins	⅝" dia.		3"	OD	2
V pins	⅝" dia.		3"	OD	2

*Cut parts oversized. Trim to finished size according to the instructions.

Materials Key: LO = laminated oak; O = oak; OD = oak dowel.

Supplies: #8 x 1¾" flathead wood screws; #8 x 1" flathead brass wood screws; stain; finish.

Drill-Press Table Plan. Plan JG–#1002, $9.95. WOOD PLANS, P.O. Box 9255, Des Moines, IA 50306.

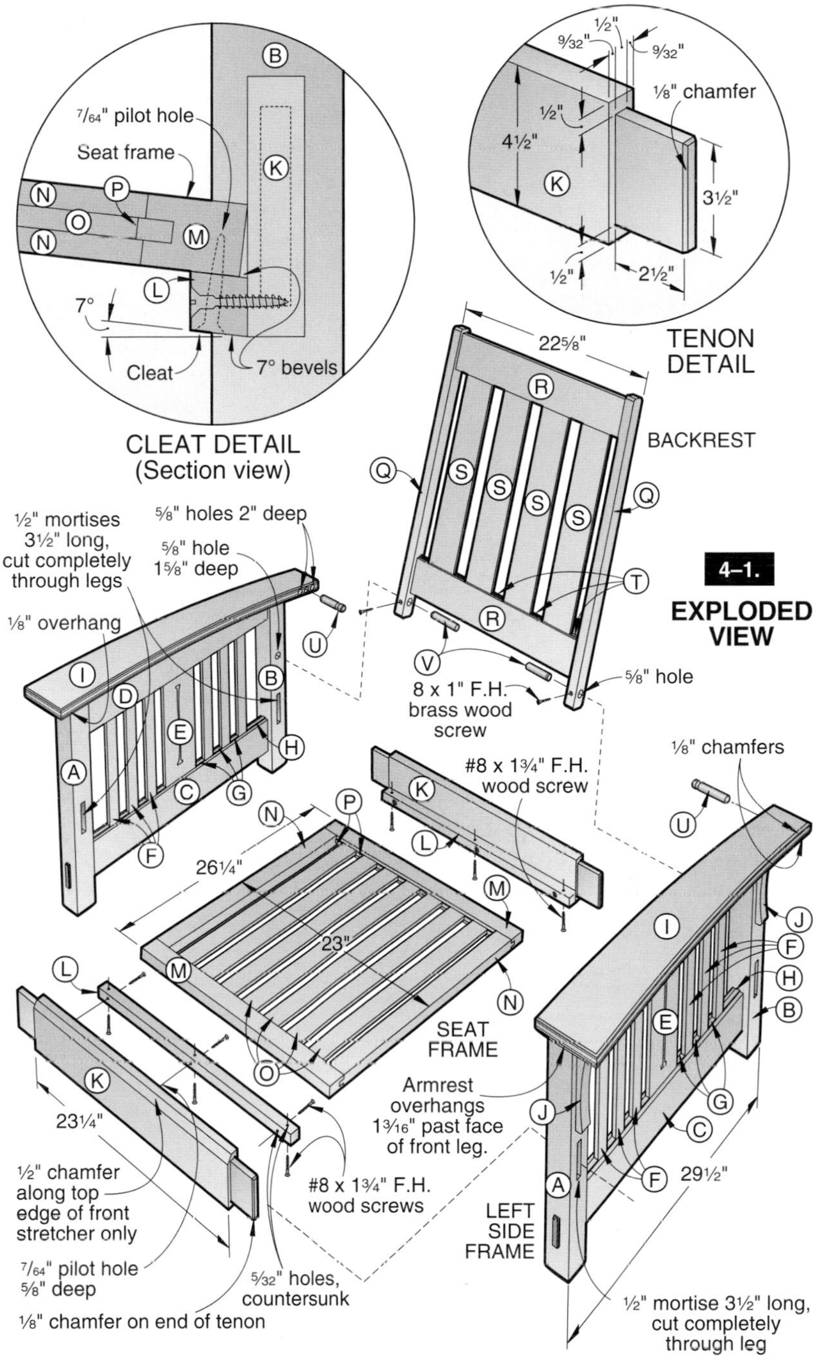

⁷⁄₆₄" pilot hole
Seat frame
7°
Cleat
7° bevels
CLEAT DETAIL (Section view)
⁹⁄₃₂"
½"
⁹⁄₃₂"
⅛" chamfer
4½"
½"
3½"
½"
2½"
TENON DETAIL
22⅝"
BACKREST
½" mortises 3½" long, cut completely through legs
⅝" holes 2" deep
⅝" hole 1⅝" deep
⅛" overhang
8 x 1" F.H. brass wood screw
⅝" hole
#8 x 1¾" F.H. wood screw
⅛" chamfers
26¼"
23"
SEAT FRAME
Armrest overhangs 1³⁄₁₆" past face of front leg.
23¼"
½" chamfer along top edge of front stretcher only
#8 x 1¾" F.H. wood screws
LEFT SIDE FRAME
29½"
⁷⁄₆₄" pilot hole ⅝" deep
⁵⁄₃₂" holes, countersunk
⅛" chamfer on end of tenon
½" mortise 3½" long, cut completely through leg

4–1.
EXPLODED VIEW

Laminate and Machine the Legs

Note: *For an authentic look, choose straight grain or rift-sawn stock, preferably white oak, for all the pieces of this project.*

1 To form the 2¼"-square chair legs (A, B), cut 12 pieces of ¾"-thick stock to 2⅜ × 22¾". (Using these dimensions, the pieces are initially ⅛" oversize in width and 1" in length so you can trim the edges and ends of the laminated legs to final dimensions later.) See **4–4** for reference.

2 Spread an even coat of glue on the mating surfaces of the three pieces making up each leg. With the edges and ends flush, glue and clamp the pieces face-to-face to form the front and rear legs.

3 Cut or plane an equal amount off both edges of each leg (A, B) for a 2¼" finished width. Then, trim an equal amount off both ends of each leg for a 21¾" finished length.

4 Using **4–4** for reference, lay out the mortises, notches, and hole centerpoints on the outside surface of each leg, where dimensioned. (To ensure any possible chip-out would be on the inside surface and covered by the rail and stretcher tenon shoulders

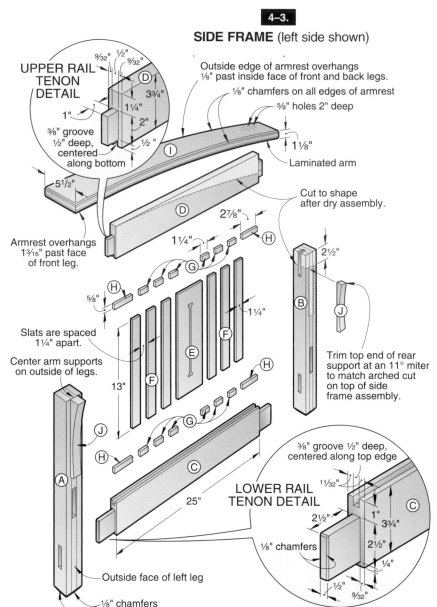

4–3.

SIDE FRAME (left side shown)

UPPER RAIL TENON DETAIL

9/32" ½" 9/32"

1"

3¾"

1¼"

2"

⅜" groove ½" deep, centered along bottom

½"

5½"

Outside edge of armrest overhangs ⅛" past inside face of front and back legs.

⅛" chamfers on all edges of armrest

⅝" holes 2" deep

1⅛"

Laminated arm

Cut to shape after dry assembly.

Armrest overhangs 1³⁄₁₆" past face of front leg.

2⅞"

1¼"

2½"

Slats are spaced 1¼" apart.

Center arm supports on outside of legs.

13"

⅝"

1¼"

Trim top end of rear support at an 11° miter to match arched cut on top of side frame assembly.

⅜" groove ½" deep, centered along top edge

LOWER RAIL TENON DETAIL

11/32"

2½"

1"

3¾"

2½"

¼"

⅛" chamfers

½"

9/32"

25"

Outside face of left leg

⅛" chamfers

4–2.

Using a fence on your drill-press table for alignment, remove the waste stock from the marked mortises on the laminated legs.

later, mark the mortises on the outside surfaces. Also drill from the outside surface so the bit comes through on the inside surface.)

5 Attach a wood top and fence to your drill-press table. Using a ⁷⁄₁₆" brad-point bit, drill holes inside the marked mortise outlines, as shown in **4–2**. Square

up the mortises with a chisel. You also could form the mortises with a mortiser.

6 Drill a ⅝" hole 1⅝" deep on the inside face of each 2¼"-square rear leg (B) to house the lower backrest pins (V) later.

7 Rout a ⅛" chamfer along the bottom end of each leg.

4–4.
LEGS

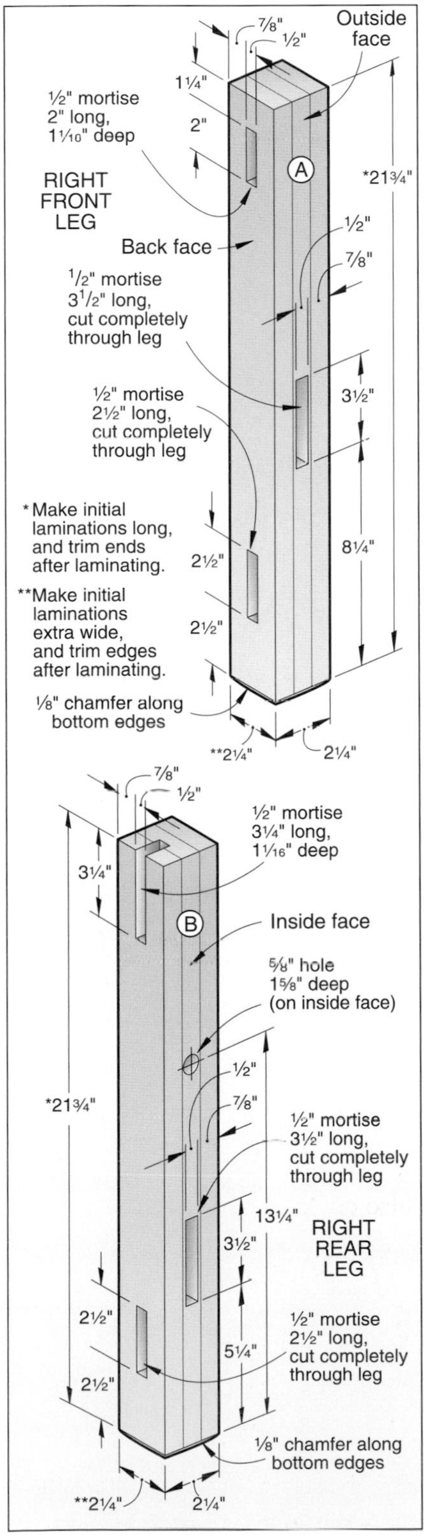

7/8"
1/2"
Outside face
1 1/4"
1/2" mortise 2" long, 1 1/16" deep
2"
RIGHT FRONT LEG
A
*21 3/4"
Back face
1/2"
7/8"
1/2" mortise 3 1/2" long, cut completely through leg
3 1/2"
1/2" mortise 2 1/2" long, cut completely through leg
*Make initial laminations long, and trim ends after laminating.
8 1/4"
2 1/2"
**Make initial laminations extra wide, and trim edges after laminating.
2 1/2"
1/8" chamfer along bottom edges
**2 1/4"
2 1/4"
7/8"
1/2"
1/2" mortise 3 1/4" long, 1 1/16" deep
3 1/4"
B
Inside face
5/8" hole 1 5/8" deep (on inside face)
1/2"
7/8"
*21 3/4"
1/2" mortise 3 1/2" long, cut completely through leg
13 1/4"
3 1/2"
RIGHT REAR LEG
2 1/2"
1/2" mortise 2 1/2" long, cut completely through leg
5 1/4"
2 1/2"
1/8" chamfer along bottom edges
**2 1/4"
2 1/4"

Machine and Assemble the Side Frames

1 Cut the lower rails (C) and upper rails (D) to the sizes listed in the Materials List from five-quarter (1 1/16") stock.

2 Fit your tablesaw with a 3/8" dado blade, and cut a 3/8" groove 1/2" deep, centered along one edge of each rail. See **4–3** and accompanying Tenon details for reference.

3 Switch to a wider dado blade on your tablesaw. Then, attach a long wooden extension to your tablesaw's miter gauge, and square the extension to the blade. Using a stop for consistency, cut rabbets to form tenons on the ends of the rails (C, D). (We test-cut scrap stock first to ensure a tight fit of the tenons into the leg mortises.) See the Upper and Lower Rail Tenon Detail accompanying **4–3** for dimensions.

4 Sand or file the chamfers on both ends of the through tenons on the lower rails (C), where shown on the Lower Rail Tenon Detail in **4–3**. If you have a small router, such as a laminate trimmer, use a chamfer bit in it to machine the tenon ends.

5 Cut the center slats (E) and narrower side slats (F) to size. Using the Center Side Slat pattern in **4–13** (*page 45*), transfer the cutout location to each center slat. Drill a blade start hole, and scrollsaw the openings to shape.

6 To form the spacers (G, H, P, T) cut six pieces of stock to 3/8" thick by 5/8" wide by 36" long. Then, crosscut the side frame spacers (G, H) to length from these strips.

7 To assemble the side frames, start by finding the center (from end-to-end) of each rail, and mark a centerline across the grain. Starting with the center slat (E) centered over the centerline on the bottom rail (C), work from the center out and add (no glue) the spacers (G, H) and slats (F). Add the top rail (D). Trim the

4–5.

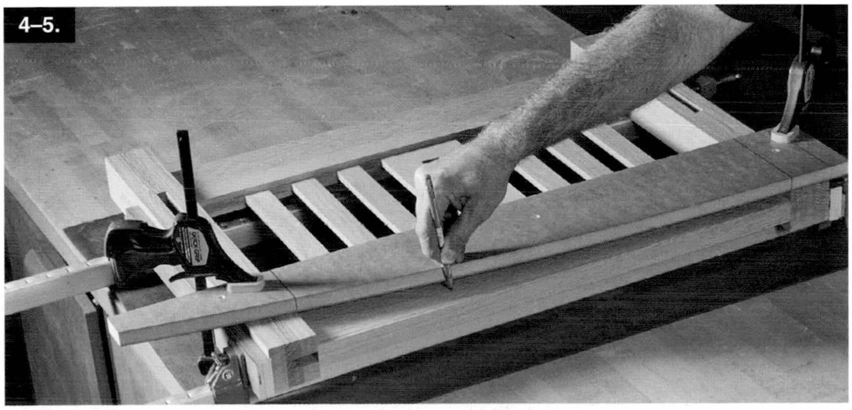

Clamp one of the template pieces to the dry-clamped (no glue) side frame, and then trace the cutline onto the top rail and leg tops. Repeat for the other chair side.

spacers if necessary. Then, fit (again, no glue) the assembly into the leg mortises to check the joinery.

8 Using the Template/Form pattern on *page 45* for reference, transfer the outline to ¾" particleboard, and cut six template/form pieces to shape. Next, as shown in **4–5**, use one of the pieces to transfer the curved cutline to each side frame.

9 Remove the clamp and separate the pieces. Band-saw along the marked lines on the leg tops and top rail from each side frame. Sand the side frame pieces. Next, assemble, glue, and clamp each side frame together, checking for square.

Create the Curved Armrests

1 With the edges and ends flush, screw the six template/ form pieces together face-to-face.

2 From ⅜" oak, cut six pieces to 6" wide by 38" long.

Spread a thin, even coat of glue on the mating surfaces of three of the pieces. With the edges and ends flush, glue and clamp them over the top, curved edge of the form, as shown in **4–6**. Immediately wipe off any excess glue with a damp cloth. Check for gaps between the boards and add more clamps if necessary. Let the assembly stand 24 hours, and then remove the clamps. When unclamping the armrests from the form, there will be a slight spring-back. This will be alleviated when gluing and clamping the armrests to the side frames later.

3 Scrape off the glue, and joint the inside edge of each armrest. Copy the Armrest pattern and transfer the cutline for the outside edge to the top face of each armrest, and band-saw to shape. Sand the armrests.

4 Glue and clamp the arched armrests to the side frames. Each armrest will overhang the front leg 1³⁄₁₆" on the front edge and ⅛" on the inside edge. Leave them clamped-up for 24 hours.

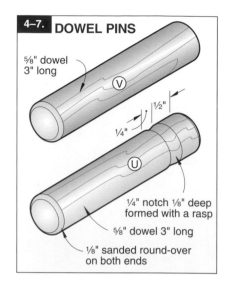

4–7. DOWEL PINS

⅝" dowel 3" long

½"

¼"

¼" notch ⅛" deep formed with a rasp

⅝" dowel 3" long

⅛" sanded round-over on both ends

5 Sand the armrests smooth, and rout a ⅛" chamfer along the top edges of each.

6 Using the enlargeable pattern on *page 45*, cut the four corbels (J) to shape. Miter-cut the top ends of the rear brackets at 11° to fit snug against the bottom side of the armrest. Glue and clamp the corbels in place, centered on the outside face of each leg.

Add the Front and Rear Stretchers and Cleats

1 Cut the stretchers (K) to size. Cut tenons on the ends of the stretchers to fit snug inside the mortises in the legs. Then, rout a ½" chamfer along the top front edge of the front stretcher. Next, cut or rout ⅛" chamfers on the ends of the tenons. See **4–1**, on *page 39*, for reference.

4–6.

Clamp the armrest form in a wood-worker's vise, and then glue and clamp the armrest pieces against the form.

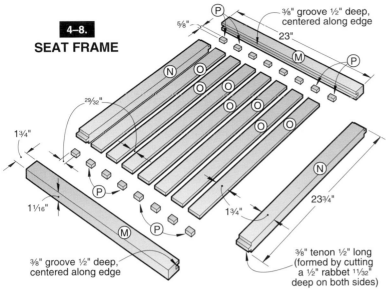

**4–8.
SEAT FRAME**

⅝" groove ½" deep, centered along edge

23"

5/8"

29/32"

1¾"

1 11/16"

⅜" groove ½" deep, centered along edge

1¾"

23¾"

⅜" tenon ½" long (formed by cutting a ½" rabbet 11/32" deep on both sides)

2 Glue and clamp the stretchers between the side frames, keeping the frames square to the stretchers.

3 Cut the cleats (L) to size, beveling opposite edges, where shown on the Cleat Detail accompanying **4–1**. Then, drill countersunk holes in each cleat, and screw them to the inside face of each stretcher (K).

Cut the Pieces and Assemble the Seat Frame

1 Cut the seat frame ends (M) and slats (N, O) to size.

2 Cut a ⅜" groove ½" deep centered along the inside edge of each end (M). Then, cut rabbets on the ends of the outside slats (N) to fit inside the grooves.

3 Cut the spacers (P) to length.

4 Assemble the seat frame (no glue), and check its fit between the stretchers (K). Then,

glue and clamp the seat frame together, checking for square.

5 Sand the seat frame smooth, and set it in place. Using the previously drilled holes in the cleats (L) as guides, drill pilot holes into the bottom of the seat frame, and screw it in place.

Construct the Backrest

1 Cut the backrest stiles (Q), rails (R), splats (S), and spacers (T) to size.

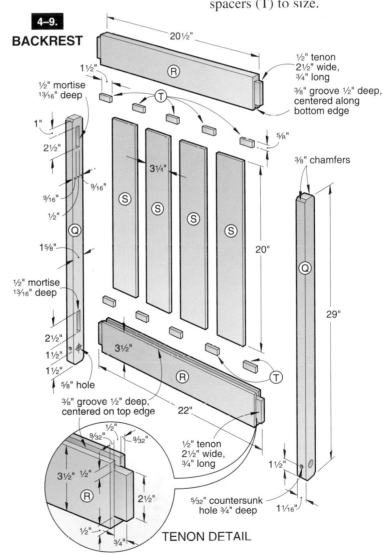

**4–9.
BACKREST**

20½"

1½"

½" mortise 13/16" deep

1"

2½"

9/16"

9/16"

½"

1⅝"

½" mortise 13/16" deep

2½"

1½"

1½"

⅝" hole

⅜" groove ½" deep, centered on top edge

½" tenon 2½" wide, ¾" long

⅜" groove ½" deep, centered along bottom edge

5/8"

⅜" chamfers

3¼"

20"

3½"

22"

½" tenon 2½" wide, ¾" long

29"

1½"

5/32" countersunk hole ¾" deep

1 11/16"

½"

9/32"

9/32"

3½"   ½"

2½"

½"

¾"

TENON DETAIL

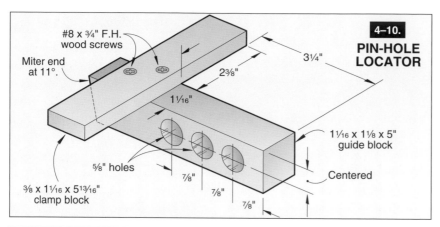

4–10.
PIN-HOLE LOCATOR

#8 x ¾" F.H. wood screws

Miter end at 11°.

3¼"

2⅜"

1¹⁄₁₆"

1¹⁄₁₆ x 1⅛ x 5" guide block

⅝" holes

Centered

⅜ x 1¹⁄₁₆ x 5¹³⁄₁₆" clamp block

⅞"   ⅞"   ⅞"

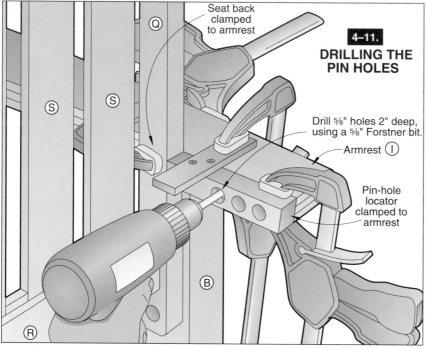

Seat back clamped to armrest

Ⓠ

4–11.
DRILLING THE PIN HOLES

Ⓢ   Ⓢ

Drill ⅝" holes 2" deep, using a ⅝" Forstner bit.

Armrest Ⓘ

Pin-hole locator clamped to armrest

Ⓑ

Ⓡ

4–12.
CUSHION CONSTRUCTION

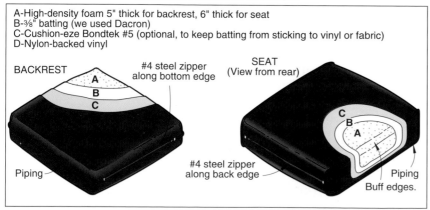

A-High-density foam 5" thick for backrest, 6" thick for seat
B-⅜" batting (we used Dacron)
C-Cushion-eze Bondtek #5 (optional, to keep batting from sticking to vinyl or fabric)
D-Nylon-backed vinyl

BACKREST

#4 steel zipper along bottom edge

A
B
C

SEAT (View from rear)

C
B
A

Piping

#4 steel zipper along back edge

Piping
Buff edges.

2 Using **4–9** for reference, mark the mortise locations and hole centerpoints on each stile. Cut the mortises and drill the holes. Then, cut chamfers along the ends of each stile.

3 Cut tenons on the ends of the rails to fit into the stile mortises. Cut a ⅜" groove along the inside edge of each rail.

4 Dry-fit the backrest together to check the fit. Once verified, glue and clamp the pieces together. Later, sand smooth.

5 Form the backrest pins (U, V) from oak dowel stock. Temporarily pin the backrest to the chair.

6 Construct the pin-hole locator, where shown in **4–10**.

7 Position the backrest on the lower pins (V), and then center the backrest between the armrests. Using the previously drilled holes in the bottom fronts of the stiles (Q) as guides, drill pilot holes into the pins. Drive screws through the stiles and into the pins.

8 Position the backrest straight up at a 90° angle to the floor, and clamp it in place. Then, clamp the pin-hole locator to the armrest and flush with the back of the backrest where shown in **4–11**. Now, use the pin-hole locator to drill three ⅝" holes 2" deep on the *inside* edge of each armrest.

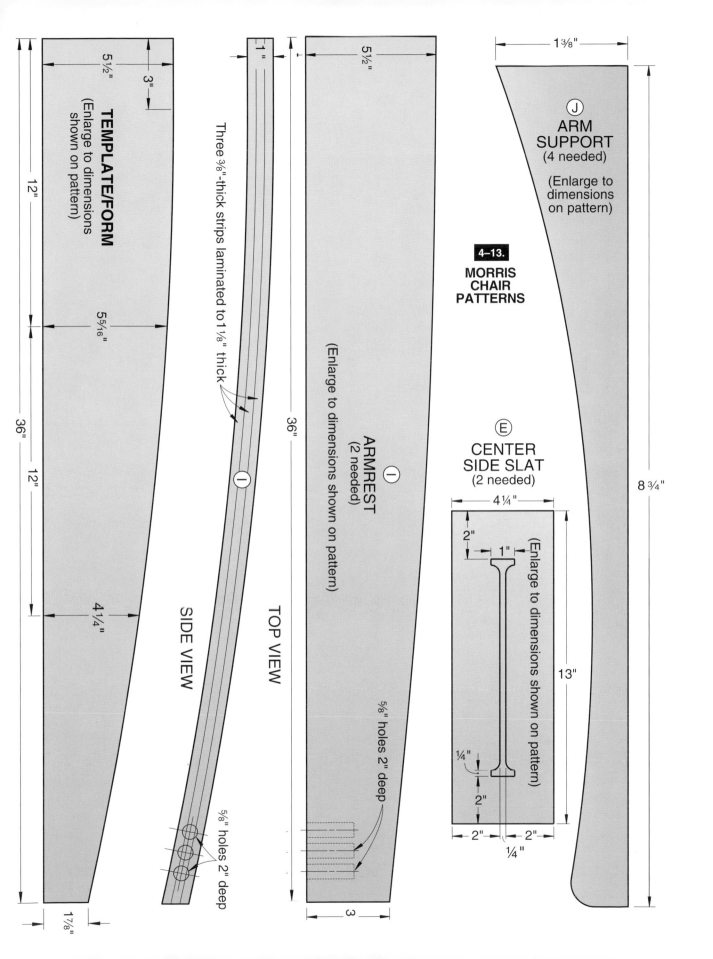

TEMPLATE/FORM
(Enlarge to dimensions shown on pattern)

5½"

3"

5⁵⁄₁₆"

12"

36"

12"

4¼"

1⅞"

SIDE VIEW

Three ⅜"-thick strips laminated to 1⅛" thick

1"

36"

Ⓘ

5⁄₈" holes 2" deep

TOP VIEW

5½"

3

ARMREST
(2 needed)

(Enlarge to dimensions shown on pattern)

Ⓘ

5⁄₈" holes 2" deep

4–13.

MORRIS CHAIR PATTERNS

Ⓙ

ARM SUPPORT
(4 needed)

(Enlarge to dimensions on pattern)

1⅜"

8¾"

Ⓔ

CENTER SIDE SLAT
(2 needed)

(Enlarge to dimensions shown on pattern)

4¼"

2"

1"

13"

¼"

2"

2"

2"

¼"

Finish-Sand the Chair and Apply a Stain and Clear Coat

1 Remove the seat and backrest from the chair frame. Finish-sand all the pieces.

2 Stain as desired, or see the fumeless finish instructions on *pages 29 to 31* of Chapter Three. Apply the finish. (The chair shown on *page 38* has several coats of satin polyurethane.)

3 Screw the seat frame in place, and pin the backrest in place.

4 To make the cushions, see **4–12** on *page 44* and the material layout at right. Because of the simulated leather (real leather if you choose), we recommend taking the assembled chair along with the drawings to a professional upholster to have the work done. For fabric, see *pages 68 to 74* for no-sew instructions.

4–14.
UPHOLSTERY PATTERNS

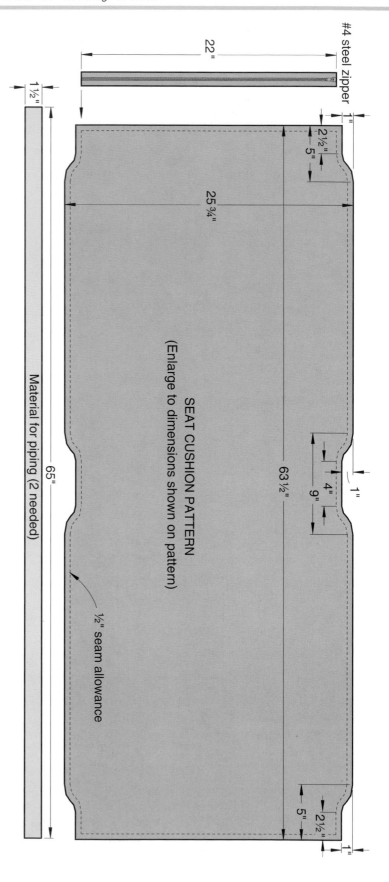

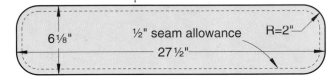

4–14.

UPHOLSTERY PATTERNS *(continued)*

SEAT CUSHION END
2 pieces needed
(Enlarge to dimensions shown on pattern)

6⅛" ½" seam allowance R=2"
27½"

> **Note:** Checking with upholsterers around the country, we learned that the supplies and the thickness of materials used very greatly. We recommend providing our drawings and your chair to your upholsterer, and having them make the cushions to fit your chair.

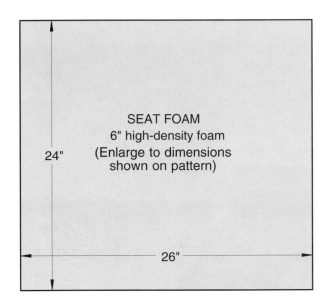

SEAT FOAM
6" high-density foam
(Enlarge to dimensions
shown on pattern)

24"

26"

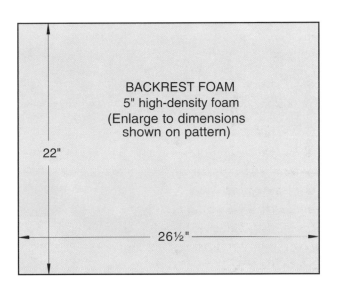

BACKREST FOAM
5" high-density foam
(Enlarge to dimensions
shown on pattern)

22"

26½"

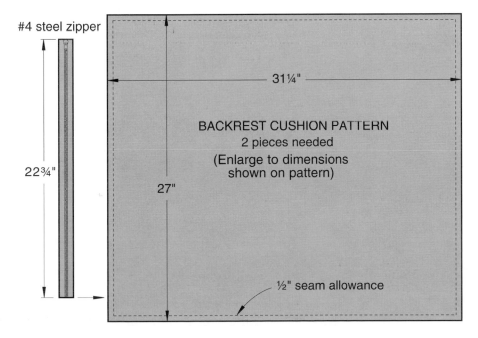

#4 steel zipper

22¾"

31¼"

BACKREST CUSHION PATTERN
2 pieces needed
(Enlarge to dimensions
shown on pattern)

27"

½" seam allowance

COFFEE TABLE AND OTTOMAN

If you liked the Morris chair project on the preceding pages, you'll want to build this pair to join it in your living room. They make a wonderful Arts and Crafts statement.

Laminate and Machine the Legs

Note: For an authentic look, choose straight grain or rift-cut stock, preferably white oak, for all the pieces of this project.

COFFEE TABLE CUTTING DIAGRAM

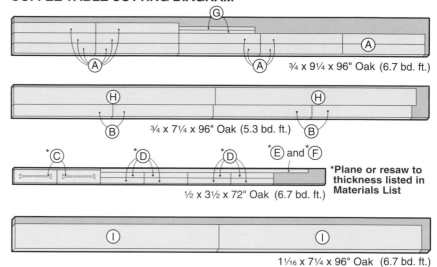

¾ x 9¼ x 96" Oak (6.7 bd. ft.)

¾ x 7¼ x 96" Oak (5.3 bd. ft.)

½ x 3½ x 72" Oak (6.7 bd. ft.)

*Plane or resaw to thickness listed in Materials List

1¹⁄₁₆ x 7¼ x 96" Oak (6.7 bd. ft.)

1¹⁄₁₆ x 7¼ x 96" Oak (6.7 bd. ft.)

Coffee table

Ottoman

MATERIALS LIST FOR COFFEE TABLE

| PART | FINISHED SIZE | | | Mtl. | Qty. |
	T	W	L		
A* legs	2¼"	2¼"	18"	LO	4
B rails	¾"	2¾"	23"	O	4
C center slats	⅜"	3"	10"	O	2
D side slats	⅜"	1¼"	10"	O	8
E* spacers	⅜"	⅝"	1¼"	O	16
F* spacers	⅜"	½"	2½"	O	8
G cleats	¾"	¾"	17¾"	O	2
H stretchers	¾"	4"	46½"	O	2
I* tabletop	1¹⁄₁₆"	22½"	46"	EO	1

*Cut parts oversize. Trim to finished size according to the instructions.

Materials Key: LO = laminated oak; O = oak; EO = edge-joined oak.
Supplies: #8 x 1¼" flathead wood screws; #8 x 1½" roundhead wood screws with flat washers; stain; clear finish.

4–15.

COFFEE TABLE EXPLODED VIEW

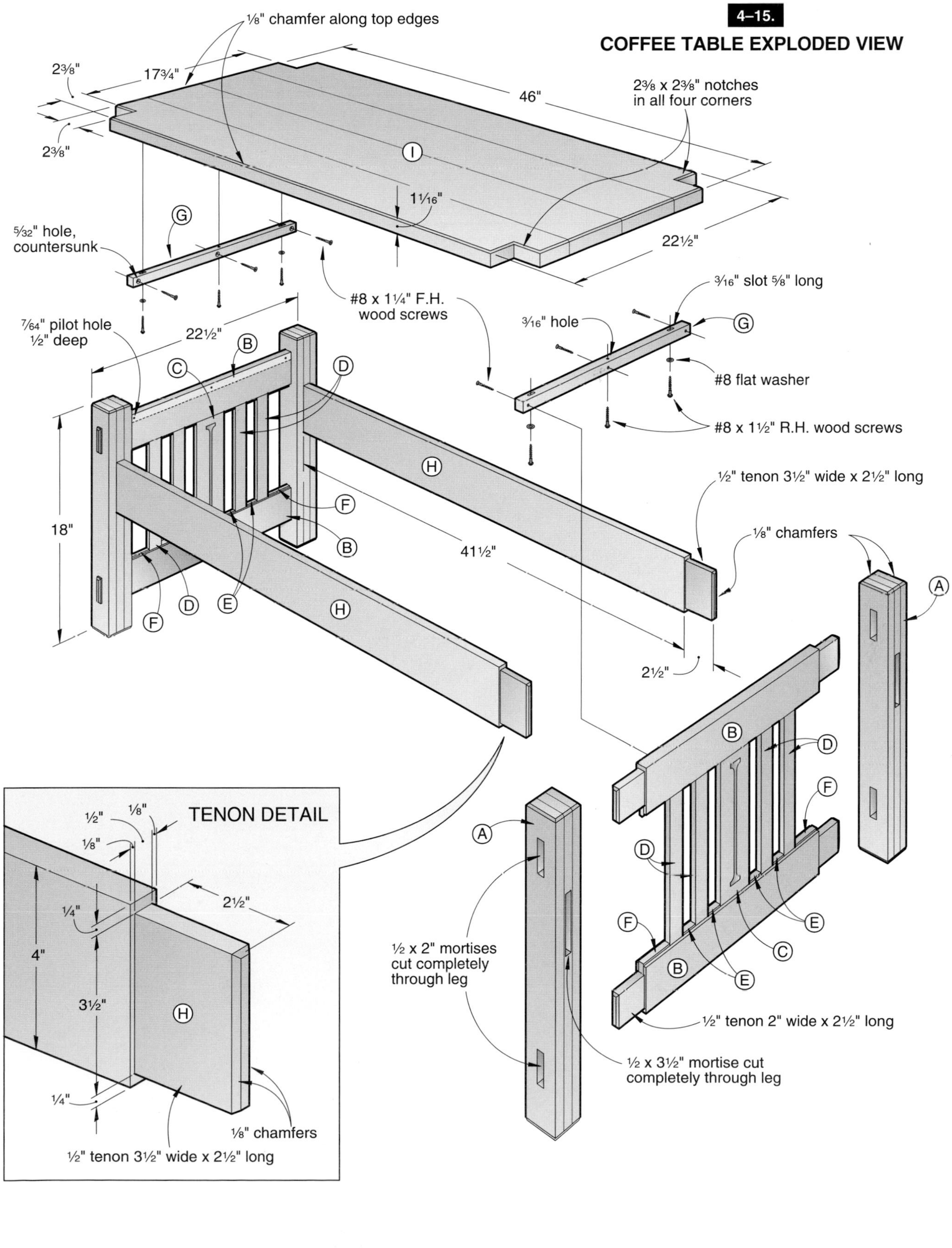
⅛" chamfer along top edges
2⅜"
17¾"
46"
2⅜ x 2⅜" notches in all four corners
2⅜"
I
1¹⁄₁₆"
22½"
G
5⁄32" hole, countersunk
#8 x 1¼" F.H. wood screws
3⁄16" slot ⅝" long
3⁄16" hole
G
#8 flat washer
#8 x 1½" R.H. wood screws
7⁄64" pilot hole ½" deep
22½"
B
C
D
H
18"
F
B
41½"
½" tenon 3½" wide x 2½" long
⅛" chamfers
A
F
D
E
H
2½"
B
D
F
TENON DETAIL
½"
⅛"
⅛"
¼"
2½"
4"
3½"
H
¼"
⅛" chamfers
½" tenon 3½" wide x 2½" long
A
½ x 2" mortises cut completely through leg
D
F
E
C
B
E
½" tenon 2" wide x 2½" long
½ x 3½" mortise cut completely through leg

1 To form the 2¼"-square legs (A), cut 12 pieces of ¾" stock to 2⅜" × 19". (Using these dimensions, the pieces are over-sized ⅛" in width and 1" in length so you can trim flush the edges and ends of the legs later.) See **4–16** for reference.

2 Spread an even coat of glue on the mating surfaces of the three pieces making up each leg. With the edges and ends flush, glue and clamp the pieces face-to-face to form the legs.

3 Cut or plane an equal amount off both edges of each leg for a 2¼" finished width. Then, trim both ends of each leg for an 18" finished length.

4 Lay out the mortises on the *outside* surface of each leg, where dimensioned. (To ensure any possible chip-out would be on the *inside* surface and covered by the rail and stretcher tenon shoulders, we marked the mortises on the outside surfaces. We also drilled from the outside surface so the bit came through on the inside.)

5 Attach a wood top and fence to your drill-press table. Using a ⁷⁄₁₆" brad-point bit, drill holes inside the marked mortises. Square-up the mortises with a chisel. You also could form the mortises with a mortiser.

6 Rout a ⅛" chamfer along the top and bottom end of each leg.

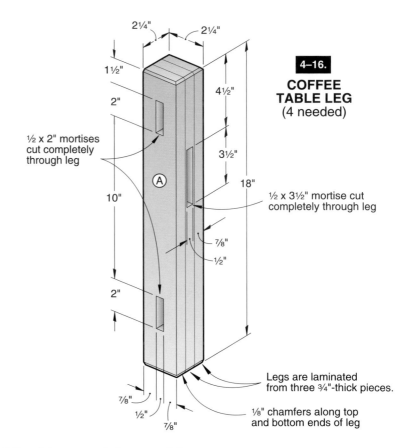

½ x 2" mortises cut completely through leg

4–16.
COFFEE TABLE LEG
(4 needed)

½ x 3½" mortise cut completely through leg

Legs are laminated from three ¾"-thick pieces.

⅛" chamfers along top and bottom ends of leg

Machine and Assemble the End Frames

1 Cut the upper and lower rails (B) to the sizes listed in the Materials List from ¾" stock.

2 Fit your tablesaw with a ⅜" dado blade, and cut a ⅜" groove ½" deep, centered along one edge of each rail. See **4–17** for reference.

3 Switch to a wider dado blade on your tablesaw. Then, attach a long wooden extension to your tablesaw's miter gauge, and square the extension to the blade. Using a stop for consistency, cut rabbets to form tenons on the ends of the rails (B). (Test-cut scrap stock first to ensure a tight fit of the tenons into the leg mortises.) See the Tenon Detail in **4–17** for dimensions.

4 Carefully sand or file the chamfers on both ends of the through tenons on the rails (B), where shown in the Tenon Detail in **4–17**. If you have a small laminate-trim router, use a chamfer bit in it to machine the tenon ends.

5 Cut the center slats (C) and narrower side slats (D) to size. Using the Center Slat Pattern in **4–21** (*page 53*), transfer the cutout location to each center slat. Drill a blade start hole, and scrollsaw the openings to shape.

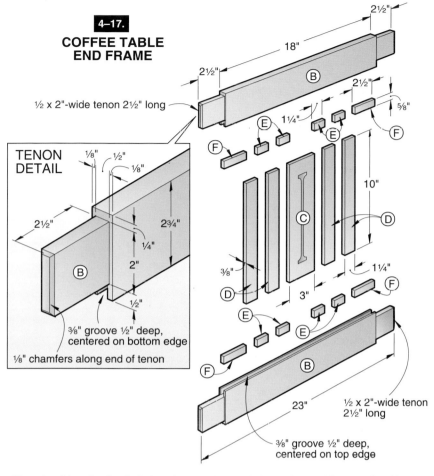

4–17.
COFFEE TABLE END FRAME

½ x 2"-wide tenon 2½" long

TENON DETAIL

⅜" groove ½" deep, centered on bottom edge

⅛" chamfers along end of tenon

23"

½ x 2"-wide tenon 2½" long

⅜" groove ½" deep, centered on top edge

6 To form the spacers (E, F) cut a piece of stock to ⅜" thick by ⅝" wide by 48" long. Then, crosscut the spacers (E, F) to length from this strip.

7 To assemble the end frames, start by finding the center (from end-to-end) of each rail, and mark a centerline across the grain. Starting with the center slat (C) centered over the centerline on the bottom rail (B) and working from the center out, add (no glue) the spacers (E, F) and the slats (D). Add the top rail (B). Trim the spacers if necessary. Then, fit (again, no glue) the assembly into the leg mortises to check the joinery.

8 Sand the legs and end frame pieces. Next, glue and clamp the two frames together, checking for square, as shown in **4–18**.

After checking the fit of all the pieces, glue and clamp the end frame, checking the assembly for square.

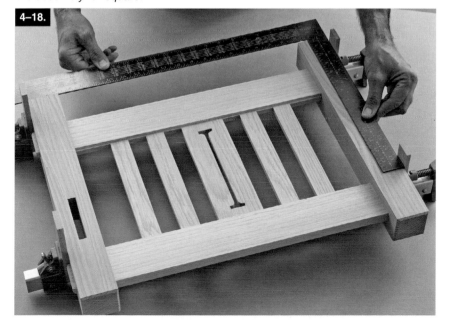

4–18.

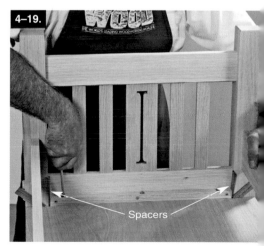

4–19.

Spacers

Notice the ⅛"-thick spacers between the end-frame legs and tabletop. We used the spacers to center the top on the base when screwing the assemblies together.

Add the Cleats and Stretchers

1 Cut the cleats (G) to size.

2 Mark the locations, and machine a pair of screw expansion slots on each cleat, where dimensioned in **4–21**. Mark the centerpoints, and drill countersunk holes through each cleat. Screw the cleats to the inside face of each top rail (B), keeping the top edge of the cleats flush with the top edge of the rails. There should be an ⅛" gap between the ends of the cleat and the legs, so you won't see the cleat when the tabletop is attached later. See the Notch Detail in **4–21** for reference.

3 Cut the stretchers (H) to size. Cut tenons on the ends of the stretchers to fit snug inside the mortises in the legs. See the Tenon Detail in **4–15** for reference. Next, cut or rout ⅛" chamfers on the ends of the tenons, as shown on the drawing.

4 Glue and clamp the stretchers between the end frames, making sure to keep the frames square to the stretchers.

Edge-Join Pieces for a Solid-Stock Top

1 Cut four pieces of 1¹⁄₁₆" stock to 5¾" wide × 47" long. Joint the edges of the four boards so that each measures 5⅝" wide.

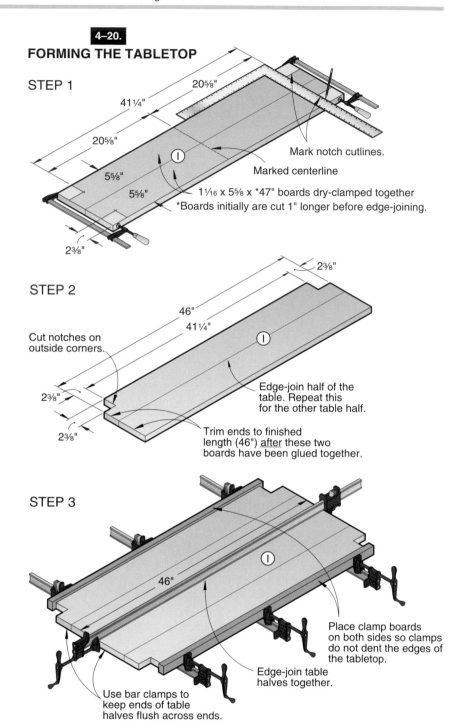

4–20.
FORMING THE TABLETOP

STEP 1

41¼"
20⅝"
20⅝"
5⅝"
5⅝"
2⅜"

Mark notch cutlines.
Marked centerline
1¹⁄₁₆ x 5⅝ x *47" boards dry-clamped together
*Boards initially are cut 1" longer before edge-joining.

STEP 2

46"
41¼"
2⅜"
2⅜"
2⅜"

Cut notches on outside corners.

Edge-join half of the table. Repeat this for the other table half.

Trim ends to finished length (46") after these two boards have been glued together.

STEP 3

46"

Place clamp boards on both sides so clamps do not dent the edges of the tabletop.

Edge-join table halves together.

Use bar clamps to keep ends of table halves flush across ends.

Note: Because of the weight and size of the tabletop, we found it more manageable to band-saw the notches before edge-joining the corner boards.

2 Mark a centerline across two of the boards. Measuring from the center out (you need to do this because the boards are cut long at this point), mark the loca-

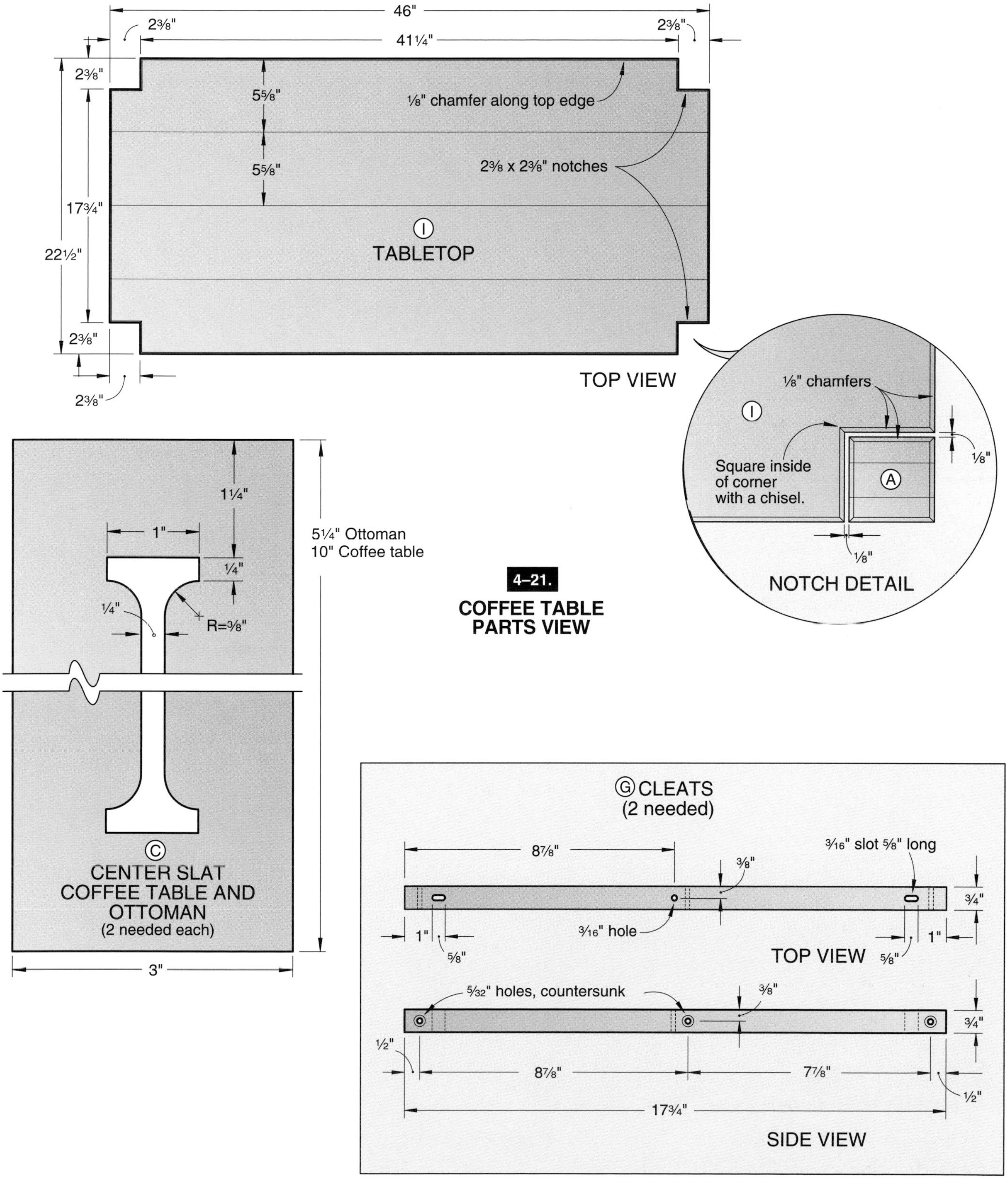
46"
41¼"
2⅜"
2⅜"
2⅜"
17¾"
22½"
2⅜"
2⅜"
5⅝"
5⅝"
⅛" chamfer along top edge
2⅜ x 2⅜" notches
I
TABLETOP
TOP VIEW
⅛" chamfers
I
Square inside of corner with a chisel.
A
⅛"
⅛"
NOTCH DETAIL
1¼"
1"
¼"
¼"
R=⅜"
5¼" Ottoman
10" Coffee table
C
CENTER SLAT COFFEE TABLE AND OTTOMAN
(2 needed each)
3"
G CLEATS
(2 needed)
8⅞"
3⁄16" slot ⅝" long
⅜"
¾"
1"
⅝"
3⁄16" hole
1"
⅝"
TOP VIEW
5⁄32" holes, countersunk
⅜"
¾"
½"
8⅞"
7⅞"
½"
17¾"
SIDE VIEW

4–21.
COFFEE TABLE PARTS VIEW

tions of the notches on one of the boards. Now, as shown in Step 1 of **4–20**, clamp two of the boards together, aligning the centerlines. Use a framing square to transfer the notch locations onto the second board. Remove the clamps, and band-saw the notches in each board to shape.

3 Edge-join one notched board against a second unnotched board, keeping the surfaces flush. See Step 2 of **4–20** for reference. Repeat this procedure for the remaining two boards.

4 Remove the clamps and scrape off the excess glue. Crosscut the ends of both table halves for a 46"-long finished length, so that the notches measure 2⅜" long. Now, being careful to keep the ends and notches aligned, as shown in Step 3 of **4–20**, glue and clamp the two tabletop halves together, again checking to see that the surfaces are flush. After the glue dries, remove the clamps, scrape off the excess glue, and sand the tabletop smooth.

5 Rout a ⅛" chamfer along the top of the tabletop (I). On the inside corners of the notches, you'll need to use a sharp chisel to square-up the chamfer.

Finish-Sand, Stain, and Add a Clear Coat to the Table

1 Finish-sand the table base and tabletop. (Sand with 100-,

150-, and finally 220-grit sand-paper, using a bright light, as, for example, a halogen, at a low angle to check the surfaces for sanding marks. Or check for sanding marks by lightly damp-ening the surface with lacquer or paint thinner, and then taking a close look at it.)

2 Place a blanket on your workbench top, and place the tabletop (I) upside down on the blanket. Center the base (also upside down) on the tabletop, keeping the gaps around the notches even. Using the holes and slots in the leg cleats as guides, drill pilot holes into the bottom side of the tabletop, and screw the assemblies together, as shown in **4–19**, as shown on *page 51*. Center the screws in the slots, tighten them, and then back them off about half a revolution. You want the screws to be able to

move back and forth in the slots as the tabletop expands and contracts with seasonal changes in the humidity.

3 Stain as desired. (We used a "provincial" color, a good choice for imitating that time period.) Or, see how to produce a fumeless Arts and Crafts finish on *page 29*. Apply the finish. (We brushed on several coats of satin polyurethane.)

Make the Ottoman

Using a construction procedure like that of the coffee table, build the Ottoman. See **4–21** on *page 53* for part C. See the Cushion Parts View on *page 57* for the material layout for the cushion. See the Ottoman Materials List for part sizes.

Ottoman

MATERIALS LIST FOR OTTOMAN

PART	FINISHED SIZE			Mtl.	Qty.
	T	W	L		
A* leg	2¼"	2¼"	12¼"	LO	4
B rails	¾"	2¾"	18"	O	4
C center slats	⅜"	3"	5¼"	O	2
D side slats	⅜"	1¼"	5¼"	O	4
E* spacers	⅜"	⅝"	1¼"	O	8
F* spacers	⅜"	⅝"	2½"	O	8
G stretchers	¾"	4"	24"	O	2
H cleats	¾"	¾"	19"	O	2
I slats	⅜"	1¼"	14½"	O	8

*Cut parts oversize. Trim to finished size according to the instructions.

Materials Key: LO = laminated oak; O = oak.

Supplies: #8 x 1" flathead brass wood screws; #8 x 1¼" flathead wood screws; stain; finish.

OTTOMAN CUTTING DIAGRAM

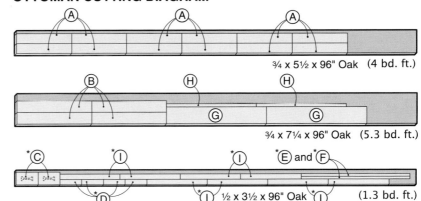

¾ x 5½ x 96" Oak (4 bd. ft.)

¾ x 7¼ x 96" Oak (5.3 bd. ft.)

½ x 3½ x 96" Oak (1.3 bd. ft.)

*Plane or resaw to thickness listed in the Materials List

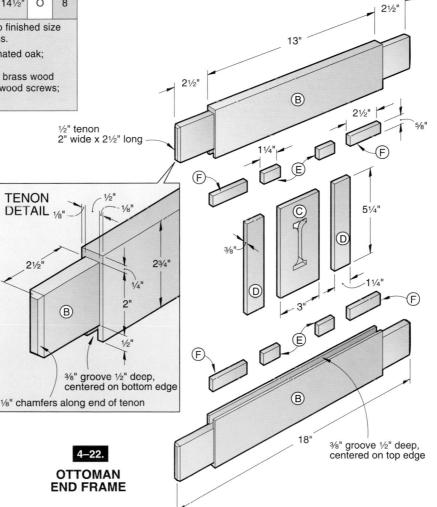

½" tenon
2" wide x 2½" long

TENON DETAIL

⅜" groove ½" deep, centered on bottom edge
⅛" chamfers along end of tenon

⅜" groove ½" deep, centered on top edge

4–22.

OTTOMAN END FRAME

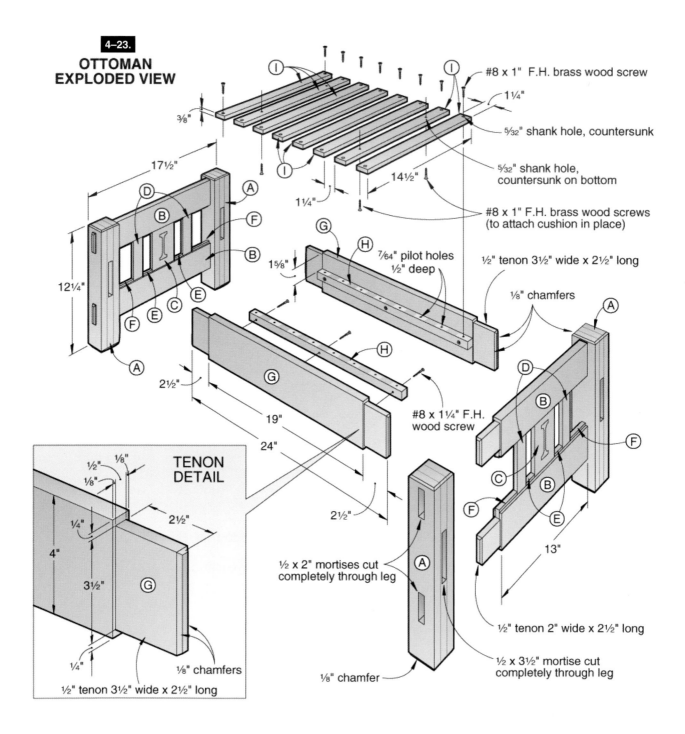

4–23.

OTTOMAN EXPLODED VIEW

#8 x 1" F.H. brass wood screw

1¼"

⁵⁄₃₂" shank hole, countersunk

⁵⁄₃₂" shank hole, countersunk on bottom

#8 x 1" F.H. brass wood screws (to attach cushion in place)

½" tenon 3½" wide x 2½" long

⅛" chamfers

⅜"

17½"

14½"

1¼"

12¼"

1⅝"

⁷⁄₆₄" pilot holes ½" deep

2½"

19"

24"

2½"

#8 x 1¼" F.H. wood screw

½ x 2" mortises cut completely through leg

½" tenon 2" wide x 2½" long

⅛" chamfer

½ x 3½" mortise cut completely through leg

13"

TENON DETAIL

⅛"

½"

⅛"

2½"

¼"

4"

3½"

¼"

⅛" chamfers

½" tenon 3½" wide x 2½" long

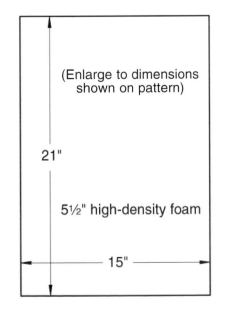

4-24.
OTTOMAN LEG
(4 needed)

2¼" 2¼"

½"

2"

3½"

½ x 2" mortises cut completely through leg

Ⓐ

3½"

5¼"

12¼"

2"

½ x 3½" mortise cut completely through leg

⅞"

½"

Legs are laminated from three ¾"-thick pieces.

⅞"

½" ⅞"

⅛" chamfer along top and bottom ends of leg

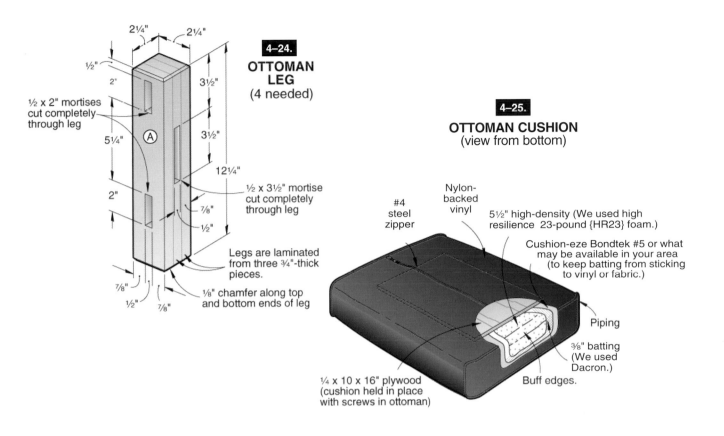

4-25.
OTTOMAN CUSHION
(view from bottom)

#4 steel zipper

Nylon-backed vinyl

5½" high-density (We used high resilience 23-pound {HR23} foam.)

Cushion-eze Bondtek #5 or what may be available in your area (to keep batting from sticking to vinyl or fabric.)

Piping

⅜" batting (We used Dacron.)

Buff edges.

¼ x 10 x 16" plywood (cushion held in place with screws in ottoman)

4-26.
CUSHION PARTS

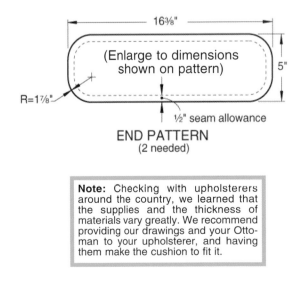

(Enlarge to dimensions shown on pattern)

21"

5½" high-density foam

15"

16⅜"

(Enlarge to dimensions shown on pattern)

5"

R=1⅞"

½" seam allowance

END PATTERN
(2 needed)

Note: Checking with upholsterers around the country, we learned that the supplies and the thickness of materials vary greatly. We recommend providing our drawings and your Ottoman to your upholsterer, and having them make the cushion to fit it.

Cushion Parts continued on next page.

4–26.

CUSHION PARTS *(continued)*

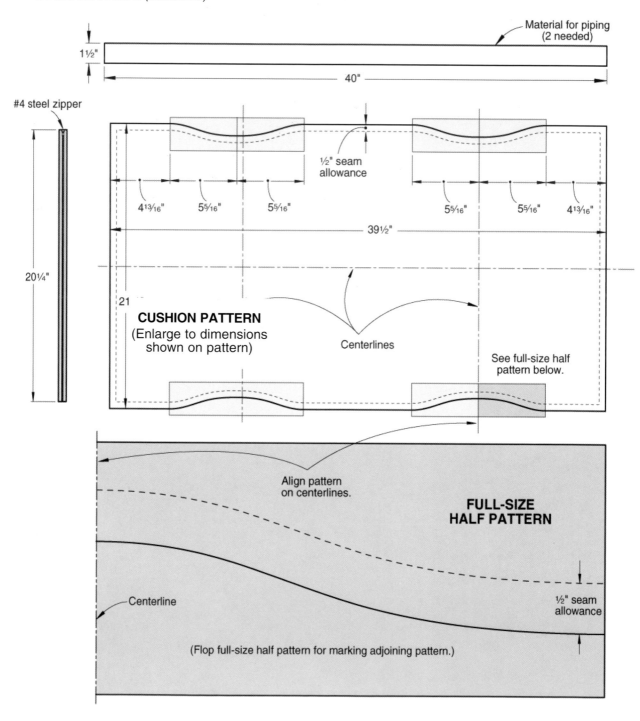

Material for piping
(2 needed)

1½"

40"

#4 steel zipper

½" seam
allowance

4¹³⁄₁₆"   5⁵⁄₁₆"   5⁵⁄₁₆"   5⁵⁄₁₆"   5⁵⁄₁₆"   4¹³⁄₁₆"

39½"

20¼"

21

CUSHION PATTERN
(Enlarge to dimensions
shown on pattern)

Centerlines

See full-size half
pattern below.

Align pattern
on centerlines.

**FULL-SIZE
HALF PATTERN**

½" seam
allowance

Centerline

(Flop full-size half pattern for marking adjoining pattern.)

Sofa. (Note the special grain on the legs.)

Matching chair

COMFORTABLE SOFA

Although authentic Arts and Crafts furniture of the early 1900s was made mostly of quartersawn white oak, for this project we chose quartersawn red oak because it's easier to cut and machine (plus less costly). To further economize, you could

CUTTING DIAGRAM FOR SOFA/CHAIR

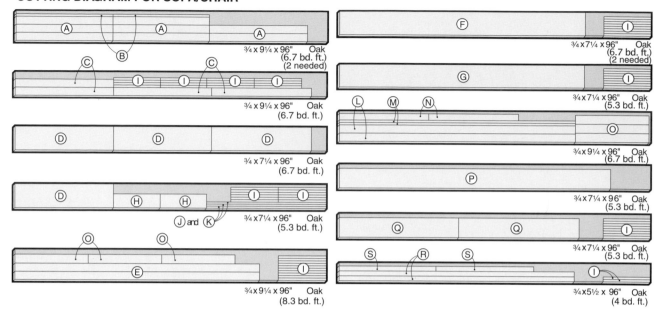

MATERIALS LIST FOR SOFA/CHAIR

| | | FINISHED SIZE | | | | | | |
| | | SOFA | | | | CHAIR | | |
PART	T	W	L	Mtl.	Qty.	L	Qty
A* leg outer wraps	¾"	2"	29¼"	O	16	29¼"	16
B* leg cores	¾"	¾"	29¼"	O	4	29¼"	4
C* **end frame upper rails	1¼"	2¼"	30½"	LO	2	30½	2
D* **end frame lower rails	1¼"	7"	30½"	LO	2	30½"	2
E* **upper back rail	1¼"	2¼"	75½"	LO	1	33½"	1
F* **lower back rail	1¼"	7"	75½"	LO	1	33½"	1
G lower front rail	¾"	7"	75½"	O	1	33½"	1
H end frame center slats	¾"	4¼"	14½"	O	2	14½"	2
I spindles	¾"	¾"	14½"	O	72	14½"	44
J spindle spacers	¾"	⅝"	¾"	O	118	¾"	82
K spindle spacers	¾"	⅝"	1¾"	O	16	1¾"	16
L seat frame supports	¾"	2½"	72¾"	O	2	30¾"	2
M seat frame cleats	¾"	¾"	72¾"	O	2	30¾	2
N spreaders	¾"	2"	27⅝"	O	3		0
O corbels	¾"	2¾"	22¾"	O	6	22¾"	6
P seat backrest	¾"	6"	83¾"	O	1	41¾"	1
Q armrests	¾"	6"	37"	O	2	37"	2
R seat-cushion frames	¾"	1½"	72½"	O	2	30½"	2
S seat-cushion end frame	¾"	1½"	28⅞"	O	2	28⅞"	2

*Cut these parts oversized. Trim to finished size according to the instructions.
**Make these parts by laminating two pieces of ¾" stock and planing to 1¼" thick.

Materials Key: LO = laminated oak; O = oak
Supplies: #8 x 1¼" flathead wood screws; #8 x ¾" roundhead wood screws; #10 and #20 biscuits; 1½" pocket screws; ¼" dowels 1½" long; stain; clear finish; 2" seat webbing 52' long; and 46 seat-webbing clips. For a complete listing of the upholstery supplies, see *page 69.*

make the parts that don't show (L, M, N, R, S and the inner laminations of D and F) from plainsawn red oak.

The following pages show you how to build the sofa. To make the chair simply shorten parts E, F, G, L, M, P, and R according to the chair's length dimensions given in the Materials List. If you plan to build both the sofa and chair, cut and machine the matching parts at the same time.

And don't be worried about upholstering the two pieces. *Pages 68 to 74* contain instructions for a no-sew technique that was used to upholster the pieces. Or, you can take the dimensions and drawings to a professional.

Construction techniques begin on *page 62.*

4–27. SOFA EXPLODED VIEW

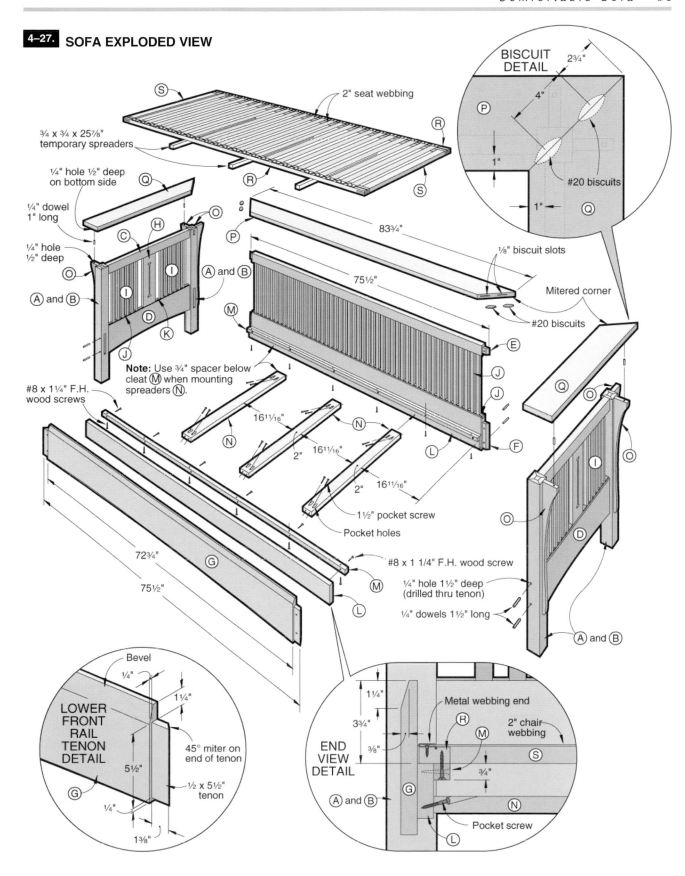

BISCUIT DETAIL
2¾"
4"
1"
1"
#20 biscuits

2" seat webbing

¾ x ¾ x 25⅞" temporary spreaders

¼" hole ½" deep on bottom side

¼" dowel 1" long

¼" hole ½" deep

83¾"

⅛" biscuit slots

Mitered corner

#20 biscuits

75½"

Note: Use ¾" spacer below cleat M when mounting spreaders N.

#8 x 1¼" F.H. wood screws

16¹¹/₁₆"

2"

16¹¹/₁₆"

2"

16¹¹/₁₆"

1½" pocket screw

Pocket holes

72¾"

75½"

#8 x 1 1/4" F.H. wood screw

¼" hole 1½" deep (drilled thru tenon)

¼" dowels 1½" long

A and B

LOWER FRONT RAIL TENON DETAIL
Bevel
¼"
1¼"
5½"
45° miter on end of tenon
½ x 5½" tenon
¼"
1⅜"
G

END VIEW DETAIL
1¼"
3¾"
⅜"
Metal webbing end
2" chair webbing
¾"
Pocket screw
A and B
G
L

Make the Legs

1 From ¾" stock 30" long, cut 16 leg outer wraps (A) to 2½" wide and four leg cores (B) to ¾" square. Set your tablesaw blade at a precise 45° angle and bevel-rip one edge of each part A face-side up.

Note: To get great-looking legs, you may want to practice the next two steps with scrap stock.

2 Using the setup shown in **4–28**, bevel-rip the other edge for a final width of 2¼".

3 Surround each core (B) with four outer wraps (A), and check the miter fit, as shown in **4–29**. Cut the core equally across its width and thickness until the miters close up.

4 Apply glue to the beveled edges and inside face of each outer wrap (A), assemble them to the leg cores, and wrap masking tape around them to hold everything in place. Clamp all four sides, using clamp pads to avoid marring the wood. When dry, cut each leg to 29¼" long.

5 Lay out the mortise locations on the legs according to **4–27** and **4–30**. Note that the front legs have only one mortise for an end frame upper rail (C). Mark the ends of the legs to keep straight their locations on the sofa ("front/right" for example).

6 Using a plunge router fitted with a ½" straight bit (spiral up-cuts work best), cut the

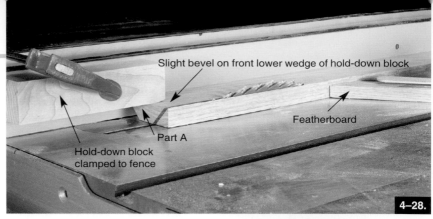

Slight bevel on front lower wedge of hold-down block

Featherboard

Part A

Hold-down block clamped to fence

4–28.

To rip the second beveled edge on the leg outer wraps, clamp a hold-down block in back of the blade and a featherboard in front of the blade.

1⅜"-deep mortises. You also could cut the mortises with a series of ½" holes made with your drill press. Or, check out the process on *page 25* of Chapter 2 for hand-chiseling the mortises.

7 Square up the mortise ends with a chisel and mallet. (If you cut the mortises with a drill bit, you'll need to square the mortise sides also.)

8 Rout a ¼" chamfer around the bottom ends of the legs.

9 Mark and drill the ¼" holes through the mortise wall where shown in **4–30**. Use a drill-press for accuracy—these holes will hold the tenon pins.

Make the Rails

1 Laminate ¾" stock to make rail stock (C, D, E, F). Add ¼" to the width and length dimensions in the Materials List so you can trim to size later. To economize, you can use plain-sawn red oak for the inside lamination of the lower rails (D, F). Plane each rail to a final thickness of 1¼".

4–29.

Wrap masking tape around the leg assemblies (A, B) to check the fit of the miters. This core is too big.

2 Cut all of the rails (C–G) to the sizes given in the Materials List. Mark the face side of each rail along with its part letter.

3 With a dado set, cut a ¾" groove, ½"-deep, centered on the bottom edge of C and E and along the top edge of D and F. Use featherboards to hold the rails tight against your saw's fence.

4 Replace the dado set with a crosscutting blade set ¼" high. Adjust the fence 1⅜" from the side of the teeth furthest from the fence. Cut the two ¼" tenon shoulders on G, as shown in the Lower Front Rail Tenon Detail in **4–27**. Use the same setup to cut the single ¼" shoulder in D and F, as shown in the Lower Back And End Rail Tenon Detail in **4–35**,

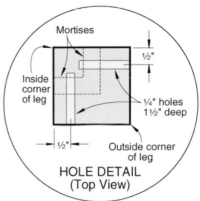

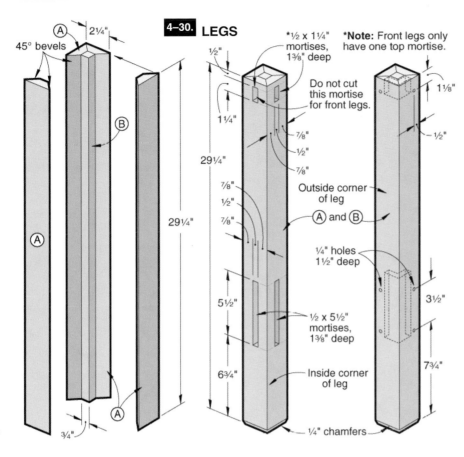

4–30. LEGS

*½ x 1¼" mortises, 1⅜" deep

Note: Front legs only have one top mortise.

45° bevels

2¼"

Do not cut this mortise for front legs.

Outside corner of leg

Ⓐ and Ⓑ

¼" holes 1½" deep

½ x 5½" mortises, 1⅜" deep

Inside corner of leg

¼" chamfers

HOLE DETAIL (Top View)

Mortises

Inside corner of leg

¼" holes 1½" deep

Outside corner of leg

7 With the blade bevel set at 45°, cut beveled ends on the tenons. Use a stopblock, as shown in **4–33**, on *page 64*. The bevel cut should not shorten the length of the tenon.

8 Angle your tablesaw blade to 17°, adjust your fence ⅜" from the blade, and cut the chamfer along the top edge of the lower front rail (G). Use a featherboard to keep the back face of the rail tight against the fence.

9 Make a mark ¾" up from the bottom edge at the center of each of the lower rails. Use a fairing stick to lay out an arc, as shown in **4–31**. Saw just outside this line with a jigsaw or bandsaw, and sand up to it with a drum sander.

on *page 65*. Use your miter gauge to keep the rails square to the blade, your fence as a work stop, and a support for the long pieces, as shown in **4–32**, on *page 64*.

5 Use the same setup, but vary the blade height to ⅜", ½", and 1¼" accordingly, to cut the remaining tenon shoulders.

6 Install a ¾"-wide dado set, and adjust it for a ¼"-deep cut. Adjust the fence 1⁵⁄₁₆" from the side of the teeth furthest from the fence. Remove the material between the ¼" shoulder cuts and the end of the rail. Adjust the height of the dado set accordingly

to repeat this step for the ⅜", ½", and 1¼" shoulders.

If you're working by yourself, you may find it hard to make the edge cuts in the long rails. In that case, use your bandsaw and the setup shown in **4–34**, on *page 64*.

4–31.

Ⓓ and Ⓖ

⅜ x ¾" fairing stick

¾"

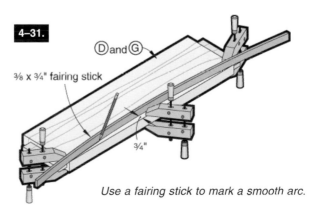

Use a fairing stick to mark a smooth arc.

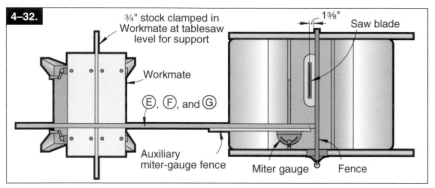

Use a supporting table to help cut tenons on long workpieces.

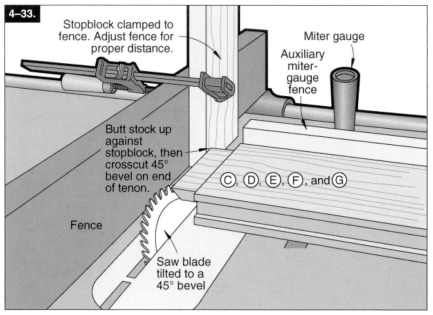

Beveling the tenon ends.

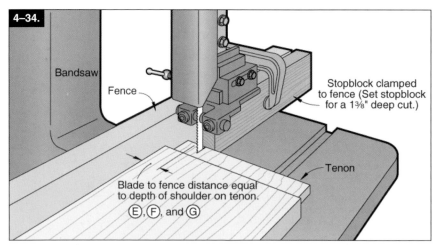

Remove the tenon waste with a bandsaw.

10 Dry-clamp the legs and rails to check for fit. Fine-tune the tenon sizes as required. Leave the assembly clamped together for now.

Saw the Slats, Spindles, and Spacers

1 Cut the end frame center slats (H) to thickness and width according to the Materials List. Determine their length by measuring between the bottoms of the end-rail grooves and subtracting ¹⁄₁₆". Now cut the center slats to length.

2 Enlarge the I-beam slat pattern (**4–38**), on *page 67*, to full size; then center and apply it to the slats. You can use a ¼" straight bit in a router table for the straight part of the pattern, and scrollcut the ends.

3 Cut a ¾ × ¾ × 14½" spindle (I). Adjust its width so it fits loosely and slides back and forth in the rail grooves. Adjust its length so you can tip it into the grooves in the upper and lower rails. Cut 71 more spindles just like it.

4 Cut two 6' lengths of ⅝ × ¾" stock for the spacers (J, K). Cut 118 spacers (J) to ¾" long. Be careful not to cut them too long—it's best to err on the side of being a hair short.

5 Finish-sand all of the parts you've made so far.

Assemble the Parts

1 Disassemble the dry-clamped frame, and glue and clamp the end frames (A/B, C, D). See **4–35**. Put the center slats (H) into place during the assembly, but do not glue them.

Note: Perform the next two steps on both end frames.

2 After the glue dries, stand the end frame upright and clamp it to your bench to keep it from falling over. Tip into position six spindles on both sides of the slat.

3 Center the slat and place glued spacers (K) on both sides of the slat, in the bottom groove only. Be sure to orient the spacers so they stand ⅝" high,

not ¾" high. Glue the spacers (J) into the bottom groove and between the spindles. Measure the length that remains for the spacers (K) at both ends of the groove. Trim these spacers and glue them in place. After the glue dries, turn the end frame upside down and glue spacers into the other groove in the same way.

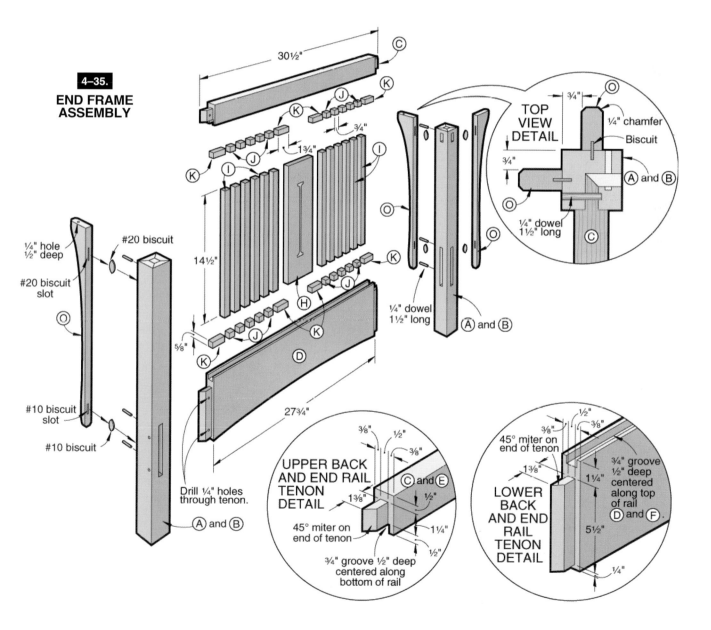

4–35.
END FRAME ASSEMBLY

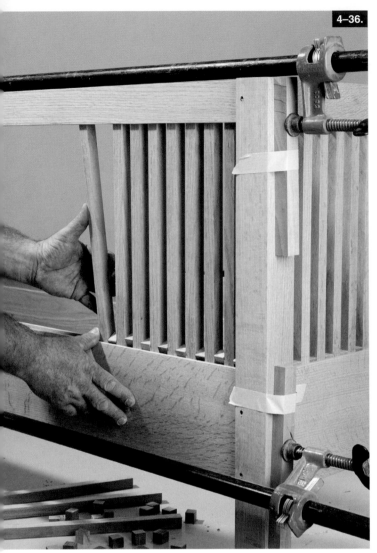

Dry-fit the back spindles and spacers, and then cut the spacers at both ends to the same length.

longer, so that you have equal-length spacers at both ends. Glue all of the spacers into the bottom and top grooves as you did with the end frames.

6 Using the ¼" leg holes as guides, drill ¼" holes 1½" deep through the tenons. Cut 22 pieces of ¼" dowel 1½" long, and sand a slight chamfer on one end of each dowel. Apply a small amount of glue to each hole, and insert the dowel, chamfer-end first. Leave just enough of the dowel protruding so you can sand it flush after the glue dries.

Make a Few More Parts, and You're Nearly Done

1 Cut the seat frame supports (L) and seat frame cleats (M) according to the Materials List. Glue and clamp the supports to the lower long rails, where shown in the End View Detail in **4–27**, on *page 61*. Attach the cleats to the supports with glue and countersunk screws (#8 wood screws require ⁵⁄₁₆" shank holes and ⁷⁄₆₄" pilot holes).

2 Cut the three spreaders (N), drill the pocket holes, and attach the spreaders with pocket screws. (Most woodworking catalogs or retail woodworking suppliers sell pocket hole jigs.)

3 Enlarge the corbel pattern in **4–37** to full size; then use it to cut the six corbels (O) to shape. Sand smooth, and rout the curved edges with a ¼" chamfer bit. (See the Top View Detail in **4–35**, on *page 65*.) Cut centered biscuit slots on the long flat edge, and drill a centered ¼" hole in the top.

4 Transfer the biscuit-slot locations to the legs, and cut centered biscuit slots in the legs. (See **4–35**.) Glue and clamp the corbels into position, flush with the tops of the legs.

5 Cut to size and miter to length the seat backrest (P) and armrest (Q). Cut biscuit slots into the mitered ends, as shown in the Biscuit Detail in **4–27**, on *page 61*. Glue and clamp the back and arms together using one long pipe clamp along the

4 Dry-fit the long rails (E, F, G) and the end-frame assemblies. There may be some glue squeeze-out in the end-frame mortises. Adjust the tenons on the long rails for a tight fit. Then glue and clamp the long rails into the mortises.

5 Place the spindles (I) and spacers (J) into the grooves between the back rails, as shown in **4–36**, but don't use glue. To make it easier to remove the spacers later, position them into the groove, as shown in the photo so they don't touch the bottom. Trim the end spacers, or make new ones slightly

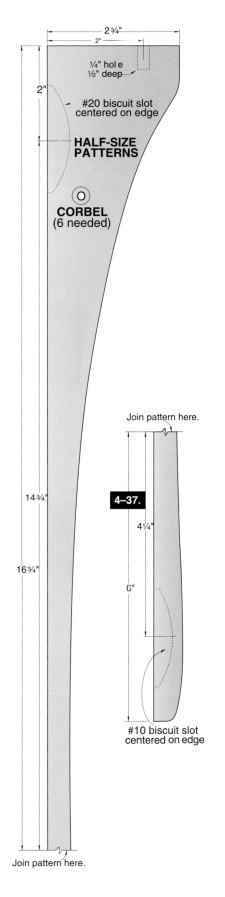

2¾"

2"

¼" hole
½" deep

~ #20 biscuit slot
centered on edge

**HALF-SIZE
PATTERNS**

◯

CORBEL
(6 needed)

2"

14¾"

16¾"

Join pattern here.

4–37.

4¼"

6"

#10 biscuit slot
centered on edge

Join pattern here.

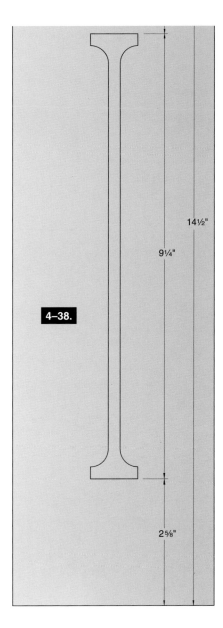

4–38.

14½"

9¼"

2⅝"

length of the seat backrest, and two shorter pipe clamps along the lengths of the armrests. Finish-sand the assembly.

6 Place ¼" dowel centers in the holes in the ends of the corbels. Carefully locate the armrest assembly in place, again referring to the Biscuit Detail in **4–27**, on *page 61* for exact positioning. Tap down to mark the dowel centers on the underside of the armrests.

7 Drill ¼" holes ½" deep at the dowel-center marks. Place ⅞"-long glued dowels into each hole. Glue and clamp the armrest assembly to the upper rails.

Make the Seat Frame

1 Cut the seat frame parts (R, S) to size according to the Materials List. Cut a centered ⅛" groove ⅛" deep along the length of the front and rear frames (R), as indicated in **4–39**. Cut the tongues and slots that join the seat frame using your bandsaw, as shown in **4–40**. Glue and clamp together, making sure the frame is square by measuring across its diagonals.

2 Cut 23 pieces of 2" webbing 26⅝" long. Install a seat-webbing clip to both ends of each piece by squeezing them together with a bench vise.

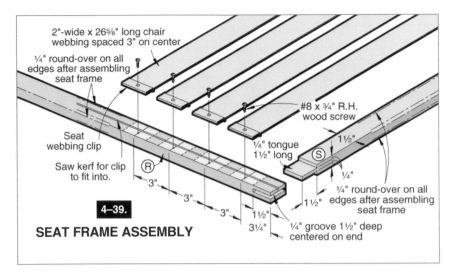

2"-wide x 26⅝" long chair
webbing spaced 3" on center

¼" round-over on all
edges after assembling
seat frame

Seat
webbing clip

Saw kerf for clip
to fit into.

#8 x ¾" R.H.
wood screw

¼" tongue
1½" long

R

1½"

S

¼"

¼" round-over on all
edges after assembling
seat frame

3"

3"

3"

1½"

3¼"

¼" groove 1½" deep
centered on end

4–39.

SEAT FRAME ASSEMBLY

5 Stretch each rubber web, and clamp it to the opposite side of the frame. Attach with screws and remove the clamp.

6 Finish the sofa. We applied one coat of dark walnut Danish oil finish topped with two coats of antique oil finish.

Apply the upholstery to the seat as described starting below. Place the upholstered seat frame into the sofa and screw it to the cleats (M). Remove the temporary spreaders.

4–40.

**CUTTING A
TONGUE-AND-SLOT
JOINT**

Tongue cuts 1 and 2

Blade positions

S

R

Slot cuts 3 and 4

Cut shoulders using tablesaw.

**TONGUE-AND-SLOT
DETAIL**

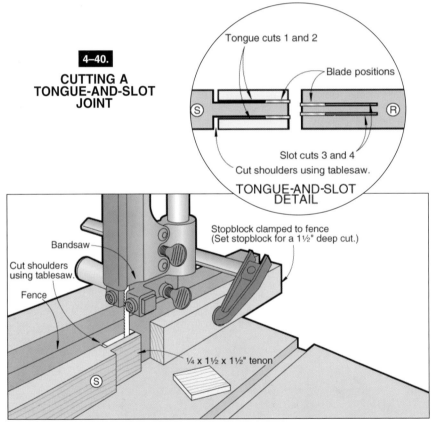

Bandsaw

Cut shoulders
using tablesaw.

Fence

Stopblock clamped to fence
(Set stopblock for a 1½" deep cut.)

S

¼ x 1½ x 1½" tenon

No-Sew Upholstery

As woodworkers, we know how to operate most any tool made for cutting, shaping, or fastening wood. But if you put many of us at the throttle of a sewing machine, we might as well be at the controls of the space shuttle.

With that in mind, we decided to seek a solution. Here and on the following pages, we'll show you the method we came up with for assembling good-looking, comfortable cushions using only tools and techniques that we as woodworkers can quickly master.

Note: In this section we'll show you step-by-step how to make a back cushion for the Arts and Crafts-style sofa or chair on the preceding pages. After making the back cushion, you'll find it a breeze to make the seat cushion.

3 Locate, drill, and screw one end of all of the webs along the length of the front or rear frame (R), making sure the tab of each clip is in the ⅛" groove.

4 Cut three ¾ x ¾ x 25⅞" temporary spreaders to fit between the front and rear frames (R). Place them equally spaced into the frame. These prevent the frame from bowing during the next two steps.

SOFA AND CHAIR CUSHION MATERIALS

PART	FINISHED SIZE			MTL.	QTY.
	T	**W**	**L**		
SOFA					
SEAT CUSHIONS (1 Required)	6"	28⅞"	72½"	HF	1
	1"	36"	73"	UB	3
	—	46"	92"	UF	1
BACK CUSHIONS (2 Required)	3"	9½"	36"	HF	2
	3"	14¼"	36"	HF	2
	1"	14"	36"	UB	4
	1"	19"	36"	UB	2
	—	30"	60"	UF	2
	—	15"	42"	UF	2
	½"	12"	36"	PW	2
	⅛"	11½"	35½"	PW	2
CHAIR					
SEAT CUSHIONS (1 Required)	6"	28⅞"	30½"	HF	1
	1"	36"	31"	UB	3
	—	46"	50"	UF	1
BACK CUSHIONS (1 Required)	3"	9½"	30"	HF	1
	3"	14¼"	30"	HF	1
	1"	14"	30"	UB	2
	1"	19"	30"	UB	1
	—	30"	50"	UF	1
	—	15"	33"	UF	1
	½"	12"	30"	PW	1
	⅛"	11½"	29½"	PW	1

Materials Key: HF = high-density foam; UB = upholstery batting; UF = upholstery fabric; PW = plywood.
Supplies: ⅜" staples; ⅝" brads; spray adhesive for foam; cloth-backed double-faced tape.

Tools and Fabric

Your woodshop probably contains all of the tools you'll need, such as a bandsaw for slicing through high-density foam. A pneumatic wide-crown stapler and brad nailer are mighty helpful, but not essential. You'll find the fabric, foam, and batting at fabric and upholstery shops.

When selecting the fabric, which typically comes in rolls 54 to 55" wide, keep in mind how you will orient it on the seat and back cushions. For example, with the sofa on *page 59*, the pattern of the fabric allowed us to run the material lengthwise on the seat cushion. As a result, we didn't have to stitch the fabric together to span the length of the seat. But with the fabric shown on the following pages, which has a striped design running along its length, the stripes need to be oriented across the width of the upholstered seat cushion for best appearance. So, if you select a fabric like this, you will need to find someone who can stitch two pieces of fabric together to span the length of the seat.

Cut and Assemble the Foam

For the sofa and chair cushions we chose a high-density foam purchased at an upholstery-supply shop. It provides a firm cushion, and holds up better over time than a lower-density foam.

To cut the foam, mark its width and length dimensions according to the list at left. Use a permanent marker and straightedge.

Although the foam pieces for the seat cushion require only square cuts, the back cushions call for some angle cuts. The foam offers little cutting resistance, so even a low-powered bandsaw will help you get the job done. Here's how to go about it.

For the sofa backs, lay out the edge and face marks shown in Seat Back (Rear Pieces) drawing in **4–46**, on *page 71,* on a piece of 3 × 9½ × 36" foam. (If you're building the chair, make the same marks on the 3 × 9½ × 30" piece.)

Angle your bandsaw table to 22° and make the beveled cuts, as shown in **4–41**. Slow the feed rate as you exit the cut—this helps

Cutting the foam for a back cushion with the bandsaw table tilted.

4–41.

4–42.

Arrange the rear pieces for the seat back in a wedge shape, and adhere them with a spray adhesive compatible with foam.

4–43.

Align and adhere the front piece of the seat back to the glued-up rear pieces.

4–44.

Stop your staples 2" from the end of the ½" plywood cushion panel when tacking the fabric in place.

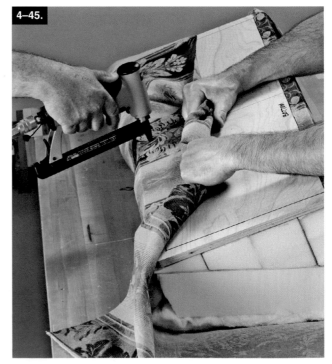

4–45.

Enlist the help of a friend to pull the fabric uniformly taut along the length of the cushion as you staple the fabric.

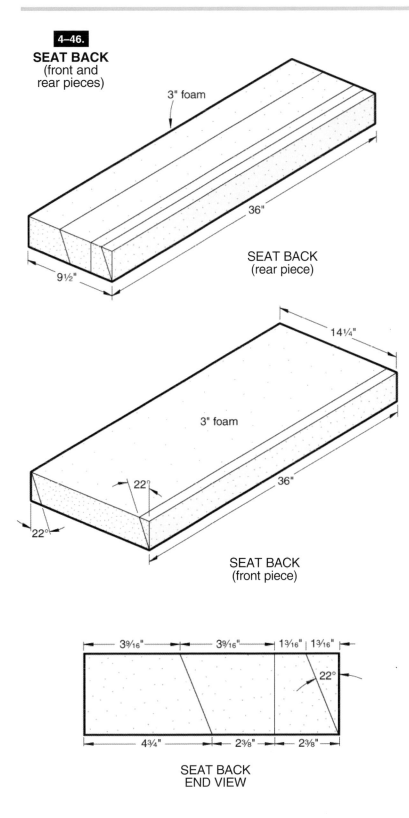

4–46.
SEAT BACK
(front and
rear pieces)

3" foam

36"

9½"

SEAT BACK
(rear piece)

14¼"

3" foam

22°

36"

22°

SEAT BACK
(front piece)

3⁹⁄₁₆"   3⁹⁄₁₆"   1³⁄₁₆" 1³⁄₁₆"

22°

4¾"   2⅜"   2⅜"

SEAT BACK
END VIEW

prevent the blade from "grabbing" the foam at the end of the cut and pulling it into the saw's throat plate.

Also cut the long edges of the 3 × 14¼ × 36" piece at a 22° angle, as shown in the Seat Back (Front Piece) in **4–46**. (Substitute the 3 × 14¼ × 30" piece if you're making the chair.) Return the table to 0° (horizontal), and make the single cut that's 90° to the faces of the rear piece.

Now, you need to glue these foam pieces together in the shape shown in **4–47**. To do this, arrange the rear pieces on a benchtop, and adhere them together in a wedge shape, as shown in **4–42**. We used a spray adhesive. Use the same glue to adhere this wedge on top of the front piece, as shown in **4–43**.

4–47.
**SEAT BACK
FOAM GLUE-UP**

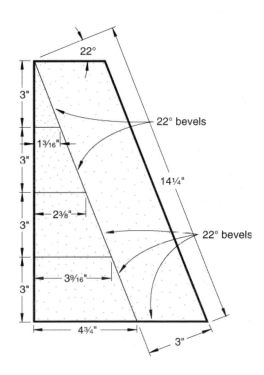

22°

3"

22° bevels

1³⁄₁₆"

3"

14¼"

2⅜"

3"

22° bevels

3⁹⁄₁₆"

3"

4¾"   3"

Cover the Foam with Batting and Fabric

Cut the ½ × 12 × 36" plywood cushion panel. Sand a ½" radius on each corner, and mark the stapling guidelines, centerline, and bottom edge, as shown in the Panel Views drawing in **4–48**.

Cut a 30 × 60" piece of upholstery fabric and staple one long edge along the stapling guideline on the bottom edge of the cushion panel, as shown in **4–44**. Use the centerline to center any design elements of your fabric. The fabric design elements should be placed symmetrically across the length of the cushion.

Note: Depending on the fabric design, you may have to take into account how the fabric will be positioned on the seat cushion before determining its best position on the back cushions. The design elements on the seat and backs should align in the finished sofa or chair.

Place the ⅜" staples every inch or two, and keep them at least ¾" from the edge of the plywood panel. Keep the end staples about 2" from the ends of the panel.

Now, arrange the foam, three pieces of upholstery batting, and the cushion panel, as shown in the Back-Cushion Assembly drawing in **4–49**. Place this assemblage, with the cushion-panel-up, on a clean benchtop.

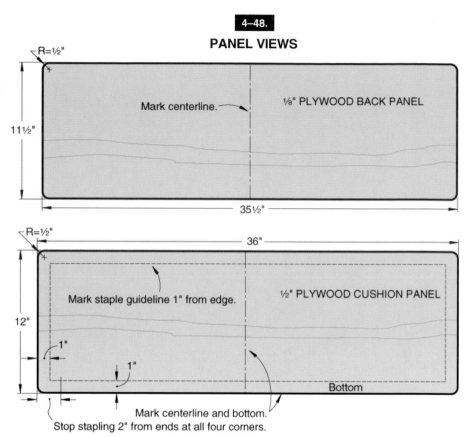

4–48.

PANEL VIEWS

R=½"

11½"

Mark centerline.

⅛" PLYWOOD BACK PANEL

35½"

R=½"

36"

12"

Mark staple guideline 1" from edge.

½" PLYWOOD CUSHION PANEL

1"

1"

Bottom

Mark centerline and bottom.
Stop stapling 2" from ends at all four corners.

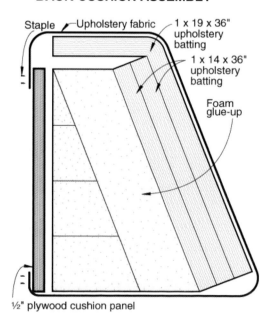

4–49.

BACK-CUSHION ASSEMBLY

Staple   Upholstery fabric   1 x 19 x 36"
upholstery batting

1 x 14 x 36"
upholstery batting

Foam
glue-up

½" plywood cushion panel

This is a good time to call in a helper if you have one. Have the helper pull the fabric taut as you staple it along the top edge of the cushion panel, as shown in **4–45**. Place the first staple in the center, being careful to center the same fabric design element that you centered at the bottom of the panel. Staple toward the ends, having your helper pull the fabric to a uniform tautness as you move along the length. Again, stop the stapling when you come within 2" of the ends.

Follow the same procedure to pull and staple the fabric to the short edges of the panel. You should be able to pull out any wrinkles in the fabric. As before, keep the end staples 2" from the edge of the panel.

To fold the fabric at the corners, take the excess fabric at the ends of the cushions and tuck it under the fabric at the top or bottom of the cushion, as shown in **4–49**. Staple the fabric at the corners. If you don't like the way the corner looks, just pull a few staples and try again. Cut away all excess fabric outside of the staples.

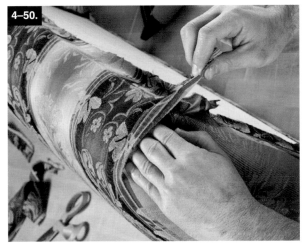

Use one hand to tuck the excess side fabric under the top or bottom fabric. Staple down and trim the extra material.

Align the back panel on the fabric, and trim the fabric so it wraps the panel edges and covers the double-faced tape.

Miter-cut the fabric at the back-panel corners, and leave enough material to fold over the point of the corner.

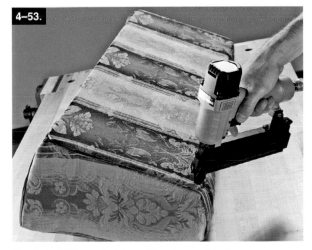

Brads hold the upholstered back panel to the upholstered cushion panel. The brad heads disappear below the fabric.

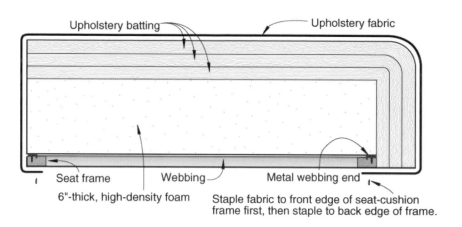

4-54.

SEAT ASSEMBLY

Upholstery batting — Upholstery fabric

Seat frame — Webbing — Metal webbing end

6"-thick, high-density foam — Staple fabric to front edge of seat-cushion frame first, then staple to back edge of frame.

Add a Back Panel and You'll Be Sitting Pretty

Cut the ⅛ x 11½ x 35½" plywood back panel. Sand a ½" radius on each corner, and mark the centerline, as shown in the Panel Views drawing in **4–48**.

Place cloth-backed, double-faced carpet tape along all four edges of the marked side of the panel. Lay your fabric face-side-down on a clean bench. Place the panel, marked side up, on top of the fabric. Center the back panel over the same fabric design element that you previously centered on the cushion panel.

Cut the fabric to width and length, as shown in **4–50**.

Pull the fabric taut, and adhere it to the double-faced tape along all four edges of the panel. Miter-cut the fabric at the corners, leaving some excess fabric at the point of each corner, as shown in **4–52**. Press down and stick the extra fabric to the double-faced tape.

Nail the back panel to the cushion panel with ⅝" brads, as shown in **4–53**. Place the brads every inch or two, and put three or four brads in each corner to securely hold down the wrinkled excess fabric on the nonexposed sides of both panels.

A Few Words About the Seat Cushions

After making the back cushions, you'll find it easy to assemble the seat cushions (**4–54**). Simply use the seat-cushion frame and its webbing in place of the ½" plywood cushion panel that you used with the seat back. The instructions for building the sofa show how to make the webbed seat-cushion frame. Be careful to position the fabric so its pattern aligns with the pattern on the back cushions.

Rocker

Chair

size listed in the Materials List. Lay out the rear legs, shown on **4–57**, on *page 78*. Bandsaw and sand the rear legs to the layout lines. Crosscut the top ends perpendicular to the legs' front faces.

Note: *The legs, as dimensioned, are the proper length for the armchair. If you are building the rocking chair, you will trim them to the proper length later.*

ROCKER/CHAIR

You can build either a handsome armchair or a rocker from the same basic plan presented here. This design, in quartersawn white oak, delivers the Arts and Crafts style's essential simple lines, while avoiding overbearing mass. We incorporated mortise-and-tenon joinery and laminate-bent rockers (should you go that route), but were able to sidestep many tricky details with our simplified construction. We'll also show you how to easily make the upholstered seat.

Start with the Legs

1 Plane 1¾"-thick stock to 1½" thick for the front legs (A) and the rear legs (B). To reduce waste, nest the front and rear legs, as shown on the Cutting Diagram, and then bandsaw individual leg blanks. Cut the front legs to the

2 Lay out the mortises on the front and rear legs, where shown in **4–56** (*page 77*). Note in the Materials List that these parts are plainsawn white oak. Because the edge grain of this stock displays quartersawn ray patterns, the front faces of the rear legs will display this pattern. Be sure to orient the front legs' ray-patterned faces to the front. Make certain that you have mirrored pairs of legs. See the Shop Tip on *page 77* for a layout tip. Drill the

MATERIALS LIST FOR ROCKER (AND ARMCHAIR)

PART	FINISHED SIZE				
	T	W	L	Mtl.	Qty.
A front legs	1½"	1½"	25¾"	WO	2
B rear legs	1½"	5¼"	45¹³⁄₁₆"	WO	2
C front rails	¾"	3"	21½"	QWO	2
D rear rails	¾"	3"	19¾"	QWO	2
E* backrest rails	1½"	3"	19¾"	QWO	2
F side rails	1¾"	3"	18³⁄₁₆"	QWO	2
G slats	½"	2"	19½"	QWO	4
H corner braces	¾"	2½"	5¼"	QWO	4
I arms	¾"	4"	21⅞"	QWO	2
J corbels	¾"	2"	6"	QWO	2
K* arm mortise plugs	1¼"	1¼"	⁵⁄₁₆"	QWO	2
L* leg mortise plugs	½"	2¾"	⁵⁄₁₆"	QWO	4
M* rockers	1"	1⅝"	37¾"	LQWO	2
N seat	½"	17½"	20¾"	P	1

*Parts initially cut oversize. See the instructions.
Materials Key: WO = plainsawn white oak; QWO = quartersawn white oak;
LQWO = laminated quartersawn white oak; P = plywood.
Supplies: #8 x 1" flathead wood screws (16); 8 x 1¼" flathead wood screws for leg-trimming jig (4); #8 x 1 ½" flathead wood screws (2); #8 x 2" flathead wood screws (6); #10 x 2 ½" panhead screws (4); ¾" particleboard for rocker form; spray adhesive; cushion foam; polyester quilt batting; upholstery fabric; upholstery thread; ⅜" staples; aniline dye; clear finish.
Bits and Blades: ¼" and 1" Forstner bits; 45° chamfer and ¼" straight router bits; stack dado set, ⅜" plug cutter.
Tools to Make the Cushion: Electric knife or serrated bread knife; sewing machine; staple gun.

CUTTING DIAGRAM FOR ROCKER (AND ARMCHAIR)

1¾ x 7¼ x 96" Plainsawn white oak (10.67 board feet) *Plane to the thickness listed in the Materials List.

1¾ x 3½ x 96" Quartersawn white oak (5.33 board feet)

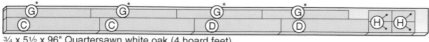

¾ x 5½ x 96" Quartersawn white oak (4 board feet)

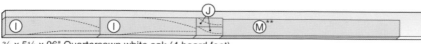

¾ x 5½ x 96" Quartersawn white oak (4 board feet)

¾ x 5½ x 96" Quartersawn white oak (4 board feet) **Resaw then plane to ¼" thick.

mortises, as shown in **4–61**, on *page 79*. Clean up the sides of the mortises, and square the ends with a chisel.

3 Chuck a chamfer bit in your table-mounted router, and rout ⅛" chamfers on the tops of the rear legs, where shown. If you are building the armchair, chamfer the bottom ends of the front legs (A) and the rear legs (B).

Make the Rails and Slats

1 Cut the front rails (C), rear rails (D), backrest rail (E) blanks, and side rails (F) to the sizes listed. Note that parts C and D are cut from ¾"-thick stock; parts E and F from 1¾"-thick stock. Set aside scrap pieces of the same thickness and width for testing your tenon cuts.

2 To cut tenons on the front rails (C) and rear rails (D), install a dado blade in your tablesaw, and attach an auxiliary extension to the miter gauge. Cut the tenons, shown on Rail Tenon detail in **4–57**, on *page 78*, on your ¾"-thick scrap, and test the fit in the legs' mortises. Then cut the tenon cheeks and shoulders on the rails.

½ x 24 x 24" Plywood

Make Layout Lines Easy to Read, Easy to Remove

Before laying out the locations of the leg mortises, cover the surface with 1½"-wide clear packaging tape. Then draw the lines on the tape with an ultra-fine-point permanent marker. The layout lines are easy to read, and peel off with the tape, as shown in 4–55, so you don't have to sand them off.

Make a mistake in your layout? Just dampen a rag with lacquer thinner, wipe away the lines, and make the necessary correction.

4–55.

3 Rout a ¼" chamfer along the edge of the upper front rail (C), where shown on **4–60**, on *page 78*. Lay out the shallow V on the bottom edge of the lower front rail (C), and bandsaw and sand to the line.

4 Without changing your saw setup, cut the tenon *shoulders* on the backrest rail (E) blanks, side rails (F), and to give you two test tenons, both ends of your 1¾"-thick scrap. Raise your dado blade to ⁵⁄₁₆", and make the first cheek cuts on these parts.

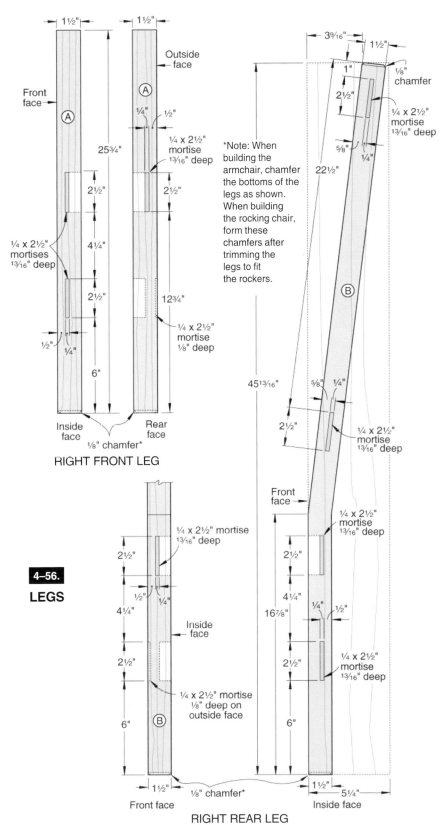

4–56.

LEGS

RIGHT FRONT LEG

RIGHT REAR LEG

*Note: When building the armchair, chamfer the bottoms of the legs as shown. When building the rocking chair, form these chamfers after trimming the legs to fit the rockers.

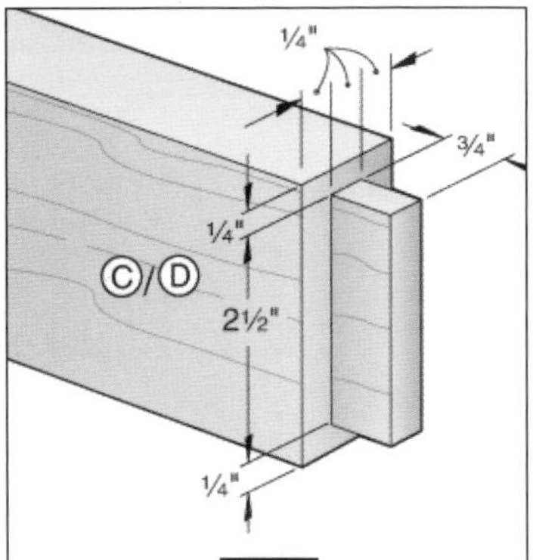
1/4"
3/4"
1/4"
C/D
2 1/2"
1/4"

4–57.
RAIL TENON DETAIL

4–58.
SLAT TENON DETAIL

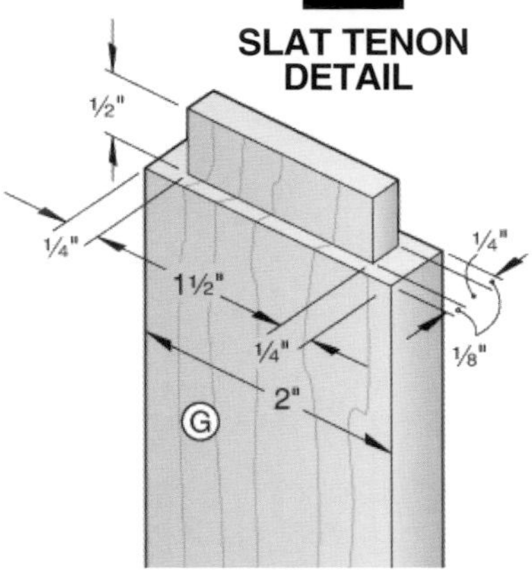
1/2"
1/4"
1 1/2"
1/4"
1/4"
1/8"
2"
G

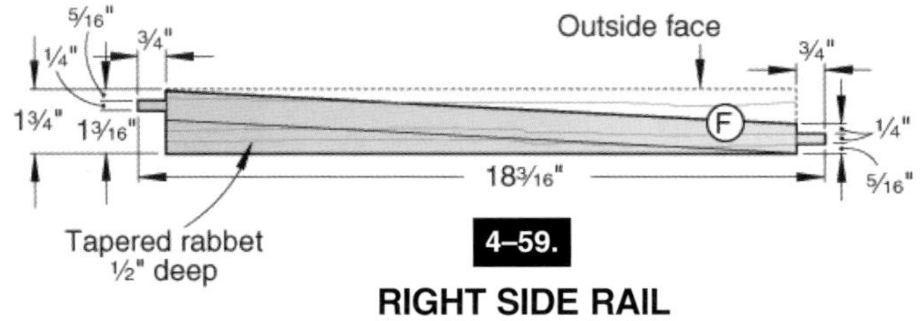
5/16"
1/4"
3/4"
Outside face
3/4"
1 3/4"
1 3/16"
F
1/4"
5/16"
18 3/16"
Tapered rabbet
1/2" deep

4–59.
RIGHT SIDE RAIL

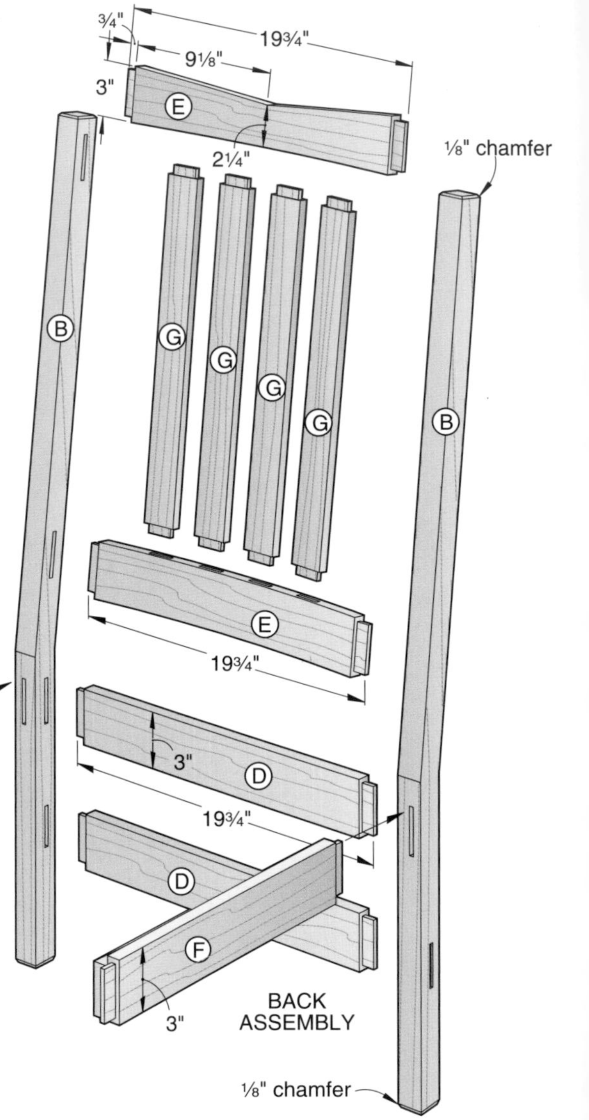
3/4"
19 3/4"
9 1/8"
3"
E
2 1/4"
1/8" chamfer
B
G
G
G
G
B
E
19 3/4"
Tapered rabbet 1/2" deep
(See 4–59 for details.)
3"
D
F
19 3/4"
18 3/16"
A
D
21 1/2"
A
F
1/4" chamfer
C
3"
BACK ASSEMBLY
2 1/4"
1/8" chamfer
C
10"
FRONT ASSEMBLY
3/4"
1/8" chamfer

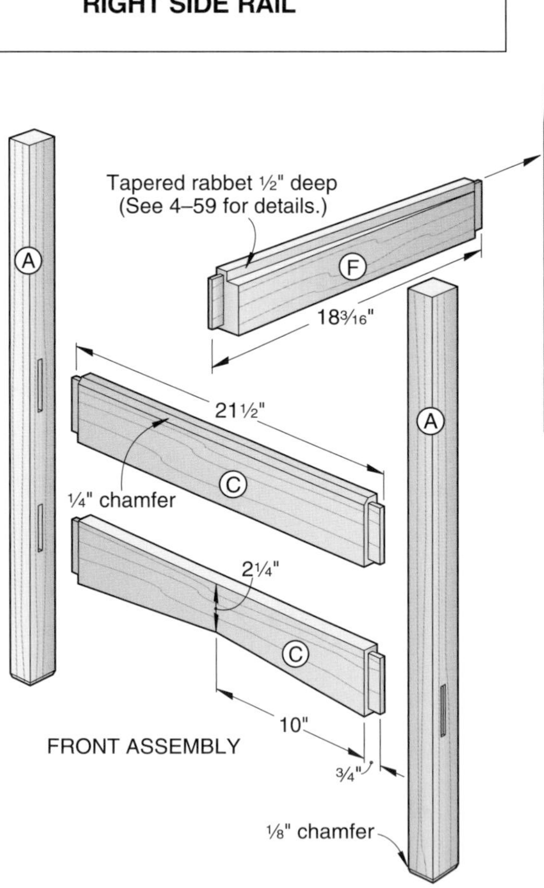

4–60.
EXPLODED VIEW

Chuck a ¼" Forstner bit in your drill press. Using the drill-press fence to position the legs, drill out the mortise slots.

With the shoulders and first cheek cut on the backrest and side rails, raise the dado blade to needed height, and cut the second cheek.

To position the backrest rails when drilling the mortises, adhere an outside waste piece to the fence with double-faced tape.

On the backrest rail blanks, make both cuts on the front faces, where shown on the Backrest Rail full-size half-patterns on *page 86*. On the side rails, make one cut on the parts' inside faces and one on the outside faces, where shown in **4–59**. Make cheek cuts at both ends of your scrap.

5 Raise the dado blade to 1³⁄₁₆", and cut a second tenon cheek in your scrap. Test the tenon's fit in the leg mortises, and make any adjustments. Cut the second tenon cheeks in the backrest (E) and side rails (F), as shown in **4–62**.

6 Make two copies of the back-rest rail full-size half-patterns on *page 86*. Using spray adhesive, adhere the patterns to the bottom edge of the top rail blank and the top edge of the bottom rail blank, joining the halves where indicated. Band-saw the rails just outside the pattern lines, and then use a random-orbit

sander to sand to the lines. Save the waste pieces.

7 Chuck a ¼" Forstner bit in your drill press, and drill the back slat mortises in the backrest rails, where shown on the patterns, and as shown in **4–63**. Clean up the sides of the mortises and square the ends with a chisel.

Sandwich the upper backrest rail between its waste pieces with double-faced tape. Draw the profile and saw to the line.

8 Band-saw the V profile in the upper backrest rail, where dimensioned in **4–60**, and as shown in **4–64**. After removing the waste pieces, sand the profile smooth.

9 To locate their tapered rabbets, pair up the two side rails (F) with the front tenons ⁵⁄₁₆" from the rails' outside faces and the rear tenons ⁵⁄₁₆" from the inside faces. Mark their inside faces and top edges. Draw the taper lines for the outside faces on their top edges, where shown in **4–59**. Band-saw to the lines, and then sand the faces smooth using a drum sander. Adjust a ⅝" dado blade in your tablesaw to cut ½" deep. Position the rip fence ¾" from the blade. With their outside faces against the fence and top edges down, make the first cut for forming the rails' tapered rabbets. Reposition the fence, and complete the rabbets. The rabbets taper from $^{15}/_{16}$" wide at the front to zero at the rear.

10 Plane material to $^{1}/_{2}$" thick for the slats (G); make an extra piece so you can test the tenon cuts. Cut the slats to the size listed in the Materials List. With a dado blade in your tablesaw, cut a tenon on your scrap, as dimensioned in **4–58**. Test the tenon's fit in the backrest rail (E) mortises. Make any necessary adjustments, and cut tenons on both ends of the slats.

Assemble the Chair

1 Glue and clamp the front rails (C) between the front legs (A), and the slats (G) between the backrest rails (E). Make certain both of these assemblies are square, by measuring the diagonals, and flat.

2 Glue and clamp the rear rails (D) and the backrest assembly (E/G) between the rear legs (B), as shown in **4–65**.

3 Join the front assembly (A/C) and the back assembly B/D/ E/G) by gluing and clamping the side rails (F) in place, where shown in **4–60**. Make certain the front legs are parallel to the straight lower portion of the rear legs. Measure diagonally between front and rear legs to check for square. Rest the assembly on a flat surface to dry.

4 Cut the corner braces (H) to the size listed. Miter the ends, where shown in **4–66**. With the faces of the miters held flat on your drill-press table, drill the countersunk $^{5}/_{32}$" holes. Turn the parts on edge, and drill the counterbored $^{5}/_{32}$" shank holes, centered on the parts' length and thickness.

5 Glue and clamp the corner braces in place, aligning their bottom edges with the rails' bottom edges, where shown in **4–67**. Using the countersunk shank holes in the braces as guides, drill pilot holes in the rails, and drive the screws.

Add Arms, Corbels, and Mortise Plugs

1 Cut two $^{3}/_{4}$ × 4 × 21$^{7}/_{8}$" blanks for the arms (I). Referring to **4–69**, on *page 82*, lay out the arms' shape and 1"-square mortise. To lay out the curves, mark the three points shown for each one. Bend a $^{1}/_{8}$"-thick strip of wood to connect the points, and then draw the curve. Make sure you have mirror-image parts. Bandsaw and sand the arms to shape. Chuck a $^{3}/_{8}$" plug cutter in your drill press, and cut two $^{3}/_{8}$"-long plugs from the edge of one of the waste pieces. You'll use these later to plug the counterbores for the screws that attach the arms to the rear legs.

Glue and clamp the backrest assembly, rear rails, and rear legs. Lay this chair back assembly on a flat surface until the glue dries.

4–65.

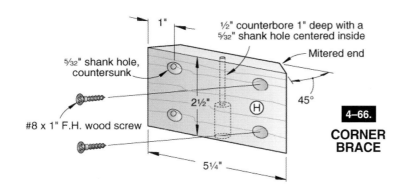

1"

½" counterbore 1" deep with a
⁵⁄₃₂" shank hole centered inside

Mitered end

⁵⁄₃₂" shank hole,
countersunk

2½"

(H)

45°

#8 x 1" F.H. wood screw

5¼"

4–66.

CORNER BRACE

them to the blanks with spray adhesive. Bandsaw and sand them to shape. Glue and clamp the corbels in place, centered on the outside face of the front legs, where shown in **4–65**.

6 Cut a 1¼ × 1¼ × 6" blank for the arm mortise plugs (K) and two ½ × 2¾ × 6" blanks for

2 Outline the mortises with a chisel. Chuck a ¼" straight bit in your handheld router, and rout the ⅛"-deep mortises close to the outlines. Finish the mortises with your chisel.

3 Drill ⁵⁄₁₆" countersunk holes, centered in the mortises. Drill ⅜" counterbores with centered ⁵⁄₃₂" countersunk holes in the arms' edges, where shown in **4–69**.

4 Draw the diagonals on the top ends of the front legs (A) to find their centers, and drill ⁷⁄₆₄" pilot holes 1⅜" deep, where shown in **4–67**. Position the arms (I), centering the shank holes in the arm mortises on the leg pilot holes. Drive the screws. Align the arms, as shown in **4–68**, and screw them to the rear legs (B). Retrieve the two ⅜" plugs cut previously, glue them into the counterbores, and sand them flush.

5 Cut blanks for the corbels (J) to the size listed. Make two copies of the corbel from the pattern on *page 86*, and adhere

4–67.

FINAL ASSEMBLY

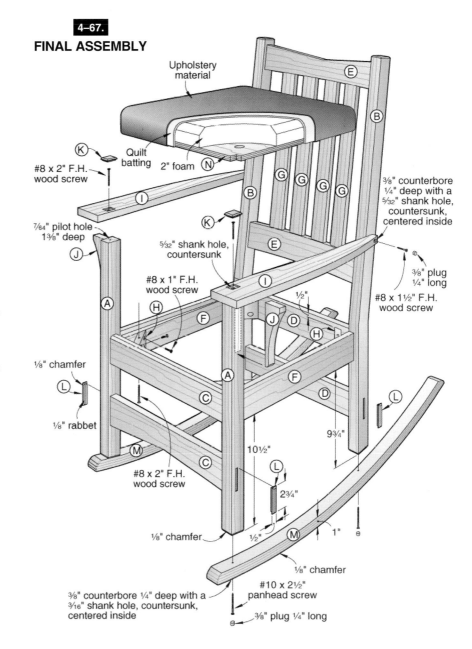

Upholstery material

(E)

(B)

(K)

Quilt batting

#8 x 2" F.H. wood screw

2" foam (N)

⅜" counterbore ¼" deep with a ⁵⁄₃₂" shank hole, countersunk, centered inside

(I)

(B)

(G) (G) (G) (G)

(K)

(E)

⁷⁄₆₄" pilot hole 1⅜" deep

(J)

⁵⁄₃₂" shank hole, countersunk

#8 x 1" F.H. wood screw

(I)

½"

⅜" plug ¼" long

#8 x 1½" F.H. wood screw

(A)

(H)

(F)

(J) (D)

(H)

⅛" chamfer

(L)

(A)

(F)

(D)

(L)

⅛" rabbet

(C)

9¾"

(M)

(C)

10½"

(L)

#8 x 2" F.H. wood screw

2¾"

(M)

1"

⅛" chamfer

½"

⅜" counterbore ¼" deep with a ³⁄₁₆" shank hole, countersunk, centered inside

#10 x 2½" panhead screw

⅛" chamfer

⅜" plug ¼" long

4–68.

Align the chair arm perpendicular to the front leg with a framing square. Using the counterbored shank hole as a guide, drill a pilot hole into the rear leg, and drive in the screw.

arm mortise plugs (K) with that of the front legs (A).

Note: If you are building the armchair, skip to the section on applying the finish, and then continue with the instructions for making the seat.

Laminate and Mount a Pair of Rockers

1 From straight-grained, knot-free stock, resaw and plane four ¼ x 3¾ x 40" strips for the laminated rocker blank, plus one additional strip to use as a clamping platen. Cut five ¾ x 8½ x 40" pieces of particleboard for the rocker form. Build your bending form from ¾"-thick particleboard pieces cut to the shape shown in **4–71**, then glued up to a thickness just a bit wider than the rockers. Cover the top of the form with tape to keep glue off the form; then glue and clamp the rocker strips to it and let dry. When the glue has dried, clean up any glue on the rockers.

2 With the rockers (M) formed, mark their overall length and

the leg mortise plugs (L). Tilt your tablesaw blade to 45°. Attach an auxiliary extension and a stop-block to the miter gauge, and chamfer all four edges of both ends of the three mortise plug blanks, where shown in Step 1 of **4–70**. Switch to a ⅛" dado blade, and cut dadoes all around each blank, where shown in Step 2.

7 To separate the mortise plugs from the blanks, fit your tablesaw with a zero-clearance throat plate. Cut the blanks where indicated in Step 2 of **4–70**.

8 Glue and clamp the mortise plugs in place, where shown in **4–70**. Align the grain of the

4–69.
ARM

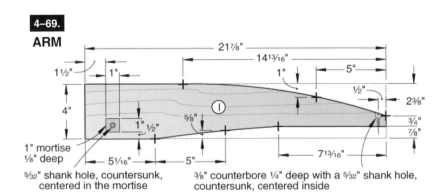

1" mortise ⅛" deep

5⁄32" shank hole, countersunk, centered in the mortise

⅜" counterbore ¼" deep with a 5⁄32" shank hole, countersunk, centered inside

4–70. **CUTTING THE MORTISE PLUGS**

STEP 1

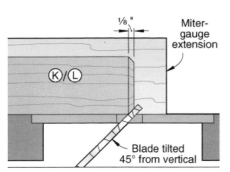

STEP 2

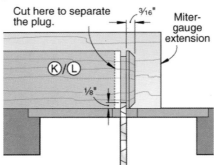

the location of the front edge of the front leg on the form, where shown in **4–71**. Match up the rockers as they were in the single bent lamination, and mark their front ends. Clamp each rocker, in turn, to the form, centered end to end with the marked end at the front. Transfer the marks from the form to the rocker. Draw the ¾" radii where shown. Bandsaw and sand the rocker to finished shape.

3 Lay the chair on its side. Mark the leg lengths, where shown in **4–67**, on *page 81*. Align the top edge of a rocker with these marks, clamp it in place, and trace the top edge of the rocker onto the legs with a pencil. Repeat on the chair's other side.

4 Make the leg-trimming jig, shown in **4–79**, on *page 85*. Clamp the jig to the first leg, aligning its edge with the marked line. Trim the leg to length, as shown in **4–80**. With the jig still in place, smooth the leg's end with a sanding block. Repeat on the other three legs.

5 Sand ⅛" chamfers on the ends of the legs with a sanding block. With the chamfer bit in your table-mounted router, rout ⅛" chamfers on the bottom edges of the rockers, where shown in **4–67**.

6 Clamp the rockers in place, and drill ⅜" counterbores ¼" deep in their bottom faces,

centered on the legs. Drill pilot and countersunk shank holes, centered in the counterbores, through the rockers into the legs. Drive the screws. Make four more ⅜"-long plugs. Glue the plugs into the counterbores, and sand them smooth.

On to the Finish

1 Sand all the surfaces to 220 grit. Ease the unchamfered edges with a sanding block. Remove the sanding dust.

2 Apply stain or dye, and topcoat with a clear finish. (We used aniline dye to bring out the wood's quartersawn figure and topcoated with aerosol shellac.)

Fashion a Seat and Cushion

1 To make the seat (N) and your own cushion, follow the instructions in the sidebar Seat Cushions Made Easy on the following page. If you do not wish to make the seat cushion yourself, take the rocker, plywood seat, and a copy of the sidebar to an upholstery shop.

4–71.
ROCKER FORM

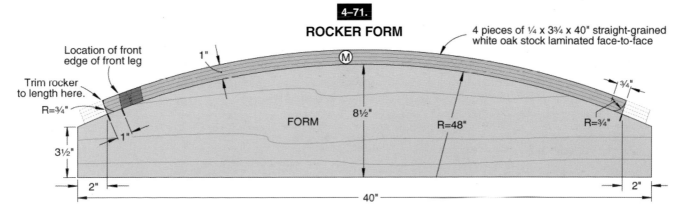

Seat Cushions Made Easy

If you have access to a sewing machine, making your own cushion is a snap. All the upholstery supplies you need are readily available at local fabric stores.

Purchase a 2 × 24 × 24" piece of urethane foam, and enough polyester quilt batting to make four 26 × 29" pieces. Select a 30 × 30" piece of upholstery material. (We chose a black imitation leather.) Buy a spool of upholstery thread to match the color of your material.

Cut a ½ × 17½ × 20¾" piece of plywood for the seat (N). Lay out the shape and the locations of the vent holes, where shown on 4–72. Drill the holes with a 1" Forstner bit, and cut the seat to shape. To keep the upholstery material from wearing on its sharp edges, rout a ⅛" chamfer on the seat's bottom edges. Now, to add the cushion, just follow the six steps shown in 4–73 to 4–78.

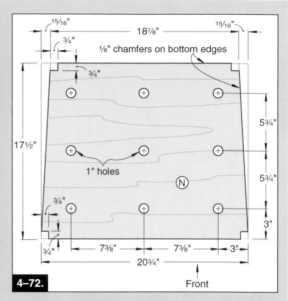

4–72.

4–73.

Step 1. *Adhere the oversize piece of foam to the seat with spray adhesive. Trim off the excess foam with an electric carving knife or serrated bread knife, guided by the seat's edges. Be sure to keep the blade perpendicular to the seat.*

4–74.

Step 2. *For the cushion to have smooth rounded edges, the foam's square top edges must be removed. To do this, first mark cutlines 1" in and 1" down from the foam's top edges with a straightedge and felt-tipped marker.*

4–75.

Step 3. *Once again using the electric knife or serrated bread knife, cut along the marked lines. Keep the knife's blade aligned with the lines marked on both the top and side to form 45° bevels on the foam's top edges.*

4–76.

Step 4. *Layer four 26 × 29" pieces of quilt batting on your workbench. Center the seat and attached cushion on the batting; now pull the batting up over the foam, and fasten it to the seat with ⅜" staples. Trim the excess batting at the corners.*

4–77.

Step 5. *Cut your upholstery material where shown on 4–81. Following the four steps in 4–82, lay out, sew, and trim two cover corners. Fold the cover on the other diagonal and repeat to form the other two corners.*

4–78.

Step 6. *Place the cover back side up, and center the cushion on it. Secure the cover to the seat at the middle of each side with one ⅜" staple. Now, working from centers to corners, pull the corner onto the seat and finish stapling it in place.*

With the leg-trimming jig clamped in place, guide your saw by pressing its blade against the jig as you crosscut the rocker leg bottom ends to length.

4–79.

LEG TRIMMING JIG

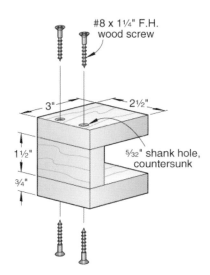

#8 x 1¼" F.H. wood screw

3" 2½"

1½"

¾"

5/32" shank hole, countersunk

4–80.

2 With the seat and cushion complete, place it on the chair, resting it on the rabbets in the side rails (F) and the corner braces (H). Using the counterbored holes in the corner braces as guides, drill pilot holes into the seat (N). Fasten the seat to the braces with screws, where shown on **4–67**, on *page 81*.

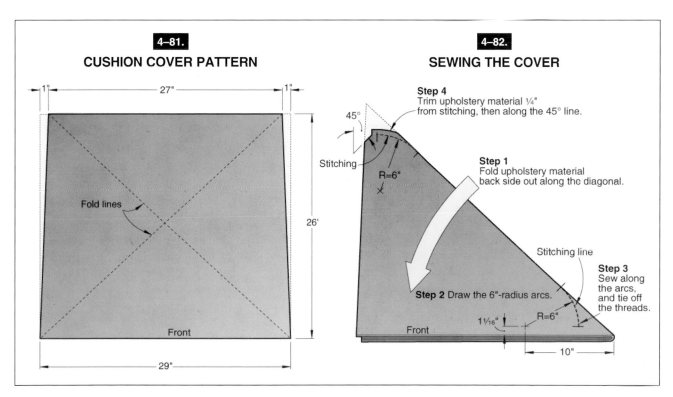

4–81.

CUSHION COVER PATTERN

1" 27" 1"

Fold lines

26'

Front

29"

4–82.

SEWING THE COVER

Step 4
Trim upholstery material ¼" from stitching, then along the 45° line.

45°

Stitching

R=6"

Step 1
Fold upholstery material back side out along the diagonal.

Stitching line

Step 3
Sew along the arcs, and tie off the threads.

Step 2 Draw the 6"-radius arcs.

Front

1 1/16" R=6"

10"

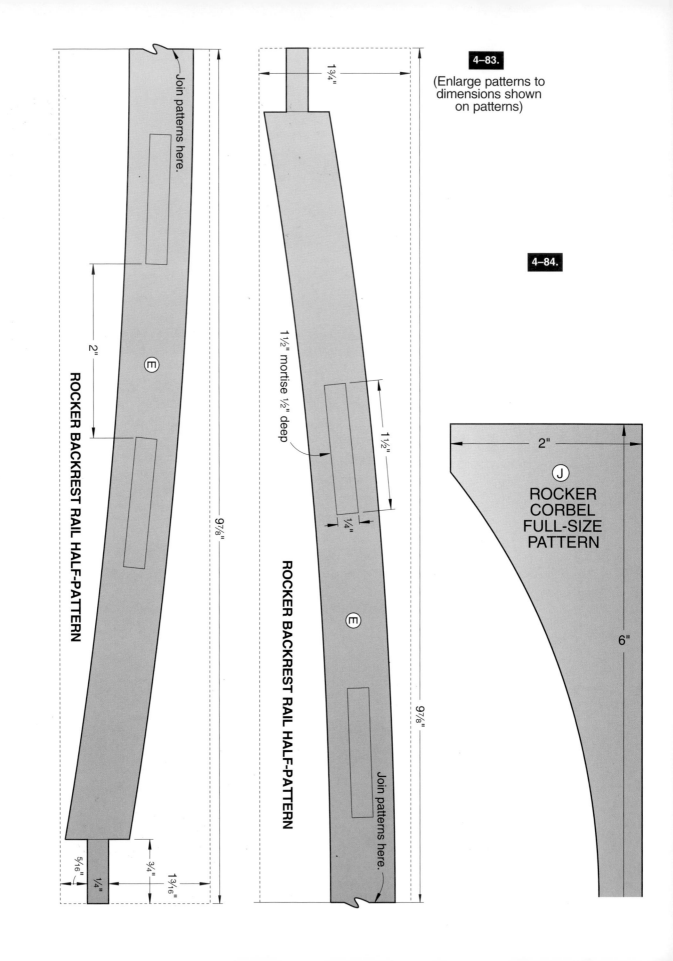

4–83.

(Enlarge patterns to dimensions shown on patterns)

4–84.

Join patterns here.

2"

E

9⅞"

ROCKER BACKREST RAIL HALF-PATTERN

5/16"   ¼"   3/4"   13/16"

1½" mortise ½" deep

1½"

¼"

E

9⅞"

Join patterns here.

ROCKER BACKREST RAIL HALF-PATTERN

1¾"

2"

J

ROCKER CORBEL FULL-SIZE PATTERN

6"

EMBELLISHED BOOKCASE

Add this stately bookcase to the furniture from the preceding pages and you'll have a roomful of craftsmanship! We embellished it with side-panel cutouts, reproduction hardware, and glass-framed doors to capture the quality and ambience of the era.

Start by Laminating and Machining the Legs

1 To form the 2⅛"-square legs (A), cut 8 pieces of 1¹⁄₁₆" stock to 2¼" by 68". (Using these dimensions, the pieces are ⅛" oversized in width and 1" in length so you can trim flush the edges and ends of the laminated legs later.) See **4–85**.

2 Spread an even coat of glue on the mating surfaces of two pieces making up each leg. With the edges and ends flush, glue and clamp the pieces face-to-face to form the front and rear legs.

3 Cut or plane an equal amount off both edges of each leg for a 2⅛" finished width. Then, trim both ends of each leg (A) for a 67" finished length.

4 Using **4–85**, lay out the mortises and grooves on each leg where dimensioned. Note the location of the joint lines when marking the mortises and grooves, and be sure the right and left legs are mirror images.

Embellished bookcase

5 Attach a fence to your drill-press table. Using a ⁷⁄₁₆" brad-point bit, drill holes inside the marked mortise outlines. Then square-up the mortises with a chisel.

6 Working from the top end down, mark the location of the shelf-hole centerpoints. The center of the top hole must be 16" from the leg tops so the top shelf

(text continues on page 89)

MATERIALS LIST FOR EMBELLISHED BOOKCASE

PART		T	W	L	Mtl.	Qty.
SIDE FRAMES						
A*	legs	2⅛"	2⅛"	67"	LO	4
B	side rails	1¹⁄₁₆"	5⅞"	11⅞"	O	2
C	top side rails	1¹⁄₁₆"	5½"	11⅞"	O	2
D	bottom side rails	¹⁷⁄₃₂"	1¼"	9¾"	O	2
E*	side panels	½"	10⅛"	48"	EO	2
RAILS AND CLEATS						
F	backrails	1¹⁄₁₆"	5⅞"	36¼"	O	2
G	bottom front rails	1¹⁄₁₆"	3"	36¼"	O	1
H	top front rails	1¹⁄₁₆"	2⅞"	36¼"	O	1
SIDE FRAMES						
I	cleats	¾"	¾"	34"	O	3
J	cleats	¾"	¾"	9⅝"	O	4
K	back	¼"	34⅞"	48"	OP	1
BOTTOM, SHELVES, AND TOP						
L*	bottom	1¹⁄₁₆"	11⅝"	36⅛"	EO	1
M*	shelves	1¹⁄₁₆"	12⁷⁄₁₆"	35¹⁵⁄₁₆"	EO	3
N*	top	1¹⁄₁₆"	16¼"	42⅜"	EO	1
O	corbels	1¹⁄₁₆"	1⅜"	5¾"	O	6
P	corbels	1¹⁄₁₆"	1½"	3"	O	4

PART		T	W	L	Mtl.	Qty.
DOORS						
Q	stiles	1¹⁄₁₆"	2½"	53"	O	4
R	top rails	1¹⁄₁₆"	2½"	17"	O	2
S	bottom rails	1¹⁄₁₆"	2¾"	17"	O	2
T	middle rails	½"	1¼"	12½"	O	2
U	mullions	½"	½"	12½"	O	2
V	mullions	½"	½"	10¼"	O	4
W	glass stops	⅜"	⅜"	48¾"	O	4
X	glass stops	⅜"	⅜"	13"	O	4
Y	stop	¾"	2⅜"	4½"	O	1

*Cut parts oversized. Trim to finished size according to the instructions.

Materials Key: LO = laminated oak; O = Oak; EO = edge-joined oak; OP = oak plywood.

Supplies: #8 x 1½" flathead wood screws; #8 x 1½" roundhead wood screws with washers; #6 x ¾" flathead wood screws; 2 pieces of 12⅞ x 48⅝" double-strength glass; ¾" x 18 brads; stain; finish.

Hardware: Two Arts and Crafts-style vertical door pulls; 3 pair of barrel hinges; 12 bracket-style shelf pins; 4 adjustable brass ball catches; ¼" oak dowel stock.

CUTTING DIAGRAM

*Plane or resaw to thickness listed in Materials List

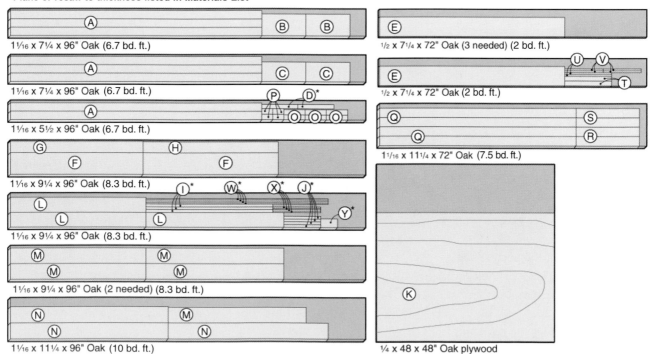

1¹⁄₁₆ x 7¼ x 96" Oak (6.7 bd. ft.)

1¹⁄₁₆ x 7¼ x 96" Oak (6.7 bd. ft.)

1¹⁄₁₆ x 5½ x 96" Oak (6.7 bd. ft.)

1¹⁄₁₆ x 9¼ x 96" Oak (8.3 bd. ft.)

1¹⁄₁₆ x 9¼ x 96" Oak (8.3 bd. ft.)

1¹⁄₁₆ x 9¼ x 96" Oak (2 needed) (8.3 bd. ft.)

1¹⁄₁₆ x 11¼ x 96" Oak (10 bd. ft.)

½ x 7¼ x 72" Oak (3 needed) (2 bd. ft.)

½ x 7¼ x 72" Oak (2 bd. ft.)

1¹⁄₁₆ x 11¼ x 72" Oak (7.5 bd. ft.)

¼ x 48 x 48" Oak plywood

will be hidden behind the door rails (T) later. Drill a ¼" hole ½" deep at each marked centerpoint. (As shown in **4–86**, we used a scrap strip of Peg Board as a guide when drilling the holes. The holes in the Peg Board are exactly 1" apart. Notice that after drilling the first hole, we slid a ¼" piece of dowel throught Peg Board into the leg to help ensure the Peg Board wouldn't move on the leg.)

7 Mount a ¼" dado blade into your tablesaw, and cut a ¼" groove ¼" deep along the edges of each leg where marked, or use a ¼" slot cutter in your router fitted with a fence.

8 Rout ⅛" chamfers along the bottom end of each leg.

Machine and Assemble the Side Frames

1 Cut the lower side rails (B) and the top rails (C) to the sizes listed in the Materials List.

2 Using **4–87** for reference, cut tenons on the ends of the rails to fit snug inside the leg mortises. To do this, fit your tablesaw with a dado blade, and attach a long wooden extension to your tablesaw's miter gauge. Square the extension to the blade. Using a stop for consistency, cut rabbets to form tenons on the ends of the

Using a piece of Peg Board, tape off the holes that won't be used, and use the remaining holes as guides to drill holes in the legs for the shelf-support pins.

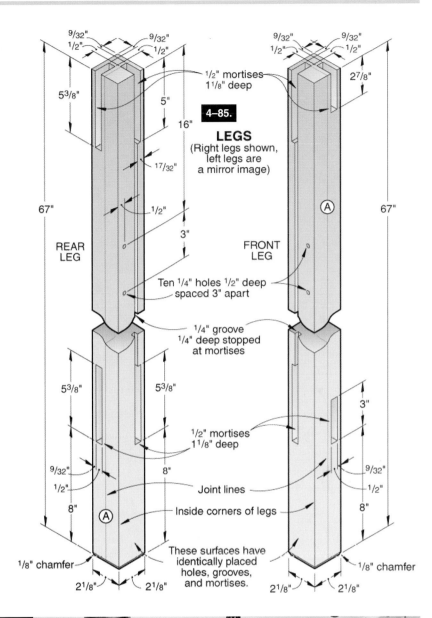

4–85.

LEGS
(Right legs shown, left legs are a mirror image)

½" mortises 1⅛" deep

Ten ¼" holes ½" deep spaced 3" apart

¼" groove ¼" deep stopped at mortises

½" mortises 1⅛" deep

Joint lines

Inside corners of legs

These surfaces have identically placed holes, grooves, and mortises.

REAR LEG

FRONT LEG

A

A

⅛" chamfer

⅛" chamfer

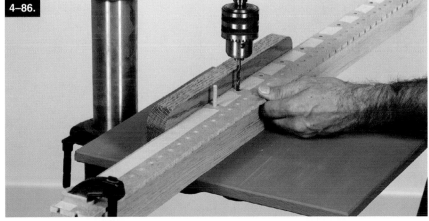

4–86.

rails. (We test-cut scrap stock first to ensure a tight fit of the tenons into the leg mortises.) Keep the long extension on the fence; you'll use it again when machining the tenons on rails (F, G, H) later.

3 Cut a ¼" groove ¼" deep along one edge of each rail (B, C), where shown on the Tenon and Groove Detail in **4–87**.

4 Cut the center side rails (D) to size.

5 Edge-join ½"-thick stock to form the side-frame panels (E). Make the panels extra long, and then crosscut the ends to finished length.

6 Rout a ½" rabbet ¼" deep along the *inside* edges and ends of each side panel (E), where shown in **4–87**.

7 For adding the center side rail (D), mark the center-points, and drill a pair of ⁹⁄₆₄" shank holes on each side panel, where shown in **4–87**.

8 Using the pattern on *page 95*, lay out the groove and shaped ends of the panel cutout on each panel, centered from side to side and 6¼" from the bottom end of each panel. Drill a ⁵⁄₁₆" hole at each end of the marked groove. (To avoid having to sand off our marks, we applied masking tape to the panels, and made our marks on that. We removed the tape after all the routing and cutting was done.)

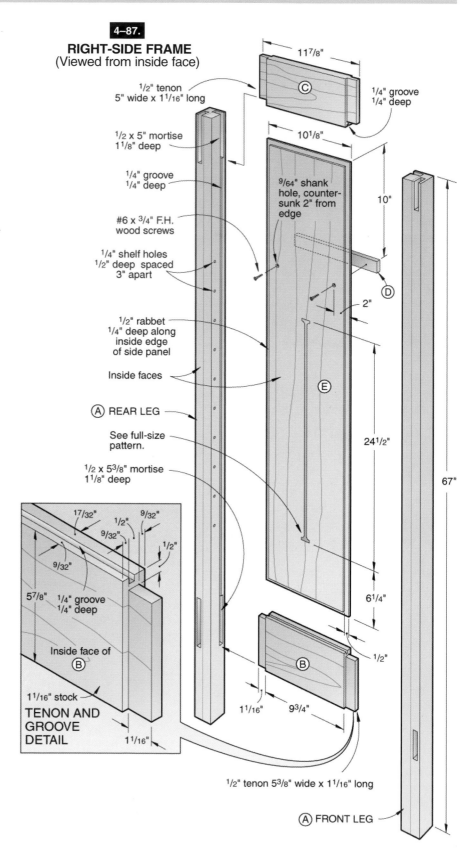

4–87.

RIGHT-SIDE FRAME
(Viewed from inside face)

9 Fit your table-mounted router with a ¼" straight bit and double fence. Position the panel so the ¼" bit fits into one of the ⁵⁄₁₆" holes. Start the router, and rout to the opposite hole, as shown in **4–88**. The double fence secures the workpiece to ensure a straight groove.

10 Scrollsaw the ends of the groove to shape.

11 Finish-sand and stain the panels. Do this to prevent unstained areas from showing should the panels shrink in the frames later.

12 Screw the rails (D) in place.

13 Assemble (no glue) the side frames (A–E) to check the fit as shown in **4–89**.

Machine the Rails and Connect the End Frames

1 Cut the back rails (F) and the front rails (G, H) to the sizes listed in the Materials List.

2 Cut rabbets to form tenons on the ends of the rails. See the Tenon Detail in **4–90**, on *page 92*.

3 Glue and clamp the rails (F, G, H) between the side frames. For proper-fitting doors later, check carefully for square.

4 Cut the cleats (I, J) to size from ¾" square stock. Drill the countersunk mounting holes and form the slots now, where shown on the Parts Views drawing on *page 96*. Screw the cleats in place where shown in **4–90**.

5 Rout the back of the cabinet to receive the ¼" back (K), using a ⅜" rabbeting bit. Square the corners with a chisel. Cut the back panel to size. Drill the countersunk mounting holes, and screw the back in place.

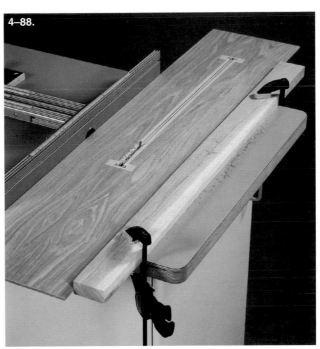

4–88.

Position the side-frame panel on your table-mounted router so the ¼" straight bit fits into one of the ⁵⁄₁₆" holes in the panel. Start the router, and rout to the opposite hole. The double fence secures the workpiece to ensure a straight groove.

4–89.

An acid brush works great for brushing glue on the mating pieces when gluing and clamping the side frames together. Use a damp cloth to wipe off excess glue immediately after clamping.

4–90.

EXPLODED VIEW

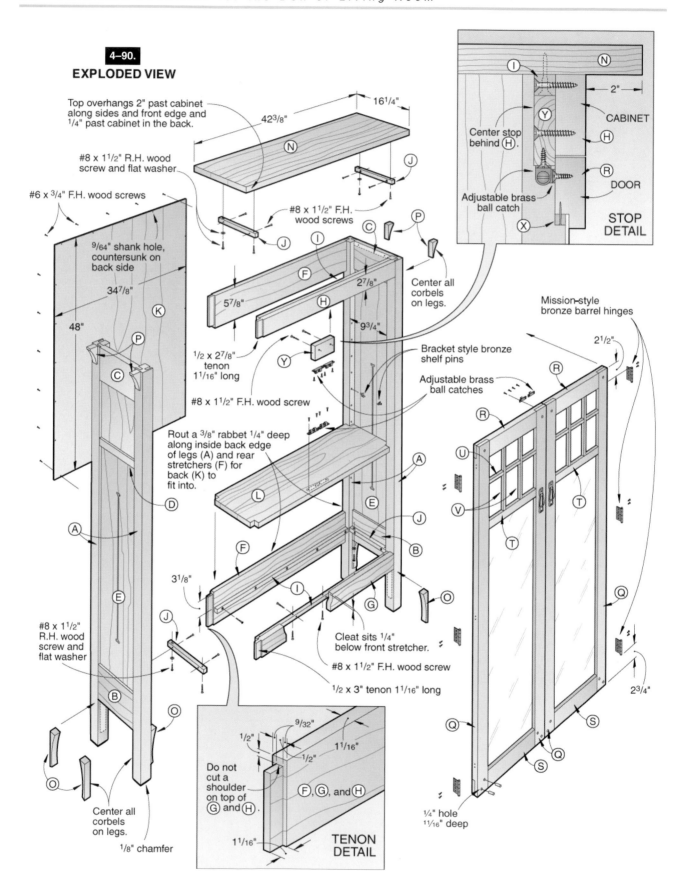

Top overhangs 2" past cabinet along sides and front edge and ¹/₄" past cabinet in the back.

16¹/₄"

42³/₈"

#8 x 1¹/₂" R.H. wood screw and flat washer

#6 x ³/₄" F.H. wood screws

#8 x 1¹/₂" F.H. wood screws

⁹/₆₄" shank hole, countersunk on back side

34⁷/₈"

48"

5⁷/₈"

2⁷/₈"

Center all corbels on legs.

9³/₄"

¹/₂ x 2⁷/₈" tenon 1¹/₁₆" long

#8 x 1¹/₂" F.H. wood screw

Bracket style bronze shelf pins

Adjustable brass ball catches

Rout a ³/₈" rabbet ¹/₄" deep along inside back edge of legs (A) and rear stretchers (F) for back (K) to fit into.

Mission-style bronze barrel hinges

2¹/₂"

#8 x 1¹/₂" R.H. wood screw and flat washer

3¹/₈"

Cleat sits ¹/₄" below front stretcher.

#8 x 1¹/₂" F.H. wood screw

¹/₂ x 3" tenon 1¹/₁₆" long

2³/₄"

Center all corbels on legs.

¹/₈" chamfer

¹/₄" hole 1¹/₁₆" deep

STOP DETAIL

Center stop behind (H).

CABINET

2"

Adjustable brass ball catch

DOOR

TENON DETAIL

9/32"

¹/₂"

1¹/₁₆"

¹/₂"

Do not cut a shoulder on top of (G) and (H).

(F), (G), and (H)

1¹/₁₆"

4–91.
SHELVES

ADJUSTABLE SHELF
(3 needed)

2"

1¹/₈"

1¹/₈"

12⁷/₁₆"

(M)

35¹⁵/₁₆"

1¹/₈"

1¹/₁₆"

1"

1¹/₁₆"

(L)

11⁵/₈"

1¹/₁₆"

36¹/₈"

BOTTOM SHELF

1"

1¹/₁₆"

Form the Edge-Joined Bottom, Shelves, and Top

1 Edge-join 1¹/₁₆"-thick stock for the bottom (L), shelves (M), and top (N). (We made our laminations extra long and wide to start, and then trimmed them to size after the glue dried.) Refer to **4–91** to cut the bottom and shelves to shape.

2 Attach the top and bottom with screws, as shown in **4–90**.

3 Using the full-size patterns on *page 89*, cut the corbels (O, P) to shape. Glue and clamp the corbels in place, centered on each leg, where shown in **4–90**. Glue the corbels to the legs only, not to the rails (B, G) or top (N).

Cut the Parts for the Half-Lapped Doors

Note: The front opening of our assembled project measures 34¹/₈" by 53¹/₈". The assembled doors have a ¹/₁₆" gap at the top and the bottom, between the doors, and between the doors and legs. The no-mortise hinges create the gap between the legs and doors.

1 Cut the door stiles (Q) and rails (R, S) to the sizes listed in the Materials List.

2 Cut laps on the ends of the stiles and rail, where shown on the Door drawing in **4–92**.

Note that the laps on the rails (R, S) are ⁹/₁₆" deep while the mating laps on the stiles (Q) are only ½" deep. (We didn't cut a true half-lap because of the ½" rabbet ½" deep routed on the back side of each door later. The depth of the laps must be the same as the depth of the rabbet for the glass. We test-cut scrap pieces first to verify the depth of cut before cutting the stiles and rails.)

3 Cut a ½" rabbet ½" deep along the inside edge of each stile and rail, where shown on the Door drawing in **4–92**.

4 Mark and cut a pair of mortises on the inside edge of each stile (Q), where shown on the Mortise Detail in **4–92**. Machine a pair of mortises in the top edge of each middle rail (T) and at the bottom edge at the door top rail (R).

5 Cut rabbets across the ends of the middle rails (T) to fit into the bottom mortise of the stiles.

6 Cut the door mullions (U, V) to size. Using the dimensions on the Parts View drawing in **4–94** (*page 96*), mark the dadoes on the pieces. Using a tablesaw and a miter gauge fitted with an auxiliary fence and stop for consistent cuts from piece to piece, cut the dadoes in the mullions (U, V).

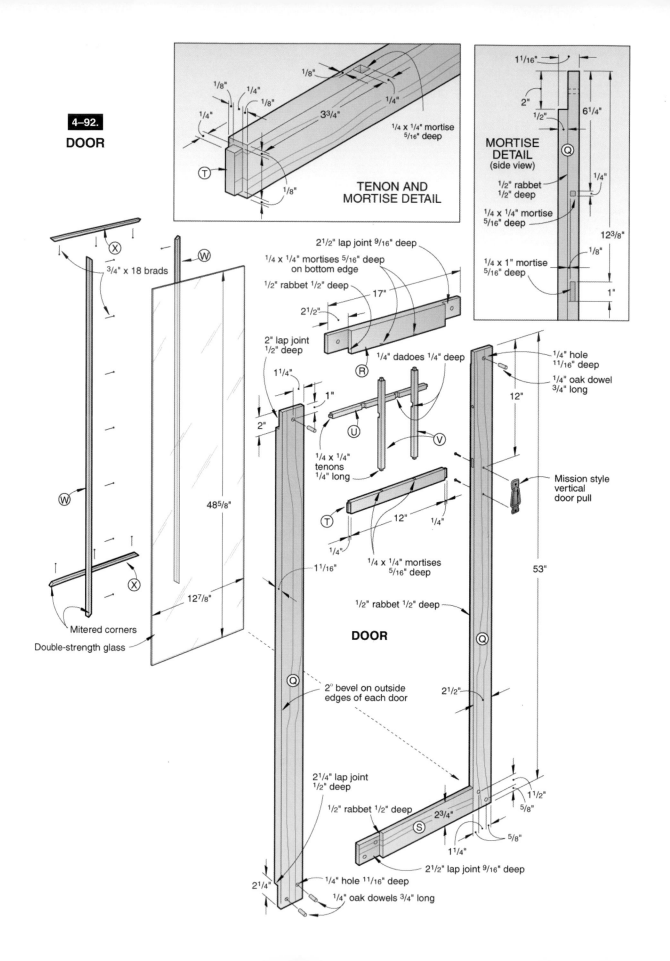

4–92.

DOOR

TENON AND MORTISE DETAIL

1/8"
1/4"
1/8"
1/4"
1/8"
1/4"
3³/4"
1/4 x 1/4" mortise 5/16" deep
1/8"
Ⓣ

MORTISE DETAIL (side view)

1¹/16"
2"
1/2"
6¹/4"
1/4"
Ⓠ
1/2" rabbet 1/2" deep
1/4 x 1/4" mortise 5/16" deep
12³/8"
1/8"
1/4 x 1" mortise 5/16" deep
1"

Ⓧ
³/4" x 18 brads
Ⓦ

2¹/2" lap joint 9/16" deep
1/4 x 1/4" mortises 5/16" deep on bottom edge
1/2" rabbet 1/2" deep
17"
2¹/2"
Ⓡ
1/4" dadoes 1/4" deep

2" lap joint 1/2" deep
1¹/4"
1"
2"
Ⓤ
1/4 x 1/4" tenons 1/4" long
Ⓥ

1/4" hole 11/16" deep
1/4" oak dowel ³/4" long
12"

Ⓦ
48⁵/8"

Ⓣ
12"
1/4"
1/4"
1/4 x 1/4" mortises 5/16" deep

Mission style vertical door pull

Ⓧ
Mitered corners
Double-strength glass
12⁷/8"

DOOR

Ⓠ
1/2" rabbet 1/2" deep
53"

Ⓠ
2° bevel on outside edges of each door
2¹/2"
1¹/16"

2¹/4" lap joint 1/2" deep
1/2" rabbet 1/2" deep
2³/4"
Ⓢ
1¹/2"
5/8"
5/8"
1¹/4"
2¹/2" lap joint 9/16" deep

2¹/4"
1/4" hole 11/16" deep
1/4" oak dowels ³/4" long

7 Machine tenons on the ends of the mullions. Glue and clamp the mullions (U, V) together, checking for square. Wipe off any excess glue with a damp cloth. (We clamped the pieces together on a piece of sheet goods to keep the grid flat.)

Assemble the Doors and Hinge Them to the Cabinet

1 Dry-assemble the door frames (Q, R, S) with the middle rail (T) and mullions (U, V) in place. Verify the fit; then glue and clamp each door together, checking for square.

2 Cut the glass stops (W, X) to size, and pre-drill the brad holes through each. (We used one of the brads for a drill bit.)

3 Lay out and mark the center-points for the ¼" oak dowels on the front of each door where dimensioned on the Door drawing in **4–92**. Drill the 1¹⁄₁₆"-deep holes, plug with ¼" dowel stock, and sand the ends of the dowels flush with the front of each door.

4 Fit the doors to the opening. (Without decreasing the width of the doors, we ripped a 2° bevel on the inside edges of the stiles [Q] to provide clearance between the doors when opening and closing, and to allow each hinge to come together without springing back.)

5 Mark the locations, drill the pilot holes, and attach the barrel hinges to the doors, where shown in **4–90**, on *page 92*. (We used no-mortise hinges.)

6 Cut the stop (Y) to size. Drill a pair of shank holes in it, where shown on Door Stop in **4–92**. Mount the stop to the cabinet; then secure the ball catches to the stop. Secure a second set of ball catches to the bottom shelf. To locate the catch

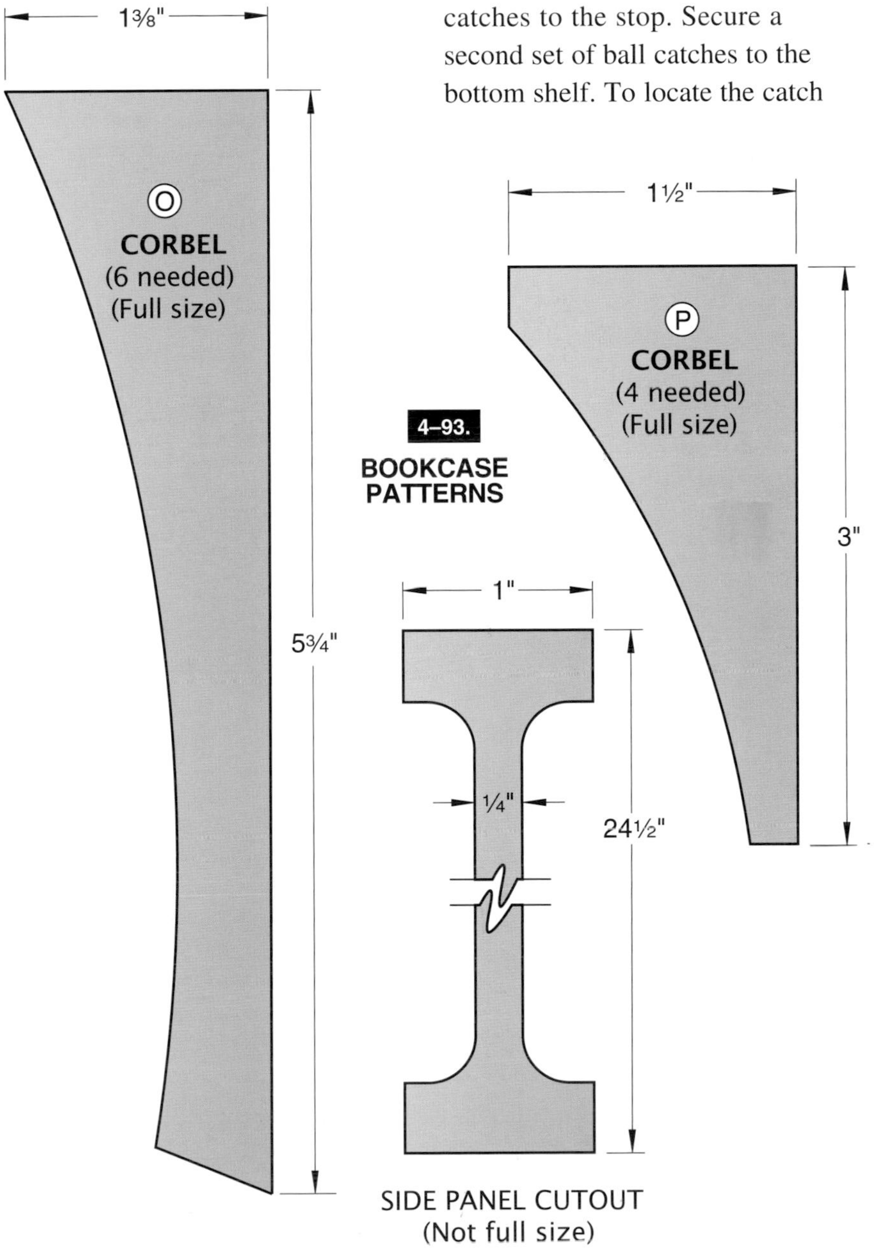

1⅜"

Ⓞ
CORBEL
(6 needed)
(Full size)

5¾"

4–93.
BOOKCASE PATTERNS

1½"

Ⓟ
CORBEL
(4 needed)
(Full size)

3"

1"

¼"

24½"

SIDE PANEL CUTOUT
(Not full size)

HORIZONTAL MULLIONS

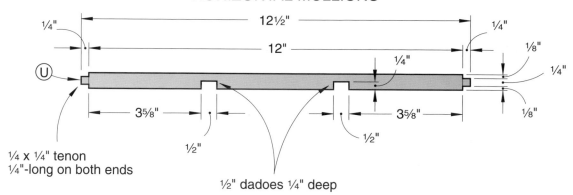

12½"

12"

¼"   ¼"   ⅛"   ¼"   ¼"

3⅝"   3⅝"

½"

¼ x ¼" tenon
¼"-long on both ends

½" dadoes ¼" deep

FRONT FACE

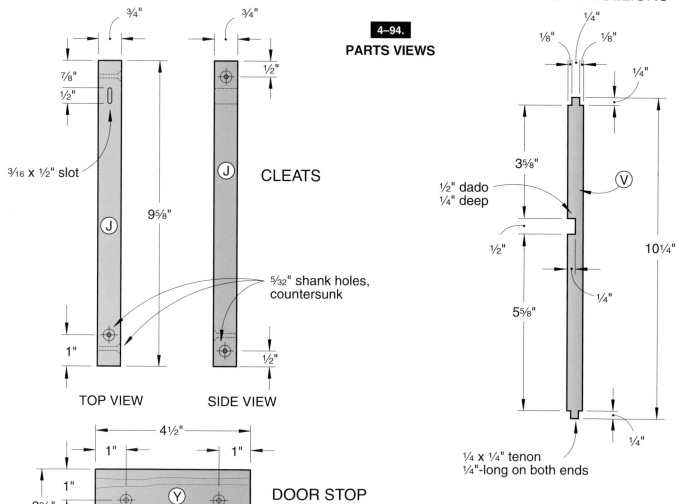

¾"   ¾"

4–94.
PARTS VIEWS

7⁄8"
½"

³⁄16 x ½" slot

9⅝"

J   J

CLEATS

½"

5⁄32" shank holes,
countersunk

1"

½"

TOP VIEW   **SIDE VIEW**

VERTICAL MULLIONS

¼"   ⅛"   ⅛"   ¼"

3⅝"

½" dado
¼" deep

V

½"

¼"

10¼"

5⅝"

¼ x ¼" tenon
¼"-long on both ends

¼"

4½"

1"   1"

1"

2⅜"

Y

DOOR STOP
(not full size)

5⁄32" shank holes, countersunk

TOP DOOR RAIL

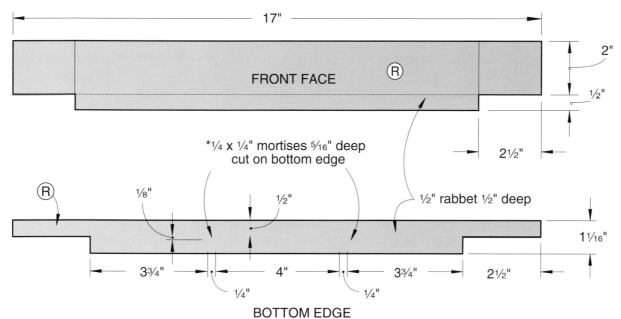

17"

FRONT FACE Ⓡ

2"

½"

2½"

*¼ x ¼" mortises ⁵⁄₁₆" deep
cut on bottom edge

½" rabbet ½" deep

Ⓡ

⅛"

½"

1¹⁄₁₆"

3¾" 4" 3¾" 2½"

¼" ¼"

BOTTOM EDGE

4–95.

PARTS VIEWS

*Note: Mortises on bottom edge
of Ⓡ are located the same as
mortises on Ⓣ. These mortises
are cut ⅛" from back edge of
stock on Ⓣ and ⅛" from edge of
rabbet on bottom edge Ⓡ.

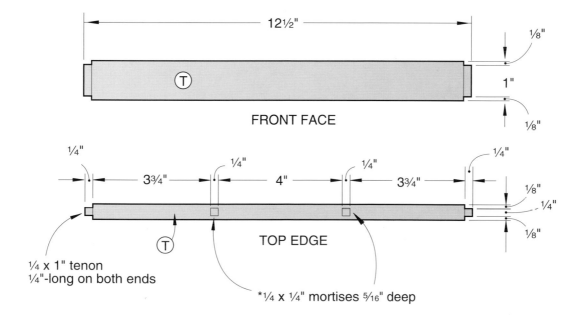

12½"

⅛"

Ⓣ

1"

FRONT FACE

⅛"

¼" ¼" ¼" ¼"

3¾" 4" 3¾"

⅛"

¼"

⅛"

Ⓣ

TOP EDGE

¼ x 1" tenon
¼"-long on both ends

*¼ x ¼" mortises ⁵⁄₁₆" deep

MIDDLE RAIL

4–96.

A piece of tablet-back cardboard protects the glass when nailing the oak glass stops to the door frame.

strikes precisely, insert a strike in the ball catch and loosen the catch until the strike can be easily pulled out. Repeat for the other catches. With the strikes in the catches, adhere a small piece of double-face tape to the back of each strike, and close the doors. Now open the doors, taking care not to pull the strikes loose from the doors, and mark the mating locations on the back side of the doors. Attach the strikes using the Stop Detail in **4–90** (*page 92*) for reference.

7 Mark the centerpoints on the doors, and drill the holes for the pulls. See **4–92** on *page 95*.

8 Remove all the hardware from the cabinet and doors.

9 Cut the glass for the doors. (We recommend taking the doors to a glass shop and having the glass cut to fit.)

10 Finish-sand all the parts. Stain as desire, or see the Arts-and-Crafts fumeless finish instruction in Chapter Three. Apply the finish. (We brushed on several coats of satin polyurethane.)

11 Position the door frames with the good face down, and set the glass panels in place. As shown in **4–96**, place a piece of thin cardboard (we used a tablet-back) on the glass and tap the brads in place. The tablet back prevents scratching the glass.

12 Reattach the hardware, and hinge the doors to the cabinet. Adjust the shelves to the desired height.

CHAPTER 5

Dining in the Arts and Crafts Style

THE FURNISHING OF AN ARTS AND CRAFTS *home doesn't end in the living room. So if you've built or are planning to build the pieces described in the last chapter— the Morris chair, coffee table, Ottoman, sofa and matching chair, the rocker/chair, and the bookcase—this chapter brings you a dining suite to complement them.*

The eight-sided table that begins on page 100 *is great for a family of four, but by expanding it with leaves, it'll seat eight easily. Its timeless style will look just as well in a more contemporary setting, too. You'll really want to build this classic for your home, and with our step-by-step instructions, we make it easy to accomplish.*

Of course, a table must have chairs. And the simply elegant lines of the ones we chose to match the table add to the set's eye-appeal. With our help, you'll effortlessly build four or more in production fashion. See how on page 107. *There's a bonus, too. The seats are a cinch to make, without the help of a professional upholsterer!*

We might have saved the best for last in this chapter. We say that because the buffet on page 114 *that we designed to go with the dining set is a masterwork, evoking a sense of craftsmanship at a glance. Build it to fill out the room, and with the easy-to-follow instructions, you'll have it done in no time!*

ELEGANT OCTAGON TABLE

This table sits four comfortably, but you can make as many leaves as you like because it's expandable. Keep in mind, though, that you'll then have to build more chairs!

Start with the Notched Feet

1 From ¾" thick stock, rip and crosscut six pieces to 3⅝" wide by 34" long for the feet (A). As dimensioned on the Foot Lamination drawing in **5–1**, the length shown (34") is 1" longer than the finished length to allow for trimming the ends in Step 5.

2 Mark and cut a pair of 2 × 2⁹⁄₁₆" notches in two of the six pieces, where shown on the Foot Lamination drawing in **5–1**. (We bandsawed the notches to shape.)

3 Spread an even coat of glue on the mating surfaces of the three pieces making one foot. With the edges and ends flush and a notched piece in the middle, glue and clamp the pieces face-to-face to form one foot (A). Remove any glue from the notches before it hardens. Repeat the process to laminate the second foot.

4 Scrape the glue from the bottom edge of each foot, and then joint or plane that edge flat, removing no more than ¹⁄₁₆" of

Arts and Crafts dining set

OCTAGON TABLE CUTTING DIAGRAM

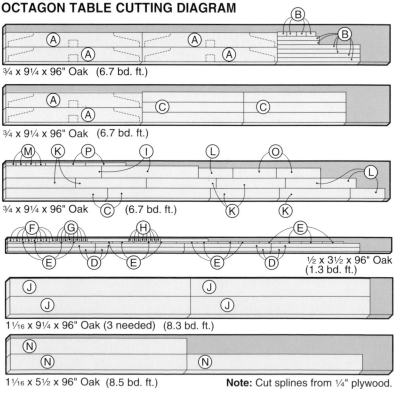

¾ x 9¼ x 96" Oak (6.7 bd. ft.)

¾ x 9¼ x 96" Oak (6.7 bd. ft.)

¾ x 9¼ x 96" Oak (6.7 bd. ft.)

½ x 3½ x 96" Oak (1.3 bd. ft.)

1¹⁄₁₆ x 9¼ x 96" Oak (3 needed) (8.3 bd. ft.)

1¹⁄₁₆ x 5½ x 96" Oak (8.5 bd. ft.)

Note: Cut splines from ¼" plywood.

MATERIALS LIST FOR THE OCTAGON TABLE

PART	T	W	L	Mtl.	Qty.
	FINISHED SIZE				
BASE					
A* feet	2¼"	3½"	33"	LO	2
B* cross members	1¹⁄₁₆"	2¼"	20½"	LO	2
C uprights	1½"	2½"	24⁹⁄₁₆"	LO	4
D slats	½"	1"	21"	O	8
E* trim	⅜"	½"	5⅛"	O	16
F* spacers	½"	¾"	1½"	O	8
G* spacers	½"	¾"	1"	O	8
H* spacers	½"	¾"	⅞"	O	8
I supports	¾"	3"	24"	O	2
TABLETOP (2 Halves)					
J* tabletop halves	1¹⁄₁₆"	22³⁄₁₆	44⅜"	EO	2
K rails	¾"	2½"	17½"	O	6
L rails	¾"	2½"	8¾"	O	4
M cleats	¾"	¾"	2½"	O	4
ONE LEAF					
N* leaf	1¹⁄₁₆"	11"	44⅜"	EO	1
O rails	¾"	2½"	11"	O	2
P cleats	¾"	¾"	10"	O	2

*Initially cut oversize. Then, trim each to finished size according to the instructions.

Materials Key: LO = laminated oak; O = oak; EO = edge-joined oak.

Supplies: ¼" x 1¾" flathead machine screws; #8 x ¾" roundhead wood screws; #8 x 1¼" flathead wood screws; #8 x 1½" flathead wood screws; #8 x ⅝" roundhead wood screws; waxed paper; stain; finish.

Table Hardware: One pair of ball-bearing steel slides, 2" high x 40" long; one pack (8/pack) of tabletop eveners; two packs of tabletop fasteners (8/pack); one pack of ½" #20 T-nuts (8/pack); ¹⁄₁₆"-diameter floor glides (4).

stock. Now, joint or plane the opposite foot edge for a 3½" finished width.

5 Cut the feet to length (33"), trimming an equal amount of stock from both ends to keep the notches equally spaced from the center.

6 Using the dimensions on the Foot drawing in **5–1** for

5–1.

DETAILS FOR BASE, FOOT LAMINATION, AND FOOT

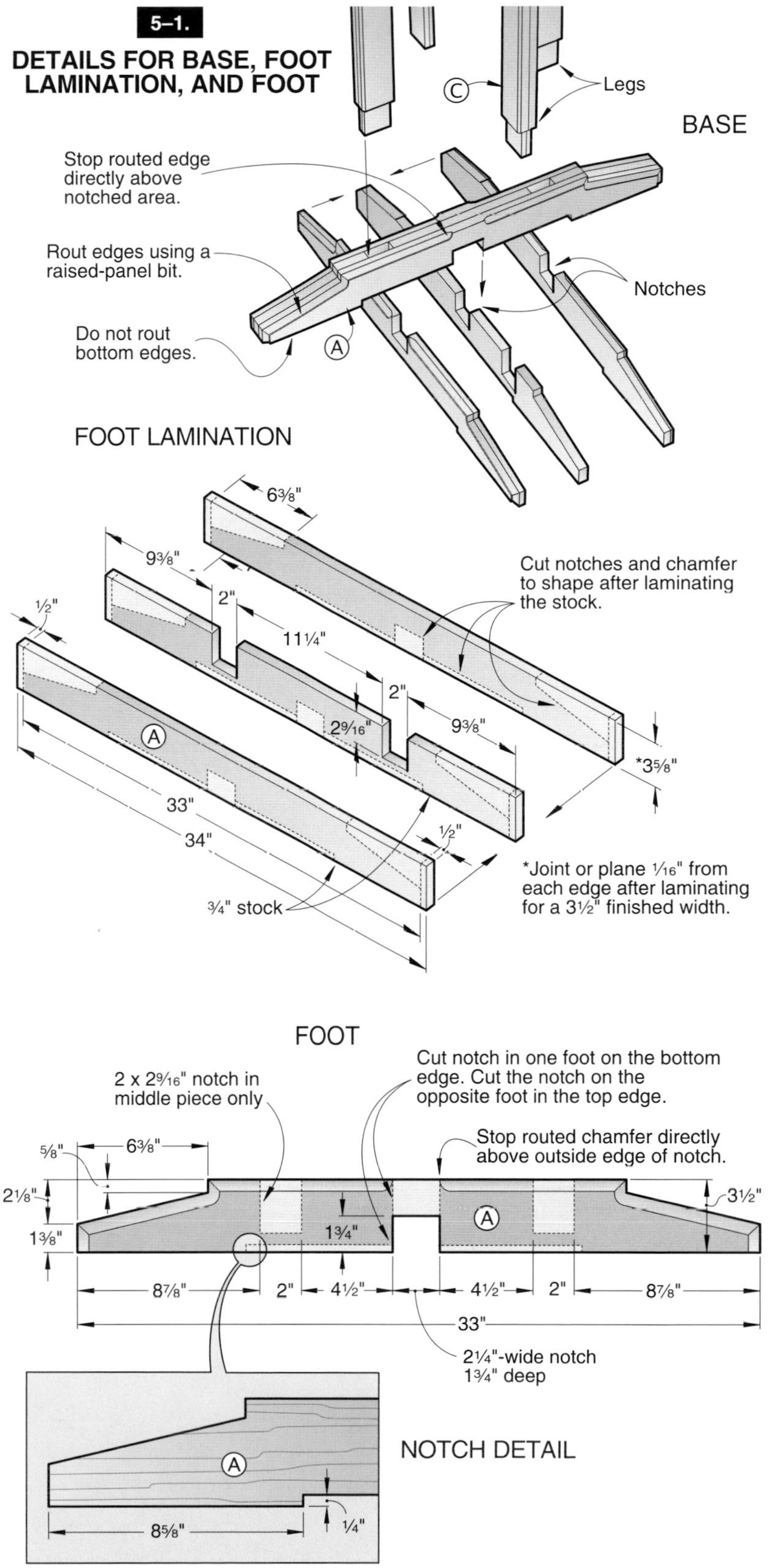

BASE
Legs
C
Stop routed edge directly above notched area.
Rout edges using a raised-panel bit.
Notches
Do not rout bottom edges.
A
FOOT LAMINATION
6⅜"
9⅜"
2"
½"
11¼"
Cut notches and chamfer to shape after laminating the stock.
2"
2⁹⁄₁₆"
9⅜"
*3⅝"
33"
34"
½"
¾" stock
*Joint or plane ¹⁄₁₆" from each edge after laminating for a 3½" finished width.
FOOT
2 x 2⁹⁄₁₆" notch in middle piece only
Cut notch in one foot on the bottom edge. Cut the notch on the opposite foot in the top edge.
Stop routed chamfer directly above outside edge of notch.
⅝"
6⅜"
2⅛"
1⅜"
1¾"
3½"
8⅞"
2"
4½"
4½"
2"
8⅞"
33"
2¼"-wide notch 1¾" deep
NOTCH DETAIL
8⅝"
¼"

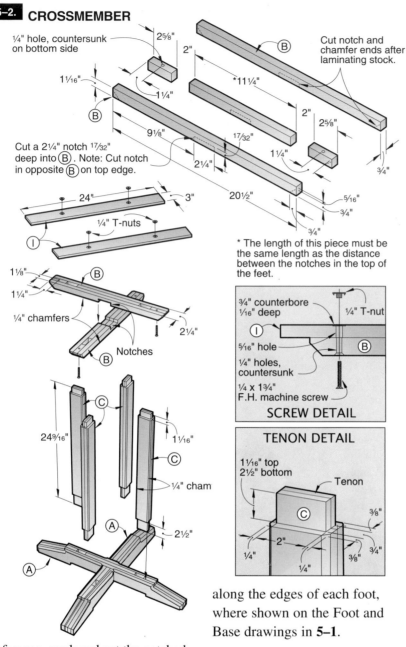

¼" hole, countersunk
on bottom side

2⅝"

2"

1¹⁄₁₆"

1¼"

B

Cut notch and
chamfer ends after
laminating stock.

B

*11¼"

2"

2⅝"

9⅛"

17⁄32"

B

Cut a 2¼" notch ¹⁷⁄₃₂"
deep into B . Note: Cut notch
in opposite B on top edge.

2¼"

1¼"

¾"

24"

3"

20½"

5⁄16"

¾"

¼" T-nuts

I

¾"

* The length of this piece must be
the same length as the distance
between the notches in the top of
the feet.

1⅛"

B

1¼"

¼" chamfers

2¼"

Notches

B

¾" counterbore
¹⁄₁₆" deep

¼" T-nut

I

⁵⁄₁₆" hole

B

¼" holes,
countersunk

¼ x 1¾"
F.H. machine screw

SCREW DETAIL

TENON DETAIL

C

24⁹⁄₁₆"

1¹⁄₁₆"

C

¼" cham

1¹⁄₁₆" top
2½" bottom

Tenon

A

2½"

C

2"

⅜"

A

¼"

¾"

⅜"

¼"

¼"

reference, mark and cut the notched
recess across the bottom, the
chamfered top ends, and the mating
1¾ x 2¼" notches on each foot.
Note that the notch in one foot is
cut in the bottom edge while the
notch in the other foot is cut in
the top surface. Sand the cut edges
smooth to remove saw marks.

7 Fit your table-mounted router
with a raised panel bit. Rout

along the edges of each foot,
where shown on the Foot and
Base drawings in **5–1**.

Add the Crossmembers and Uprights to Finish the Base

1 Using the dimensions on **5–2**,
cut 10 pieces for the two
crossmembers (B). As noted on
the drawing, the length of the
middle piece must be the same as
the distance between the notches
in the top of the feet.

2 With the edges and ends
flush, dry-clamp each crossmember. Check the alignment of
the mortises in the crossmembers
against the notches in the feet.
Trim the crossmember parts if
necessary for alignment. Laminate the pieces to form the two
crossmembers.

3 Cut the mating ¹⁷⁄₃₂ x 2¼"
notches centered from end to
end in the crossmembers. When
mating the crossmembers together
at the notches, the top and bottom
surfaces of the crossmembers
must be flush.

4 Miter-cut a ¾" chamfer across
the ends of each crossmember.

5 For mounting the tabletop
to the crossmembers later,
drill and countersink a pair
of ¼" mounting holes in each
crossmember, 1¼" from the
ends, where shown on the
Crossmember drawing and
accompanying Screw Detail in
5–2. Spread glue in the notches,
and clamp the crossmembers
together.

6 Cut the four uprights (C)
to size. (We laminated two
¾"-thick pieces to create each
1½"-thick upright.) Referring to
the Tenon Detail accompanying
the Crossmember drawing in
5–2, cut a tenon on both ends of
each upright.

7 Rout a ¼" chamfer along
each edge of each upright.

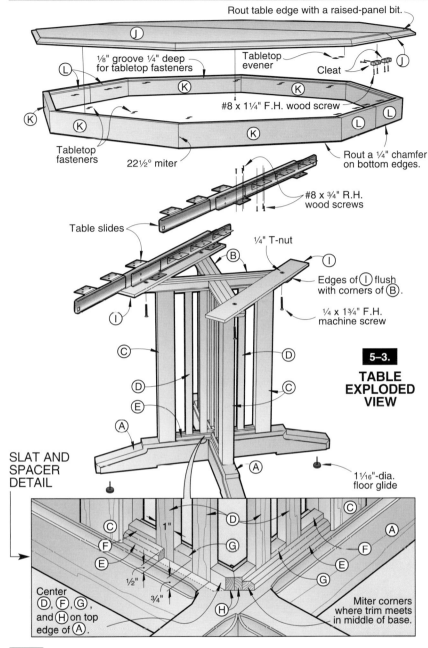

Rout table edge with a raised-panel bit.

J

¹⁄₈" groove ¹⁄₄" deep for tabletop fasteners

L

Tabletop evener

Cleat

J

K

K

K

K

K

#8 x 1¹⁄₄" F.H. wood screw

L

L

Tabletop fasteners

22¹⁄₂° miter

K

Rout a ¹⁄₄" chamfer on bottom edges.

#8 x ³⁄₄" R.H. wood screws

Table slides

¹⁄₄" T-nut

B

I

Edges of I flush with corners of B.

C

I

¹⁄₄ x 1³⁄₄" F.H. machine screw

D

C

5–3.

TABLE EXPLODED VIEW

D

E

A

C

A

1¹⁄₁₆"-dia. floor glide

SLAT AND SPACER DETAIL

C

D

C

A

F

G

F

E

G

E

H

Center D, F, G, and H on top edge of A.

1"

¹⁄₂"

³⁄₄"

Miter corners where trim meets in middle of base.

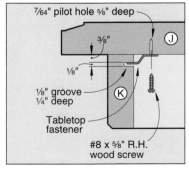

5–4. **TABLETOP FASTENER**

⁷⁄₆₄" pilot hole ⁵⁄₈" deep

J

³⁄₈"

¹⁄₈"

¹⁄₈" groove ¹⁄₄" deep

K

Tabletop fastener

#8 x ⁵⁄₈" R.H. wood screw

until it forms a tough skin and remove it with a chisel.

3 Cut the slats (D) to size, as dimensioned on the Materials List.

4 To form the slat trim (E), cut a piece of stock to ³⁄₈ x ¹⁄₂ x 48". Cut or rout a ¹⁄₈" chamfer along one edge of the strip. See **5–3**.

5 Cut the spacers (F, G, H) to size. (For safety, we made the double miter-cuts on the ends of a long piece of stock for parts H, miter-cutting the parts on a hand miter box. Then, we crosscut the spacers to length from the ends of the long stock.)

6 Dry-fit the slat assembly (D, E, F, G, H) between the feet and crossmembers to check the fit. Then, glue and clamp the pieces in place, where shown on the Slat and Spacer Detail in **5–3**.

7 Next, cut the table-slide supports (I) to size. Position and clamp them on the top of the crossmembers, where shown in **5–3**. Using the previously drilled ¹⁄₄" mounting holes in the crossmembers (B) as guides, mark the centerpoints and drill the ⁵⁄₁₆" mounting holes and T-nut depressions in each support. See the Screw Detail in **5–2** for reference.

Assemble the Base and Add the Slats

1 Dry-fit the base pieces (A, B, C) to check the fit. Trim if necessary, and then sand smooth.

2 Glue and clamp the base (A, B, C) together, checking for square. Remove any excess glue now with a damp cloth, or wait

Now, Edge-Join Narrower Stock for the Tabletop

1 To form the two halves (J) for the tabletop, cut 1¹⁄₁₆"-thick stock to the sizes listed in **5–5**. Only one half is shown, so be sure to cut two pieces for every one shown.

2 Lay out the pieces for the best grain match. Mark the edges that will receive the splines. See **5–5** for the location.

3 Fit your router with a ¼" slotting cutter. Rout ¼" slots centered along the marked edges of the tabletop pieces, stopping 1¾" from the ends. See the Spline Detail in **5–5** for reference.

4 From ¼" stock (we used plywood), cut ¹⁵⁄₁₆"-wide splines to the lengths listed in **5–5**. (Before cutting, make sure the ¼" plywood fits snugly in the ¼" slots. We've found some ¼" plywood is undersize, making for a sloppy fit.) Now, cut or sand the ends of each spline to the shape shown on the full-size Spline End pattern in **5–5**.

5 Glue, spline, and clamp one tabletop half together, checking that the top remains flat. Repeat for the other tabletop half. Remove excess glue.

6 Mark the layout lines, and cut the tabletop halves to shape. See the Tabletop Assembly and Tabletop Half drawings in **5–5**.

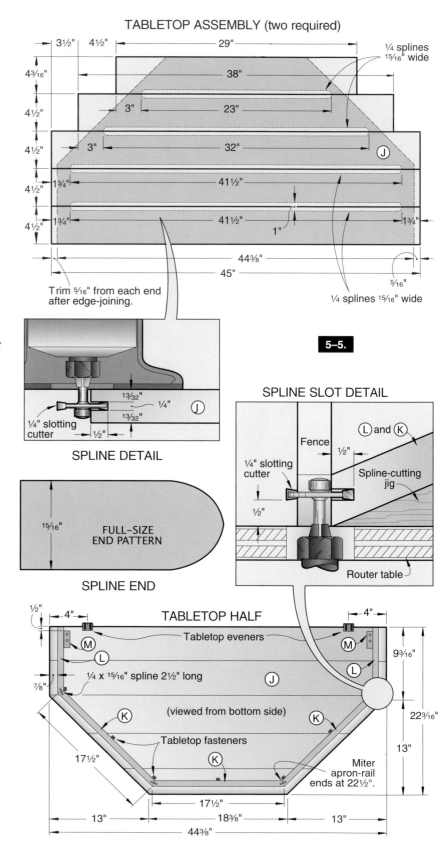

TABLETOP ASSEMBLY (two required)

¼ splines ¹⁵⁄₁₆" wide

Trim ⁵⁄₁₆" from each end after edge-joining.

¼ splines ¹⁵⁄₁₆" wide

5–5.

SPLINE DETAIL

¼" slotting cutter

SPLINE SLOT DETAIL

Fence

¼" slotting cutter

Spline-cutting jig

Router table

FULL-SIZE END PATTERN

SPLINE END

TABLETOP HALF

Tabletop eveners

¼ x ¹⁵⁄₁₆" spline 2½" long

(viewed from bottom side)

Tabletop fasteners

Miter apron-rail ends at 22½°.

5–6.

SPLINE-CUTTING JIG

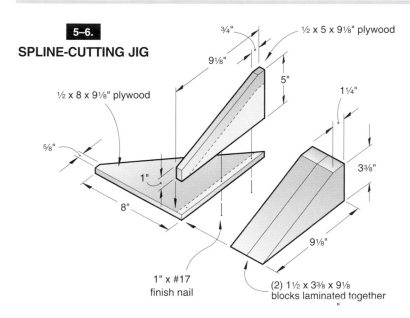

½ x 8 x 9⅛" plywood

¾"

9⅛"

½ x 5 x 9⅛" plywood

5"

1¼"

⅝"

1"

3⅜"

8"

9⅛"

1" x #17
finish nail

(2) 1½ x 3⅜ x 9⅛
blocks laminated together
"

5–7

Using the spline-cutting jig for support, rout slots across the ends of the apron rails. To make the cut, raise the slotting cutter ½" above the top surface of the router table.

Add the Apron Rails and Hardware

1 Cut the apron rails (K, L) to the sizes listed in the Materials List. Miter the ends at the angle shown on the Tabletop Half drawing in **5–5**.

2 Cut a ⅛" groove ¼" deep along the top inside edge of each apron rail where shown on the Tabletop Fastener Detail (**5–4**).

3 Rout a ¼" chamfer along the bottom edges of each apron rail.

4 Build the spline-cutting jig, referring to **5–6**.

5 Raise the bottom edge of the slotting cutter ½" above the top surface of the router table. Using the spline-cutting jig, as shown in **5–7**, rout a slot across both ends of each long apron rail (K) and across the mitered end of each short apron rail (L).

6 Lay a blanket on top of your workbench. Then, position the tabletop halves upside down and edge to edge with the ends aligned. Attach the tabletop eveners, where shown on the Tabletop Half drawing in **5–5**. The eveners align with each other on each half.

7 Set the apron rails (K, L) on the tabletop halves, positioning the square-cut ends of the short apron rails (L) with the inside edge of the tabletop half. To keep glue off the tabletop bottom, slide waxed paper between the apron rails and tabletop. Glue and spline the apron rails together. Use masking tape to hold the mitered-splined joints tight and the pieces in place until the glue has dried. (We used large handscrew clamps to temporarily clamp the pieces to the tabletop bottom until the glue dried.) Later, remove the clamps, waxed paper, and masking tape.

8 Carefully position the apron assembly on the tabletop bottom. Slide one end of each tabletop fastener into the ⅛" groove you cut in the apron rails, and screw the opposite end of the fastener to the tabletop bottom.

9 With the ends flush and the slides parallel to each other, attach the slides to the base supports, where shown in **5–3**, on *page 103*.

10 With the tabletop still upside down, position the base (also upside down) on the bottom side of the tabletop. Position the slides so they are perpendicular to the joint line of the tabletop halves. Drill mounting holes, and fasten the slides to the tabletop.

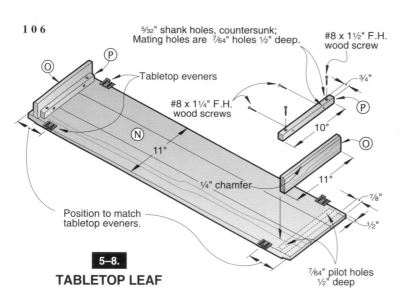

5/32" shank holes, countersunk; Mating holes are 7/64" holes 1/2" deep.

#8 x 1½" F.H. wood screw

Tabletop eveners

#8 x 1¼" F.H. wood screws

O

P

N

P

O

¾"

10"

11"

11"

¼" chamfer

7/8"

½"

Position to match tabletop eveners.

7/64" pilot holes ½" deep

5–8.
TABLETOP LEAF

5–9.

Attach the metal slides to the slide supports (I), and then secure them to the bottom of the tabletop halves.

Build a Leaf (or Two, or Three)

1 Edge-join stock for each 11"-wide leaf (N), cutting the pieces 1" extra in length. Crosscut the ends square, trimming the leaves to the same length as the tabletop. (To ensure the correct length, we positioned our leaves next to the tabletop halves to mark the cutoff lines.)

2 Turn the table right side up, and position the leaves on the slides between the tabletop halves (J). Attach the tabletop eveners to the leaves mating them to the eveners already attached to the tabletop halves. Keep the leaves in place for routing in the next step.

3 Using the same raised-panel bit used earlier to rout the feet, rout the top edges of the tabletop and the ends of the leaf or leaves.

4 Cut the leaf apron rails (O) to size, and chamfer the bottom outside edge of each rail.

5 Cut the apron-rail cleats (P) to size. Drill mounting holes through them to the sizes stated in **5–8**. Fasten the cleats to the apron rails, and then attach the apron rail/cleats to the bottom of the leaf, making sure the leaf apron rails align with the tabletop apron rails.

Finishing Up

1 With the table leaves in place, sand the top surface of the tabletop assembly absolutely flush and smooth.

2 Remove the slides from the tabletop and base. (To maintain alignment between the tabletop and leaves, we didn't remove the eveners.) Finish-sand the base, tabletop, and leaves, going to 220-grit.

3 Stain the pieces. Apply the finish. (We applied a fast-drying, clear, gloss polyurethane, followed by a final coat of fast-drying, clear, semigloss polyurethane.) To help prevent warping later due to moisture absorption from the atmosphere, add as many coats of finish to the bottom of the tabletop and leaf as you do to the top.

4 Allow the finish to dry thoroughly; then reattach the slides to the supports and tabletop halves as shown in **5–9**.

5 Nail the floor glides to the bottom of the feet, install the table in your dining room, set it with your best china, and invite the gang for dinner. Their enthusiasm for your handiwork probably will send you back to the shop to construct the complementary chairs coming on the following pages.

CHAIRS FOR THE OCTAGON TABLE

The distinguished-looking table on the preceding pages cries out for four, six, or even eight of these Arts and Crafts chairs. Mortise-and-tenon joinery makes for rock-solid construction, and the padded-seat design guarantees an oh-so-comfortable dining experience for your guests.

Note: *The instructions, Materials List, and Cutting Diagram are for one chair. Adjust for the number of chairs you plan to build.*

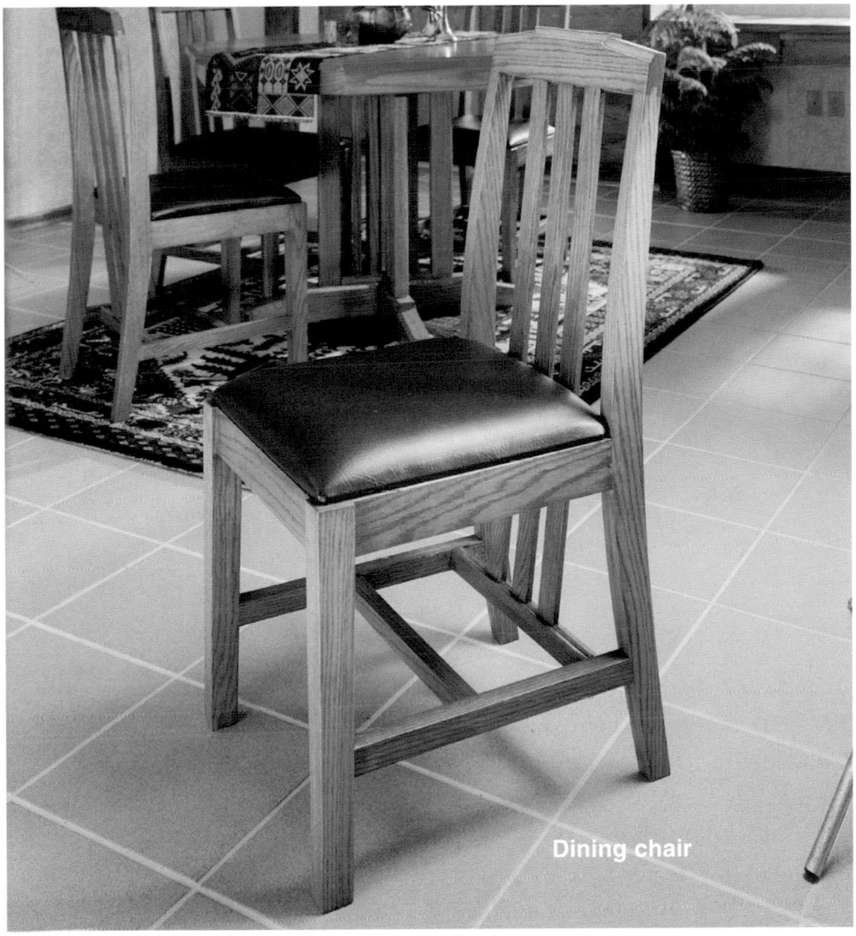
Dining chair

MATERIALS LIST FOR ONE CHAIR

	FINISHED SIZE				
PART	T	W	L	Mtl.	Qty.
A* front legs	1½"	1¾"	17½"	LO	2
B* rear legs	1 1/16"	4"	35"	O	2
C upper side rails	1 1/16"	2½"	16⅞"	O	2
D* lower side rails	1 1/16"	1¼"	15 5/16"	O	2
E front rail	1 1/16"	2½"	15 1/16"	O	1
F back rail	1 1/16"	2½"	13¼"	O	1
G stretcher	1 1/16"	1"	13¼"	O	1
H stretcher	1 1/16"	1⅛"	13¼"	O	1
I slats	⅜"	1½"	29 3/16"	O	3
J spacers	⅜"	⅝"	1⅛"	O	4
K spacers	⅜"	⅝"	3¼"	O	4
L top rail	1 1/16"	3"	15⅜"	O	1
M brace	1 1/18"	1 1/16"	3 ⅝"	O	4
N seat	¾"	15¼"	15½"	PW	1

*Initially cut parts oversize. Trim to finished size according to the instructions.
Material Keys: LO = laminated oak; O = oak; PW = plywood.
Supplies: spray adhesive; double-faced tape; ⅜" dowel pins 1½" long; #8 x 1¼" flathead wood screws; #10 x 1½" flathead wood screws; 1"-thick foam; ⅝" x #18 nails for webbing; ⅜" staples for seat cover; vinyl or fabric for seat cover; stain; clear finish.

CUTTING DIAGRAM FOR ONE CHAIR

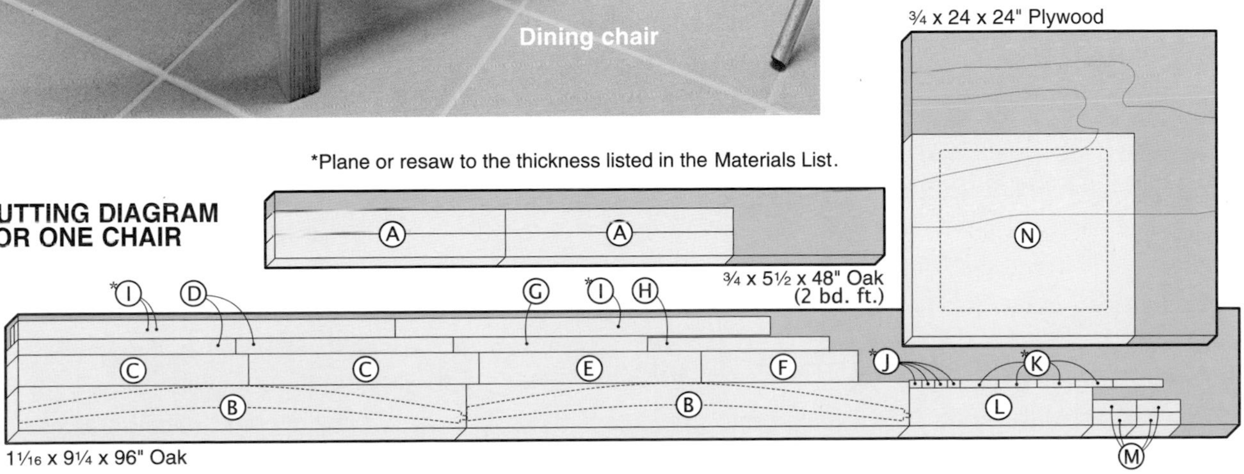
¾ x 24 x 24" Plywood
N
*Plane or resaw to the thickness listed in the Materials List.
A
A
¾ x 5½ x 48" Oak
(2 bd. ft.)
*I
D
G
*I
H
C
C
E
F
*J
*K
B
B
L
M
1 1/16 x 9¼ x 96" Oak

Start with the Front Legs

1 Use 1½"-thick stock for the front legs (A) if you have it. If not, rip and crosscut four pieces of ¾"-thick stock to 1⅞" wide × 18" long. To allow for trimming later, these dimensions are slightly larger in length and width than those on **5–10**.

2 Spread an even coat of glue on the mating surfaces. With the edges and ends flush, glue and clamp two pieces face-to-face to form each leg. Repeat the process to laminate the second front leg.

3 Scrape the glue from one edge of each leg, and then joint or plane that edge flat, removing no more than ¹⁄₁₆" of stock. Now, rip the opposite edge for a 1¾" width. Crosscut both ends of each leg for a finished length of 17½".

4 Mark the locations for the mortises and dowel holes, where shown on **5–10**. Be sure to lay out the legs in pairs.

5 Cut the mortises, and drill the dowel holes in each leg. (To form the mortises, we drilled overlapping holes to remove most of the waste stock, and then chiseled the mortises square. As an alternative you can leave the ends of the mortises round, and use a rasp to round the ends of the mating tenons.)

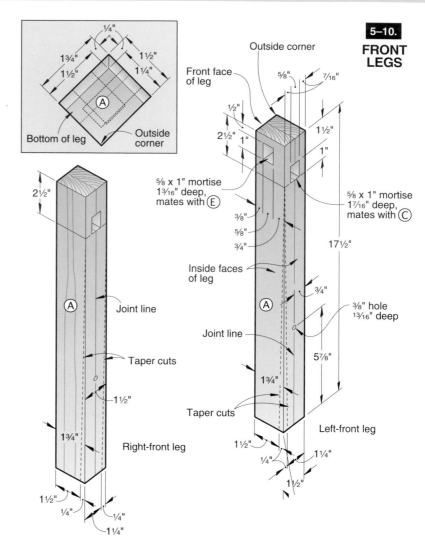

5–10. FRONT LEGS

6 Mark a pair of taper lines on two surfaces (the same surfaces as the mortises) of each leg, where shown on **5–10**. Bandsaw the tapers where marked. (You also could make the cuts using a taper jig.) Sand the tapered surfaces smooth to remove the saw marks.

Lay Out, Cut, and Machine the Rear Legs

1 From 1¹⁄₁₆"-thick stock, cut two pieces 4" wide × 35" long for the rear legs (B). Cut a piece of thin plywood or hardboard or stiff cardboard to the same size for use as a template, which you'll make in a later step.

2 Photocopy and enlarge the Rear Leg pattern, on *page 110*. Due to the length of the leg, you'll need to copy the two patterns in several sections, and then cut and assemble them to form the complete pattern. In doing so, refer to the dimensions in the pattern to ensure that the

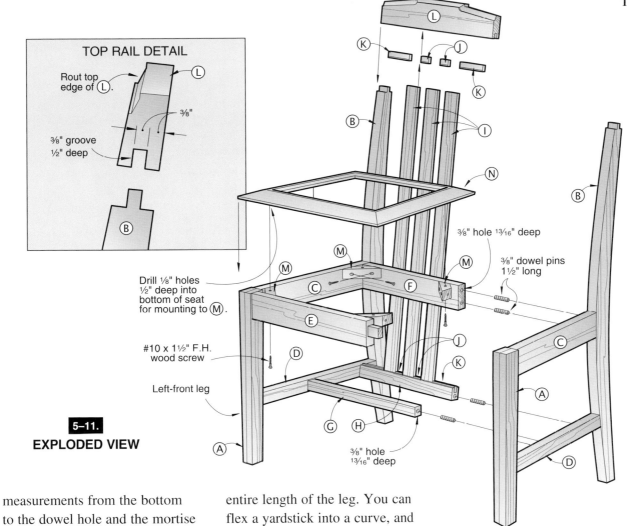

TOP RAIL DETAIL

Rout top edge of Ⓛ.

⅜"

⅜" groove ½" deep

Ⓑ

Drill ⅛" holes ½" deep into bottom of seat for mounting to Ⓜ.

⅜" hole 13/16" deep

⅜" dowel pins 1½" long

#10 x 1½" F.H. wood screw

Left-front leg

5–11.
EXPLODED VIEW

⅜" hole 13/16" deep

measurements from the bottom to the dowel hole and the mortise are correct. Also ensure that the curve flows smoothly along the

entire length of the leg. You can flex a yardstick into a curve, and lay it against the leg outlines on the pattern sections to check

the curvature. Once you have arranged the pattern sections correctly, tape them together.

3 Using spray adhesive, adhere the pattern to the 4 x 35" template stock. Cut the template to shape.

4 Using double-faced tape, temporarily laminate the two rear leg blanks together face-to-face, with the edges and ends flush. Next, position the template on the side of the stacked blanks, and apply spring clamps to hold the template in place, as shown in **5–12**.

5–12.

Transfer the mortise location, dowel-hole centerline, and leg outline to the rear leg blanks from the template.

5–13.
REAR LEG PATTERN

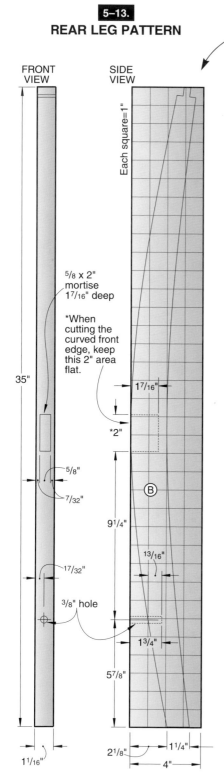

FRONT VIEW | SIDE VIEW

Each square=1"

5/8 x 2" mortise 1 7/16" deep

*When cutting the curved front edge, keep this 2" area flat.

35"

1 7/16"

*2"

5/8"

7/32"

9 1/4"

Ⓑ

13/16"

17/32"

3/8" hole

1 3/4"

5 7/8"

2 1/8" | 1 1/4"

1 1/16"

4"

(Enlarge to dimensions shown on pattern)

5–14.
TENON DETAIL

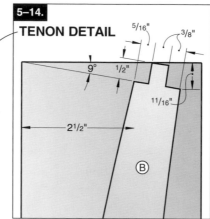

5/16" 3/8"

9° 1/2"

11/16"

2 1/2"

Ⓑ

5 As shown in **5–12**, use a square to transfer the mortise location and dowel-hole centerlines to the rear leg blanks. Next, transfer the leg outline. Separate the template from the leg blanks. Drill the dowel holes. (We did this on our drill press, using a brad-point bit.) Next, chisel the mortises to shape.

6 Bandsaw the rear legs to shape, and bandsaw the tenons to shape. (We used a ¼" blade.) Sand the edges of the legs smooth. Using a tapered wood wedge, pry the legs apart.

The Upper Rails Come Next

1 From 1¹⁄₁₆"-thick stock, cut the upper side rails (C) to the size listed in the Materials List.

2 Using the dimensions on the Front Tenon and Rear Tenon Details in **5–15**, on *page 111*, carefully lay out a tenon on each end of the upper side rails (C).

3 Cut the tenons on the rails. (We cut them out of scrap

stock first to verify the settings. We did this on a tablesaw using a miter gauge fitted with an auxiliary fence and stopblock. The stopblock helped ensure even-length tenons.) Check the fit of the tenons in their mating mortises, and trim if necessary. For reference when gluing the same joints later during assembly, make matching marks across each mating piece.

4 Mark the pair of dowel-hole centerpoints on the inside face, rear end of each upper rail (C), where dimensioned on the Rear Tenon Detail in **5–15**.

Now, Cut the Lower Rails

1 From 1¹⁄₁₆"-thick stock, cut the lower side rails (D) to size plus 1" in length.

2 Using the dimensions in **5–15** and angles shown on the Section View drawing in **5–15**, mitercut the ends of the lower side rails. Mark the centerpoints, and drill dowel holes in the inside face of each rail, where shown on the Section View drawing.

3 To drill the hole in each end of the rails, mark their centerpoints. To do this, extend a reference line parallel to the top and bottom edges of the rail. Secure the rail in a bench vise. Chuck a ⅜" brad-point bit into your portable drill. Align the bit with the marked lines, and drill the holes ¹³⁄₁₆" deep.

4 Mark the centerpoints, and drill the dowel holes for the stretchers (G, H), where located on the Section View drawing in **5–15**.

5 Dry-clamp the side frame rails (C, D) between the legs (minus the dowels) to check the fit, and trim if necessary.

Shape the Rails and Stretchers

1 Cut the front rail (E) to size. Using the Stretcher Tenon Detail in **5–16**, on *page 112*, machine a tenon on both ends of the rail.

2 Cut the back rail (F) to size, as dimensioned in the Materials List (*page 107*).

3 To transfer the dowel-hole centerpoints to the ends of the back rail (F), position ⅜" dowel centers (you'll need four) in the previously drilled dowel holes in the back inside surface of the

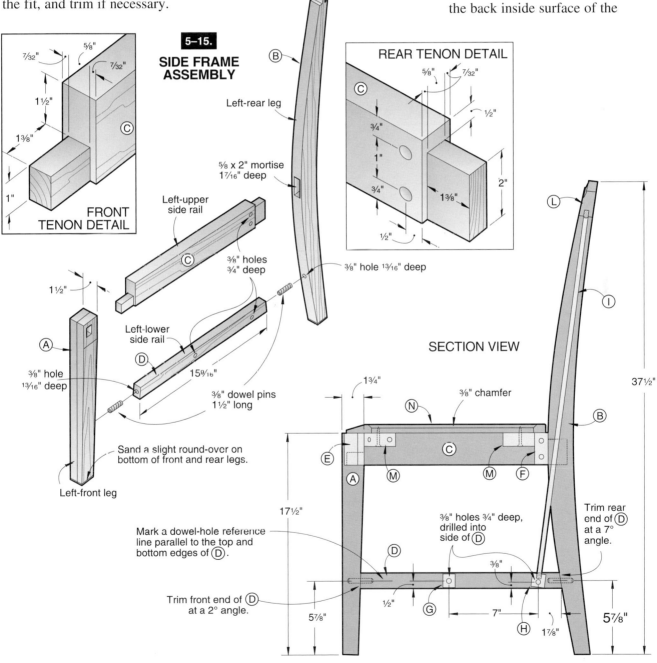

5–15.
SIDE FRAME ASSEMBLY

⅝"
7/32"   7/32"
1½"
1⅜"
Ⓒ
1"
FRONT TENON DETAIL

Ⓑ
Left-rear leg
⅝ x 2" mortise 1⁷⁄₁₆" deep

Left-upper side rail
Ⓒ
⅜" holes ¾" deep
1½"
Left-lower side rail
Ⓓ
15⁹⁄₁₆"
⅜" dowel pins 1½" long
Ⓐ
⅜" hole 1³⁄₁₆" deep
Sand a slight round-over on bottom of front and rear legs.
Left-front leg

REAR TENON DETAIL
Ⓒ
⅝"   7/32"
¾"   ½"
1"
¾"
2"
1⅜"
½"
⅜" hole 1³⁄₁₆" deep

SECTION VIEW
Ⓛ
Ⓑ
Ⓘ
37½"
1¾"   ⅜" chamfer
Ⓝ
Ⓒ
Ⓔ
Ⓐ   Ⓜ   Ⓜ   Ⓕ
17½"
Mark a dowel-hole reference line parallel to the top and bottom edges of Ⓓ.
Ⓓ
⅜" holes ¾" deep, drilled into side of Ⓓ
⅜"
Trim rear end of Ⓓ at a 7° angle.
Trim front end of Ⓓ at a 2° angle.
5⅞"
½"
Ⓖ
7"
Ⓗ   1⅞"
5⅞"

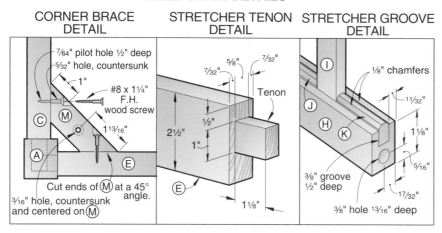

5–16. **CHAIR DETAILS**

CORNER BRACE
DETAIL

STRETCHER TENON
DETAIL

STRETCHER GROOVE
DETAIL

5–17. **CUTTING THE LOWER RAILS**

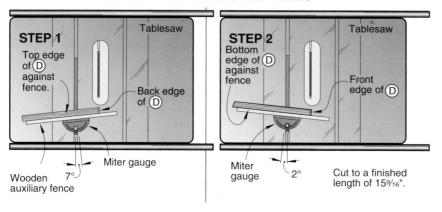

5–18. **PART VIEW**

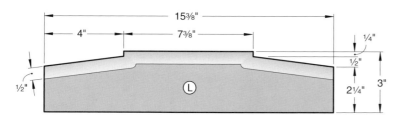

Slip in the Slatted Backrest

1 Cut and sand the backrest slats (I) to size. They're easier to sand now than when glued in place.

2 Cut a piece of stock to $\frac{3}{8} \times \frac{5}{8} \times 20$" for the spacers (J, K). Cut or rout a pair of $\frac{1}{8}$" chamfers along one edge of the 20" strip, where shown on the Stretcher Groove Detail in **5–16**. Then, crosscut the middle spacers (J) to length from the long strip.

3 Using **5–18** for reference, cut the backrest top rail (L) to shape.

4 Fit your table-mounted router with a raised-panel bit with a $\frac{1}{2}$" cutter. Rout along the top front edges of the backrest top rail (L). Do not rout the ends, bottom, or back of the rail.

5 Cut a $\frac{3}{8}$" groove $\frac{1}{2}$" deep along the bottom edge of the backrest top rail (L) and along the top edge of the rear stretcher (H). The top rail groove is cut $\frac{3}{8}$" from the back face. The groove in the rear stretcher is centered.

6 Stain the slats and back surface of the back rail (F). It's easier to do this now than with the chair assembled.

7 Glue, dowel, and clamp the stretchers (E, F, G, H) between the side frames. To angle the rear stretcher (K), stick one end of a slat in the groove in the rear stretcher, and align the top end of the slat with the rear

upper rails (C). Clamp the front and back rails (E, F) between the side frame assemblies.

4 With the assembly dry-clamped, cut the front stretcher (G) and rear stretcher (H) to fit snugly between the chair's lower rails (D).

5 Drill a dowel hole centered in each end of the front stretcher (G). Mark the dowel-hole centerpoints on the ends of the rear stretcher (H), where dimensioned on the Stretcher Groove Detail in **5–16**. Drill the holes.

leg tenons. (To give us a bit more working time, we used white woodworker's glue.)

8 Working from the center of the chair out, glue and clamp the slats, spacers, and top rail (L) in place. Doing this now will angle the rear stretcher (H) automatically. (We used masking tape to hold the spacers in place until the glue dried.)

9 Miter-cut the braces (M) to length. Drill the holes, then glue and screw them to the chair frame. See the Corner Brace Detail in **5–16** for reference.

10 Finish-sand and stain the chair, and apply a durable clear finish. (We applied two coats of fast-drying, clear, gloss polyurethane, followed by a coat of fast-drying, clear, semigloss polyurethane.)

Add the Padded Seat

1 From ¾" fir plywood, cut the seat frame (N) to shape. The outside edges of the seat should

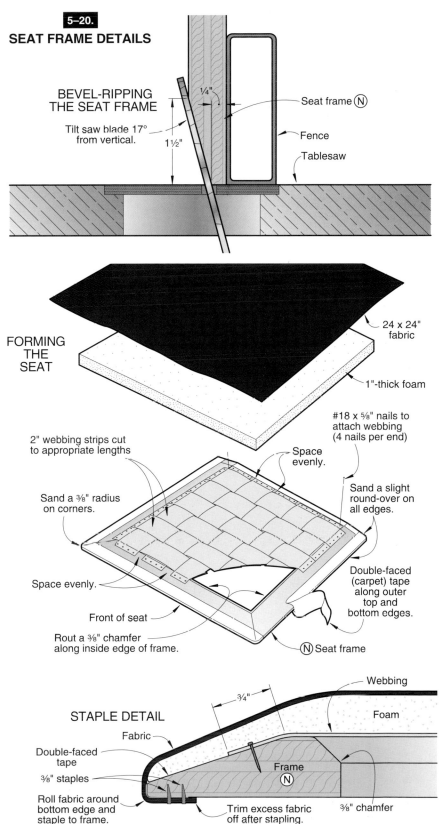

5–20.
SEAT FRAME DETAILS

BEVEL-RIPPING THE SEAT FRAME

Tilt saw blade 17° from vertical.

¼"

1½"

Seat frame Ⓝ

Fence

Tablesaw

FORMING THE SEAT

24 x 24" fabric

1"-thick foam

2" webbing strips cut to appropriate lengths

Sand a ⅜" radius on corners.

Space evenly.

Front of seat

Rout a ⅜" chamfer along inside edge of frame.

Space evenly.

#18 x ⅝" nails to attach webbing (4 nails per end)

Sand a slight round-over on all edges.

Double-faced (carpet) tape along outer top and bottom edges.

Ⓝ Seat frame

STAPLE DETAIL

¾"

Webbing

Foam

Fabric

Double-faced tape

⅜" staples

Roll fabric around bottom edge and staple to frame.

Frame Ⓝ

Trim excess fabric off after stapling.

⅜" chamfer

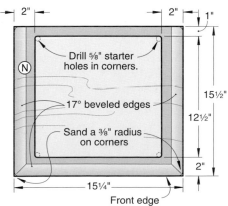

5–19.
SEAT FRAME

2"

2"

1"

Drill ⅝" starter holes in corners.

Ⓝ

17° beveled edges

15½"

12½"

Sand a ⅜" radius on corners

2"

15¼"

Front edge

be ⅛" in from the outside edges of the top rails (C, E, F).

2 Using **5–19**, lay out and cut the border for the opening with a jigsaw. (We drilled ⅝" blade start holes first.) Sand the cut edges.

3 Tilt your tablesaw blade 17° from vertical, and rip the front and side top edges of the seat frame, where shown on the Bevel-Ripping the Seat Frame drawing in **5–20**.

4 Rout a ⅜" chamfer along the inside top edge of the seat-frame opening. Sand a ⅜" radius on the sharp front corners of the seat frame to round them off. Sand a slight round-over on all other edges.

5 Starting at the center and working out, nail one end of the center piece of webbing to the seat frame, pull the opposite end tight, nail it in place, and cut off the excess. Nail the other four front-to-back strips in place. Then, starting at the front and working back, weave and nail the remaining webbing in place, where shown on the Forming the Seat drawing and accompanying detail in **5–20**. (Buy webbing at upholstery supply shops.)

6 To help hold the 1"-thick seat foam in place when applying it in the next step, cover all four edges of the plywood seat frame with double-faced tape. (We purchased our foam at an upholstery

supply store. You'll need 16" marble, multiplied by the number of chairs you'll be building.) Left untaped, the foam tends to pull away from the edges.

7 Lay the seat frame on a piece of 1" foam. Use a utility knife with a sharp blade to trim the edges of the foam flush with the edges of the seat frame.

8 Cut a piece of vinyl (or fabric), both available at upholstery suppliers, to 24" square, and lay it good side down on your workbench. Position the seat frame, foam side down, centered over the vinyl.

9 Staple the back edge of the vinyl to the bottom side of the seat frame. Pull the front edge of the vinyl tight over the frame to remove any ripples, and staple the vinyl in place. (See the Staple Detail in **5–20**.) Fold the corners until they're smooth, pull tight, and staple the sides of the vinyl to the frame. Trim the vinyl on the bottom side of the seat frame, where shown on the detail.

10 Position and center the seat on the chair frame. Use the previously drilled holes in the braces as guides to drill pilot holes in the bottom side of the seat frame. Drive screws through the four braces into the seat frame to fasten it securely to the chair.

A BEAUTIFUL BUFFET

Either as a stand-alone project or as a complement to the table and chairs, you'll find this buffet a worthy addition to your home's decor. Made from oak and accented with reproduction brass hardware, you'll especially appreciate the buffet's ample spaces.

Begin with the Carcase Assembly

1 Cut the carcase top and bottom (A) and the sides and dividers (B) to the sizes listed in the Materials List from ¾" oak plywood.

2 Mark the locations of the dadoes and rabbets on the pieces just cut (A, B), where dimensioned in **5–21**, on *page 116*. Cut or rout the rabbets and dadoes where marked.

3 Carefully mark the hole centerpoints on the inside face of the sides and dividers (B), where shown in **5–21**, for the shelf-clip holes. Clamp a fence to your drill press, set the depth gauge, and drill ¼" holes ⅜" deep, where marked.

4 For mounting the solid-oak top (G) to the carcase top (A) later, drill four ³⁄₁₆" holes in the back edge of the carcase top, where shown in **5–21**. Using the same detail for reference, form four ³⁄₁₆" slots ½" long along the

Buffet

MATERIALS LIST FOR BUFFET

PART	FINISHED SIZE			Mtl.	Qty.
	T	W	L		
CARCASE					
A top and bottom	¾"	15½"	44½"	OP	2
B sides and dividers	¾"	15½"	15¾"	OP	4
C back	¼"	44½"	16¾"	OP	1
Face Frame and Guides					
D rails	¾"	¾"	44½"	O	2
E stiles	¾"	¾"	15¼"	O	4
F guides	½"	⁷⁄₁₆"	15½"	O	6
Top					
G* top	1¹⁄₁₆"	18"	50"	EO	1
End-Panel Assemblies					
H legs	1¾"	1¾"	32"	O	4
I rails	¾"	2"	15"	O	6
J* panels	⅜"	14⅞"	13⅝"	EO	2
K slats	⅜"	1¾"	9¾"	O	6
L* spacers	⅜"	⅝"	1¾"	O	8
M* spacers	⅜"	⅝"	2⅜"	O	8
Doors					
N stiles	¾"	2½"	15⅛"	O	4
O rails	¾"	2½"	7⅝"	O	4
P* panels	¼"	7½"	11"	EO	2
Drawers					
Q fronts	¾"	5"	17⅞"	O	3
R sides	½"	5"	16"	O	6
S backs	½"	4¼"	17⅜"	O	3
T bottoms	¼"	13½"	17⅜"	OP	3
Shelves and Spacers					
U shelves	¾"	14⅞"	11⅝"	OP	2
V banding	½"	¾"	11⅝"	O	2
W spacers	½"	2"	13½"	O	4

*Initially cut parts oversized. Trim to finished size according to the instructions. Length is measured with the grain.

Materials Key: OP = oak plywood; O = oak; EO = edge-joined oak.
Supplies: 4d finish nails; 16 x ¾" nails; #8 x ¾", #8 x1½", #8 x 1 ¾" flathead wood screws; shelf clips; #10 x 1½" roundhead wood screws and #10 flat washers; stain; clear finish.

front edge and one centered at each end of the carcase top. The slots allow the screws used to secure the top (G) to the carcase top (A) to move as the top expands and contracts with seasonal humidity changes.

5 Glue, screw, and clamp the carcase pieces (A, B) together, checking for square.

6 Cut the back (C) to the same overall dimensions as the length and height of the assembled carcase and cut it to size from ¼" oak plywood. Set the back aside for now; you'll attach it later.

Add the Face Frame and Drawer Guides

1 Cut the face frame rails (D) and stiles (E) to size. Because ¾" plywood can vary in thickness slightly, be sure to cut or plane the stiles and rails to the same exact thickness as the plywood used for

the carcase. For an authentic look, we recommend quartersawn oak.

2 Cut the drawer guides (F) to fit snugly into the dadoes and protrude ³⁄₁₆".

3 Glue and clamp the guides in place, being careful not to let the guides bow out at the middle. (For even clamping pressure, we placed a piece of ¾ x 2 x 15½" stock over each guide when gluing it in place.)

BUFFET CUTTING DIAGRAM

*Plane or resaw to the thickness listed in the Materials List

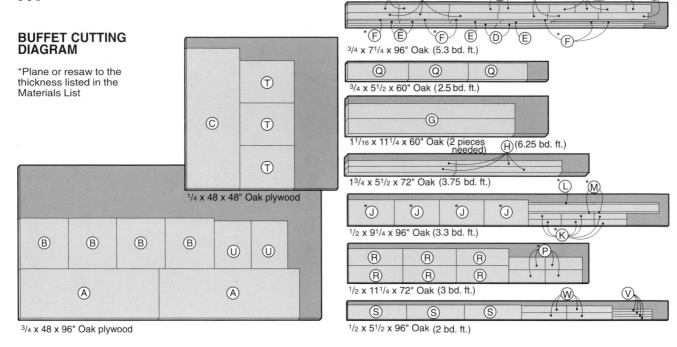

1/4 x 48 x 48" Oak plywood

3/4 x 48 x 96" Oak plywood

3/4 x 7 1/4 x 96" Oak (5.3 bd. ft.)

3/4 x 5 1/2 x 60" Oak (2.5 bd. ft.)

1 1/16 x 11 1/4 x 60" Oak (2 pieces needed) (6.25 bd. ft.)

1 3/4 x 5 1/2 x 72" Oak (3.75 bd. ft.)

1/2 x 9 1/4 x 96" Oak (3.3 bd. ft.)

1/2 x 11 1/4 x 72" Oak (3 bd. ft.)

1/2 x 5 1/2 x 96" Oak (2 bd. ft.)

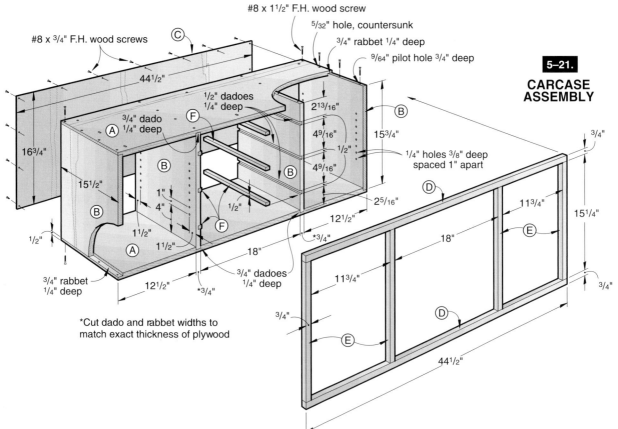

5–21.

CARCASE ASSEMBLY

*Cut dado and rabbet widths to match exact thickness of plywood

4 Glue and clamp the rails and stiles to the front of the carcase. (We placed masking tape on the adjoining oak-plywood surfaces for easier removal of the glue squeeze-out.)

5 Being careful not to sand through the veneer, use a sanding block to sand the surfaces of the stiles and rails flush with the oak plywood.

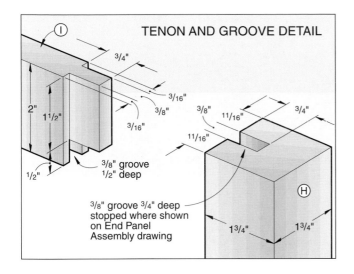

TENON AND GROOVE DETAIL

3/8" groove 1/2" deep

3/8" groove 3/4" deep stopped where shown on End Panel Assembly drawing

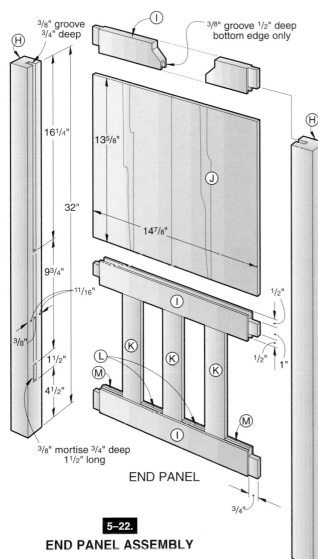

3/8" groove 3/4" deep

3/8" groove 1/2" deep bottom edge only

3/8" mortise 3/4" deep 1 1/2" long

END PANEL

5–22.
END PANEL ASSEMBLY

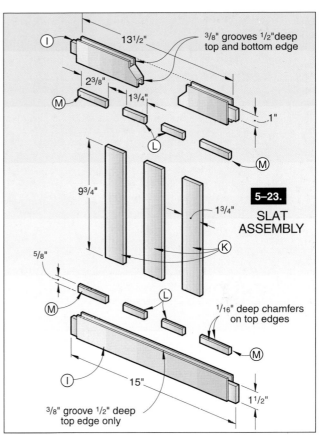

3/8" grooves 1/2" deep top and bottom edge

5–23.
SLAT ASSEMBLY

1/16" deep chamfers on top edges

3/8" groove 1/2" deep top edge only

Now Add the Solid-Oak Top

1 From 1 1/16"-thick oak (commonly called five-quarter stock), edge-join enough stock for a panel 19 × 52" for the top (G). Later, remove the clamps, scrape off the excess glue, and crosscut both ends for a 50"-long panel. (Leave the panel wide for now.)

2 Fit your router with a raised-panel bit. Rout along the ends and front (not the back) edges of the top (G).

3 Now, rip the back edge of the top (G) for a finished width of 18". By leaving the top wide at first, you'll remove any tear-out caused when routing the back corners of the ends. Set the top aside for now; you'll add it later.

End Panels Add the Arts-and-Crafts Look

1 Cut the four legs (H) to size. Carefully mark the locations of the groove and mortise on one surface

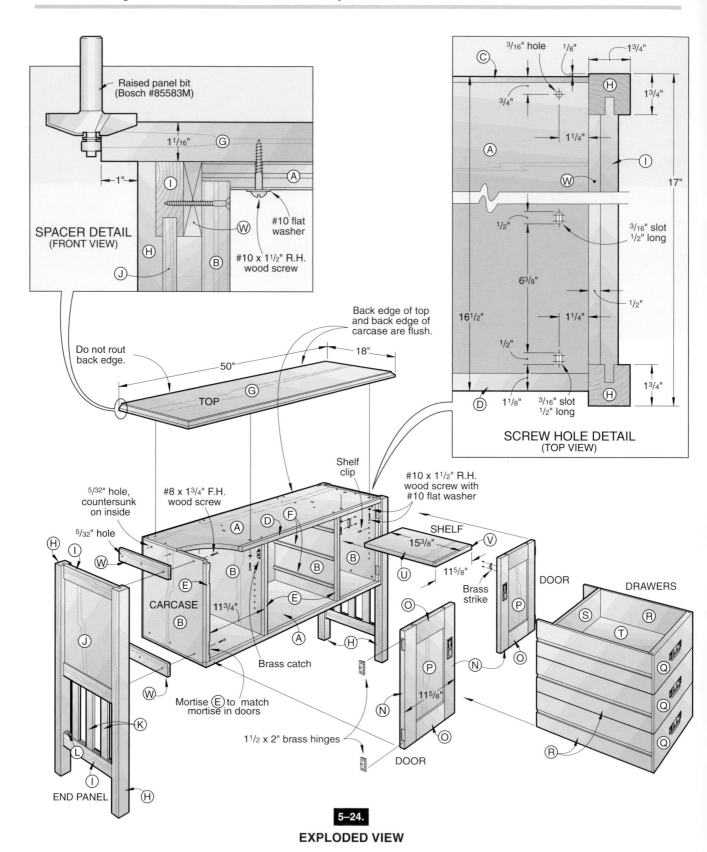

Raised panel bit
(Bosch #85583M)

$1^{1}/_{16}$" Ⓖ

1"

Ⓘ

Ⓐ

SPACER DETAIL
(FRONT VIEW)

Ⓗ

Ⓦ

Ⓙ

Ⓑ

#10 flat
washer

#10 x $1^{1}/_{2}$" R.H.
wood screw

Ⓒ

$3/16$" hole $1/8$" $1^{3}/_{4}$"

$3/4$"

Ⓗ

$1^{3}/_{4}$"

Ⓐ

$1^{1}/_{4}$"

Ⓦ

Ⓘ

17"

$1/2$"

$3/16$" slot
$1/2$" long

$6^{3}/_{8}$"

$16^{1}/_{2}$"

$1^{1}/_{4}$"

$1/2$"

$1/2$"

$1^{1}/_{4}$"

$1/2$"

Ⓓ $1^{1}/_{8}$" $3/16$" slot
$1/2$" long

Ⓗ

$1^{3}/_{4}$"

SCREW HOLE DETAIL
(TOP VIEW)

Back edge of top
and back edge of
carcase are flush.

Do not rout
back edge.

50"

18"

Ⓖ

TOP

$5/32$" hole,
countersunk
on inside

#8 x $1^{3}/_{4}$" F.H.
wood screw

Shelf
clip

#10 x $1^{1}/_{2}$" R.H.
wood screw with
#10 flat washer

$5/32$" hole

Ⓗ   Ⓘ

Ⓦ

Ⓐ   Ⓓ   Ⓕ

SHELF

$15^{3}/_{8}$"

Ⓥ

Ⓑ

Ⓑ

Ⓑ

Ⓑ

Ⓤ

$11^{5}/_{8}$"

DOOR

DRAWERS

Ⓟ

Ⓢ   Ⓡ

Ⓣ

Ⓔ

CARCASE

$11^{3}/_{4}$"

Ⓔ

Brass
strike

Ⓞ

Ⓑ

Ⓐ

Ⓗ

Ⓙ

Ⓟ

Ⓝ

Ⓞ

Ⓠ

Brass catch

Ⓦ

Ⓝ

$11^{5}/_{8}$"

Ⓡ

Ⓠ

Mortise Ⓔ to match
mortise in doors

Ⓦ

Ⓚ

$1^{1}/_{2}$ x 2" brass hinges

Ⓞ

DOOR

Ⓡ

Ⓠ

Ⓛ

Ⓘ

END PANEL

Ⓗ

5–24.

EXPLODED VIEW

of each leg where dimensioned on the End Panel Assembly drawing in **5–22**.

2 Cut or rout the grooves and mortises. (We used our tablesaw fitted with a dado blade to cut most of each groove. Then, we used our drill press fitted with a fence and mortising attachment to finish forming each groove and to form the mortises. You also can use your drill press to drill out most of the waste stock, and then remove the remaining stock with a sharp chisel.)

3 Cut the six rails (I) to size. Cut a ⅜" groove ½" deep centered along one top edge of the top and bottom rails and along both edges of the middle rails. See **5–23**, on *page 117*, for reference.

4 From ⅜" stock (we planed thicker stock), edge-join enough stock for the two end panels (J). Form the panels slightly oversized and trim them to size later. Sand smooth.

5 Cut a pair of ¾" rabbets ³⁄₁₆" deep across both ends of each rail (I) to form a ⅜" tenon ¾" long, where shown on the Tenon and Groove Detail in **5–22**.

6 Cut the end panel slats (K) to size.

7 Cut a piece of stock to ⅜ × 2 × 20" for the spacers (L, M). Cut or rout a pair of ¹⁄₁₆" chamfers along both edges of the 20"-long strip. See the chamfers in **5–23**.

Rip a ⅝"-wide strip from both edges of the 20"-long strip, and then, crosscut the spacers (L, M) to length from the ⅜ × ⅝ × 20" strips.

8 Dry-clamp each end panel assembly (H–M) to check the fit of all the parts. Adjust if necessary. Glue and clamp each end panel, checking for square as shown in the directional. (Allow the end panels to float in the grooves, as shown in **5–25**. An inch or two of glue along the top center and bottom center of each panel is all that's needed to keep the panels from rattling in the grooves.)

Construct the Two Frame-and-Panel Doors

1 Cut the door frame stiles (N) and rails (O) to size from ¾"-thick stock.

2 Cut or rout a ¼" groove ½" deep along one edge of each

piece where shown on **5–26**, *(page 120)*.

3 Cut rabbets across the ends of the rails (O) to form ¼" tenons ½" long, where shown on the Tenon Detail on **5–26**.

4 Edge-join ¼"-thick stock to form the door panels (P). Trim the panels to finished size.

5 Finish-sand and then stain both panels.

6 Dry-clamp each door to check the fit. Then, glue and clamp each door, checking for square.

7 Mark one door R (for right) and the other L. Lay out and mark the hinge location lines, and chisel the mortises in the door stiles (N) and the carcase stiles (E). Drill the pilot holes, and attach the hinges to check the fit of the doors in the openings. Adjust if necessary, and remove the hinges.

5–25.

Glue and clamp each end panel, using a framing square to check for square and flatness.

Time for the Three Drawers

1 Cut the drawer fronts (Q) to size from ¾"-thick stock. Then, from ½" stock, rip and crosscut the drawer sides (R) and backs (S) to the sizes listed in the Materials List.

2 Follow Steps 1 and 2 of the Cutting the Drawer Corner Joint Detail in **5–26** to machine the ends of the drawer fronts. Then, follow Step 3 on the drawing to machine the mating end on the drawer sides.

3 Cut all of the remaining dadoes and grooves in the drawer fronts and sides where dimensioned on **5–27** (*page 121*).

4 From ¼" oak plywood, cut the drawer bottoms (T) to size.

5 Temporarily attach the carcase back (C) to the carcase. Then, fit each drawer together (no glue) to check the fit on the glides (F) and against the back of the cabinet. Note that the cabinet back (C) provides the stop for the drawers. Adjust if necessary, and glue and clamp each drawer, checking for square. Note that the back edge of the drawer bottoms are nailed to the bottom edge of the drawer backs (S).

Build the Shelves and Assemble the Components

1 Cut the shelves (U) and front banding strips (V) to size. Make sure to cut the banding strips to the same thickness as the shelves.

2 Glue and clamp the banding strips to the front of the shelves with the ends and surfaces flush.

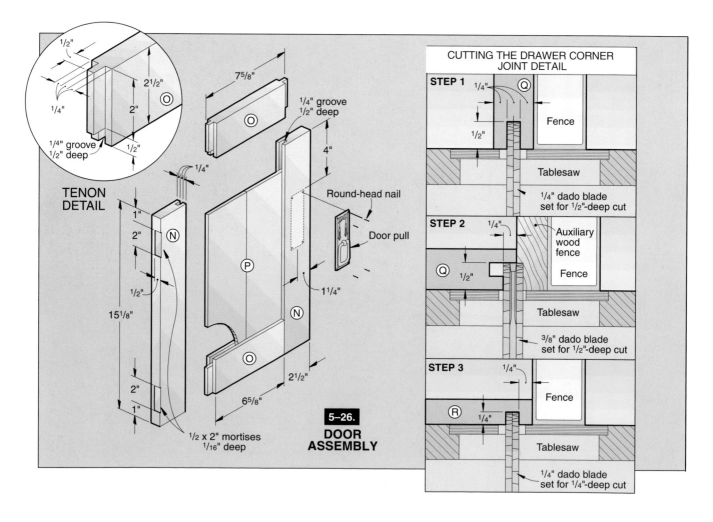

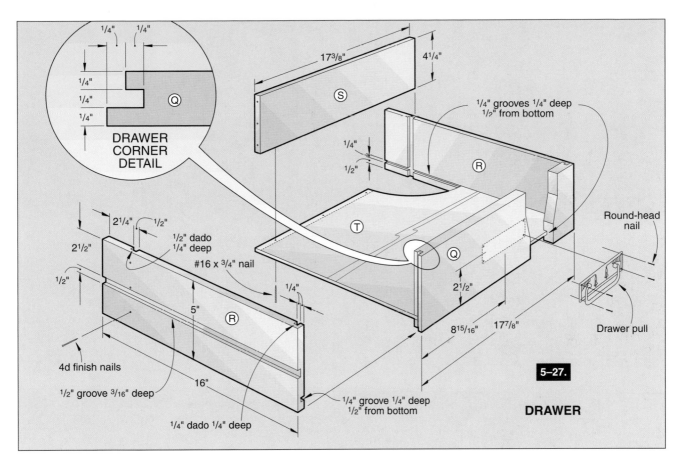

DRAWER CORNER DETAIL

1/4"
1/4"
1/4"
1/4"
1/4"

Q

17³⁄₈"

4¹⁄₄"

S

1/4" grooves 1/4" deep
1/2" from bottom

1/4"
1/2"

R

R

Round-head
nail

Drawer pull

2¹⁄₄"
1/2"

2¹⁄₂"

1/2" dado
1/4" deep

#16 x ³⁄₄" nail

1/2"

5"

R

1/4"

T

Q

2¹⁄₂"

4d finish nails

1/2" groove ³⁄₁₆" deep

16"

8¹⁵⁄₁₆"

17⁷⁄₈"

5–27.

1/4" groove 1/4" deep
1/2" from bottom

1/4" dado 1/4" deep

DRAWER

3 Cut the spacers (W) to size, and glue them to the inside face of the rails (I). See **5–24** and the accompanying Screw-Hole Detail on *page 117*.

4 Finish-sand, stain, and apply finish to the carcase, end-panel assemblies, doors, drawers, and shelves. (We used a fast-drying polyurethane for the top coat.) Even though they're not exposed, seal the inside face of the panels (J) and the bottom side of the top (G). Sealing both sides of these panels, will help prevent warping later.

5 Set the carcase upside down on your workbench. Clamp the end-panels to the ends of the carcase so the back edge of the back legs (H) protrude ⅛" beyond the back edge of the carcase back (C) where shown on the Screw Hole Detail in **5–24**. Working from the inside of the cabinet, screw the end panels to the carcase. See the Spacer Detail in **5–24** for reference.

6 Attach the pulls to the doors and drawers. Attach the doors to the cabinet.

7 Set the carcase/end panel assembly right-side up, and position the top (G) on top of the carcase/end panel assembly with an even overhang on both ends and flush with the back edge of the rear legs (H). Drive four #10 x 1½" roundhead screws through the ³⁄₁₆" holes along the back edge of the carcase top (A) and into the bottom side of the top (G). Drive roundhead screws with washers through the center of the six ³⁄₁₆" slots in the carcase top into the bottom surface of the top (G). Tighten the screws in the slots, and then back them off about half a turn to allow the screws to move in the slots with the expansion and contraction of the solid-wood top.

8 Secure the catches to the dividers (B) ¹³⁄₁₆" back from the front edge of the face frame. Now, attach the mating strike to the back side of each door, then you're done.

CHAPTER 6

Stout and Stylish Bedroom Furniture

IN THE EARLY 1900S WHEN THE ARTS AND *crafts movement was at its peak, most of the attention was focused on living and dining rooms. That's because it was in those rooms that most family activities and entertaining occurred. Also, they were open spaces just barely separated from one another.*

The furniture in them, as you've seen in the last two chapters, was simple of line but hearty, even massive in appearance. Made of oak and stained (fumed) dark, the furniture complemented the wood beams, paneling (or wainscotting), and naturally-finished woodwork that were normally part of Arts and Crafts decor. Wallcovering and fabrics featured designs from nature and earthy colors. Pottery and attractive lamps were much in evidence.

Bedrooms, however, seem to have taken a back seat to the living and dining room showplaces. Rooms on the upper floors were meant to be restful places for relaxation, and of course, sleep, so were not accorded the same attention to visual appeal. But there's no reason at all to not bring Arts and Crafts into the bedroom. In this chapter we present a bed perfect for a guest or teenager's room, or doubled up, as a bunkbed for a children's room. See how to build it starting on the next page. Then on page 131 we'll tell you how to make what is actually a multipurpose table, but we think it works pretty well as a nightstand.

Twin bed

This bed can be used as a twin bed (above) and as a bunk bed (below).

DOUBLE-DUTY BED

Bunk bed

Looking for a stylish, original bunk bed design? How about just a terrific-looking twin bed? This versatile project suits both interests. For bunk beds, simply invert one bed on top of the other, and reposition its plywood mattress support. Best of all, this size fits kids and adults alike.

Note: *Our bed was designed to fit a 39 × 75" twin mattress. Adjust accordingly for a different size mattress. The how-to instructions are for one bed. The Materials List and Cutting Diagram on the next page tell you what you need for making two beds.*

CUTTING DIAGRAM FOR TWO BEDS

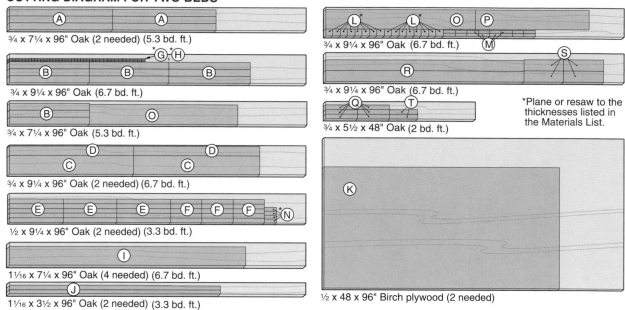

¾ x 7¼ x 96" Oak (2 needed) (5.3 bd. ft.)

¾ x 9¼ x 96" Oak (6.7 bd. ft.)

¾ x 7¼ x 96" Oak (5.3 bd. ft.)

¾ x 9¼ x 96" Oak (2 needed) (6.7 bd. ft.)

½ x 9¼ x 96" Oak (2 needed) (3.3 bd. ft.)

1¹⁄₁₆ x 7¼ x 96" Oak (4 needed) (6.7 bd. ft.)

1¹⁄₁₆ x 3½ x 96" Oak (2 needed) (3.3 bd. ft.)

¾ x 9¼ x 96" Oak (6.7 bd. ft.)

¾ x 9¼ x 96" Oak (6.7 bd. ft.)

¾ x 5½ x 48" Oak (2 bd. ft.)

*Plane or resaw to the thicknesses listed in the Materials List.

½ x 48 x 96" Birch plywood (2 needed)

MATERIALS LIST FOR TWO BEDS

PART	FINISHED SIZE			Mtl.	Qty.
	T	W	L		
LEGS					
A* headboard legs	2¼"	2¼"	33½"	LO	4
B* footboard legs	2¼"	2¼"	26"	LO	4
HEADBOARD AND FOOTBOARD					
C rails	¾"	6"	40½"	O	4
D rails	¾"	3"	40½"	O	4
E slats	½"	1½"	17½"	O	30
F slats	½"	1½"	10"	O	30
G spacers	¼"	⅝"	1"	O	112
H spacers	¼"	⅝"	1¼"	O	16
SIDE RAILS					
I rails	1¹⁄₁₆"	6"	76½"	O	4
J cleats	1¹⁄₁₆"	1"	68½"	O	4
K bottom	½"	40"	76⅜"	BP	2
POST CAPS					
L caps	⅝"	2¼"	2¼"	O	16
M supports	¾"	¾"	3⅜"	O	16
N bolt covers	⅜"	1⅛"	4"	O	8
SIDE AND HEAD SAFETY RAIL					
O side rails	¾"	6⅜"	48"	O	2
P headboard rail	¾"	6⅜"	37"	O	1
Q supports	¾"	1½"	10¼"	O	6
LADDER					
R sides	¾"	3½"	64"	O	2
S steps	¾"	3⅝"	12¾"	O	4
T catches	¾"	1½"	7"	O	2

*Parts initially cut oversize. See the instructions.

Materials Key: LO = laminated oak; O = oak; BP = birch plywood.
Supplies: ⅜" bolts 4" long with ⁵⁄₁₆" flat washers and ⅜" nuts (4); #8 x 1¼", #8 x 1½"; #10 x 1¼" flathead wood screws; ⅜" dowel stock; 4 pieces of ¾" dowel 6" long for stacking beds; stain; clear finish.

Start with the Legs

1 From ¾" oak, cut six headboard-leg parts (A) to 2⅜ x 34½" and the footboard-leg parts (B) to 2⅜ x 27". (Using these dimensions, the pieces are ⅛" oversized in width and 1" in length so you can trim flush the edges and ends of the laminated legs later. (See **6–2** for reference.)

2 Using **6–2**, lay out the notches and mortises on each piece, where dimensioned. Remember that you're making a matching pair of headboard and footboard legs, with each pair having a left and right member. Verify the marked locations before cutting.

3 Using a drill press fitted with a ½" Forstner bit and a fence with a stop, drill holes inside the marked mortise outlines. Square-up the mortises with a chisel.

You also could cut the mortises to shape with a jigsaw.

4 Cut the three notches in the center pieces. (To expedite our notch-making process, we marked centerlines on each end of each middle piece, where shown in **6–3**, on *page 126*. Then, we used a ¾" Forstner bit, and drilled a hole centered over each center-point. As shown in **6–4**, we set the fence on our bandsaw, and cut to the hole to finish forming the mortises. The round bottom on our mortises did not affect the structural integrity of the project.)

5 Mount a dado blade to your tablesaw, and cut the ¹³⁄₁₆ x 6" notch in each center piece.

6 As shown in **6–5**, on *page 126*, spread an even coat of glue on the mating surfaces of the three pieces making up each leg.

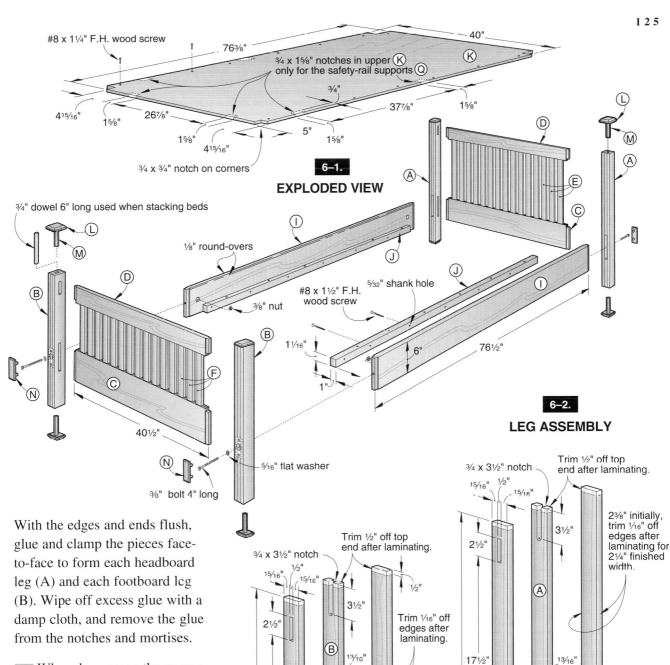

#8 x 1¼" F.H. wood screw

¾ x 1⅝" notches in upper Ⓚ only for the safety-rail supports Ⓠ

76⅜"

40"

¾"

4¹⁵⁄₁₆" 1⅝" 26⅞" 37⅞" 1⅝"

1⅝" 5" 1⅝"

4¹⁵⁄₁₆"

¾ x ¾" notch on corners

6–1.

EXPLODED VIEW

Ⓓ

Ⓐ Ⓔ

Ⓒ

Ⓛ

Ⓜ

Ⓐ

¾" dowel 6" long used when stacking beds

Ⓛ

Ⓜ

⅛" round-overs

Ⓘ

Ⓙ

⅜" nut

#8 x 1½" F.H. wood screw

⁵⁄₃₂" shank hole

Ⓙ

Ⓘ

Ⓑ

Ⓓ

Ⓑ

Ⓕ

Ⓒ

Ⓝ

1¹⁄₁₆"

1"

6"

76½"

40½"

Ⓝ

⁵⁄₁₆" flat washer

⅜" bolt 4" long

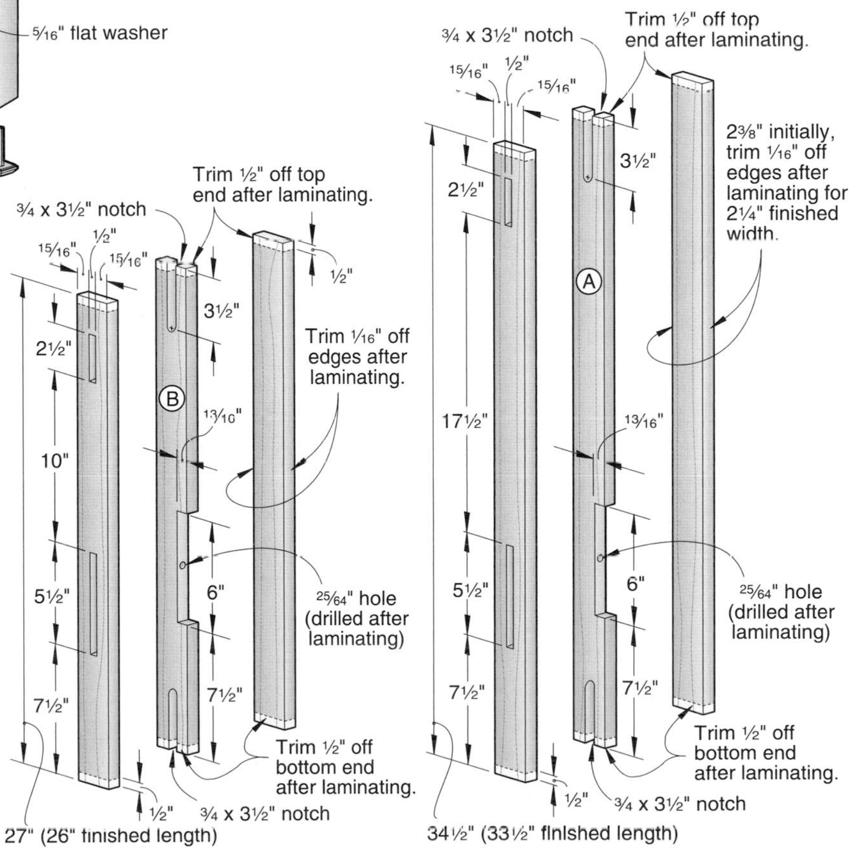

6–2.

LEG ASSEMBLY

With the edges and ends flush, glue and clamp the pieces face-to-face to form each headboard leg (A) and each footboard leg (B). Wipe off excess glue with a damp cloth, and remove the glue from the notches and mortises.

7 When dry, scrape the excess glue from the legs' edges. Then, joint or plane ¹⁄₁₆" from each laminated edge for a 2¼"-square lamination.

8 Crosscut ½" from each end so the headboard legs (A) measure 33½" long and the footboard legs (B) measure 26" long. For level side rails later, make sure when trimming the legs to

¾ x 3½" notch

Trim ½" off top end after laminating.

15⁄16" ½" 15⁄16"

2½"

Ⓑ

10"

Trim ¹⁄₁₆" off edges after laminating.

13⁄16"

5½"

6"

²⁵⁄₆₄" hole (drilled after laminating)

7½"

7½"

½"

Trim ½" off bottom end after laminating.

¾ x 3½" notch

27" (26" finished length)

¾ x 3½" notch

Trim ½" off top end after laminating.

15⁄16" ½" 15⁄16"

2½"

3½"

Ⓐ

2⅜" initially, trim ¹⁄₁₆" off edges after laminating for 2¼" finished width.

17½"

13⁄16"

5½"

6"

²⁵⁄₆₄" hole (drilled after laminating)

7½"

7½"

½"

Trim ½" off bottom end after laminating.

¾ x 3½" notch

34½" (33½" finished length)

6-3.

Using a Forstner bit in your drill press, drill a ¾" hole at the marked center-point on each leg centerpiece.

6-4.

Position your bandsaw fence to cut to the hole, creating ¾"-wide notches in the center leg pieces.

6-5.

Spread an even coat of glue on the mating surfaces, and glue the three pieces together to form each leg.

2 Fit your tablesaw with a ¼" dado blade, and cut a ¼" groove ½"deep centered along one edge of each rail (C, D). See **6–6** for reference.

3 Switch to a wider dado blade on your tablesaw. Then, attach a long wooden extension to your tablesaw's miter gauge, and square the extension to the blade. Using a stop for consistency, cut rabbets to form tenons on the ends of the rails (C, D) and slats (E, F).

4 To assemble the headboard and footboard assemblies, start by finding the center (from end-to-end) of each rail, and mark a centerline across the grain. Starting with a slat centered over the centerline and working to the ends, dry-clamp (no glue) the headboard and footboard assemblies together, checking for square. Now, check the fit of the clamped-together assemblies into the mortises of their respective legs. After verifying the fit, glue and clamp the headboard and footboard assemblies together between the legs.

Cut the Side Rails, Cleats, and Bottom to Size

1 From 1¹/₁₆"stock, cut the side rails (I) and cleats (J) to size.

2 Using the dimensions in **6–7**, cut the ¾"-thick tenons on both ends of all four side rails.

final length that the bottom of the mortise in each leg is 7" from the bottom trimmed end of each leg.

9 To form the bolt-access holes, attach a fence and stop to your drill-press table. Then, drill a 1" hole ½" deep with a ²⁵/₆₄" hole centered inside and 10" from the bottom end of each leg, where shown on **6–2**. Sand the legs smooth.

The Slatted Headboard and Footboard Come Next

1 Cut the headboard and footboard rails (C, D), slats (E, F), and spacers (G, H) to the sizes listed in the Materials List. (For the spacers, we cut four pieces of stock to ¼ × ⅝ × 40", and crosscut the spacers from the long strips.)

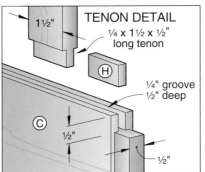

TENON DETAIL

1½"

¼ x 1½ x ½" long tenon

Ⓗ

¼" groove ½" deep

Ⓒ

½"

½"

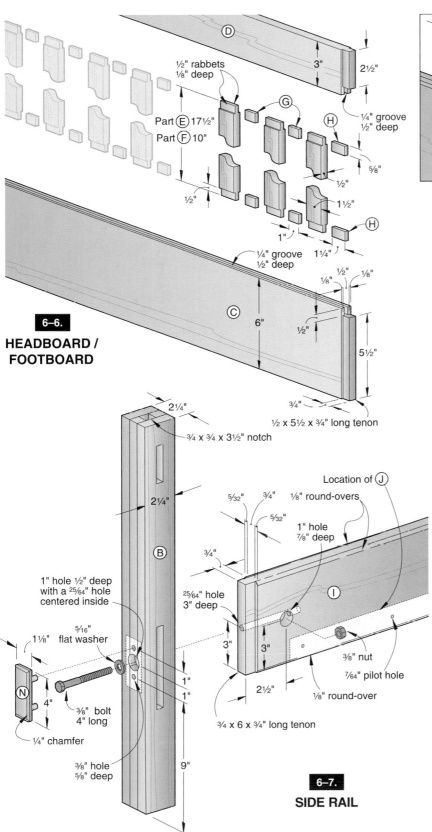

½" rabbets ⅛" deep

Part Ⓔ 17½"
Part Ⓕ 10"

Ⓓ

3"

2½"

¼" groove ½" deep

Ⓖ

Ⓗ

½"

5/8"

½"

1½"

Ⓗ

½"

1"

1¼"

¼" groove ½" deep

Ⓒ

6"

⅛"

½"

½"

⅛"

½"

5½"

¾"

½ x 5½ x ¾" long tenon

6–6.
HEADBOARD / FOOTBOARD

2¼"

¾ x ¾ x 3½" notch

2¼"

Ⓑ

1" hole ½" deep with a 25/64" hole centered inside

5/16" 1⅛" flat washer

Ⓝ

4"

⅜" bolt 4" long

¼" chamfer

⅜" hole 5/8" deep

9"

Location of Ⓙ

5/32"

¾"

⅛" round-overs

5/32"

1" hole 7/8" deep

¾"

25/64" hole 3" deep

Ⓘ

3"

3"

⅜" nut

7/64" pilot hole

2½"

⅛" round-over

¾ x 6 x ¾" long tenon

1"

1"

6–7.
SIDE RAIL

3 Mark the centerpoint, and drill a 1" hole 7/8"deep on the inside face of each side rail, where shown on the drawing. To prevent boring through the side rail, you must use a flat-bottomed bit, such as a Forstner, and a depth stop on your drill press.

4 Dry-clamp the side rails (I) into the mortises in the headboard and footboard assemblies, checking for square. Using the previously drilled 25/64" holes in each leg as a guide, chuck a twist-drill bit into your portable drill, and drill as far as possible into the tenoned end of each side rail. Then, separate the leg from the side rail, and continue drilling into the tenoned ends of the side rails until the bit goes through the 1" nut-access hole for a 3" total depth.

5 Drill countersunk mounting holes in each cleat (J), clamp them in place, and use the holes as guides to drill pilot holes in the inside face of the sideboard rails. Screw the cleats in place.

6 Reinstall the tenoned side rails into the mortised legs. Place a 5/16" washer on each ⅜" bolt (it's a tight fit, but a ⁵⁄₁₆" washer does fit onto a ³⁄₈" bolt). Slide a bolt through the hole in the leg and into the hole in the end of the side rail. Fit a ³⁄₈" nut into the nut-access hole, thread the bolt through the nut, and tighten the bolts until the bed frame is wobble free. Without the ⁵⁄₁₆" washer, the head of the bolt would cut into the wood in each leg.

7 From ½" birch plywood, cut the bottoms (K) to size. Mark and cut a notch in each corner, as dimensioned on **6–1**, on *page 125.* Cut notches in one of the bed bottoms for the side- and headboard-rail supports (Q) to be used on the upper bunk later.

8 Drill countersunk mounting holes through the plywood bottom pieces (K) for securing to the cleats (J) later.

Cut the Post Caps and Bolt Covers Next

1 From ⁵⁄₈"-thick stock, cut eight caps (L) to 2¼" square. Drill a ¾" hole ½" deep centered on the bottom of each cap, where shown in **6–8**.

2 Tilt the blade on your tablesaw to 45° away from the fence, and bevel-cut each top edge of each 2¼"-square cap, as shown in Step 1 of **6–9**. Then, follow Step 2 of the detail to cut the decorative rabbets.

3 To make the cap supports (M), cut two pieces of oak to ¾ x ¾ x 15". Then, bevel-rip

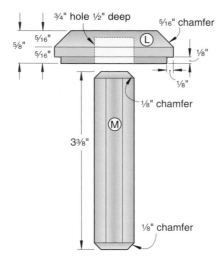

6–8.
POST CAP

¾" hole ½" deep
⁵⁄₁₆" chamfer
⁵⁄₈"
⁵⁄₁₆"
⁵⁄₁₆"
⅛"
⅛"
⅛" chamfer
3⅜"
⅛" chamfer

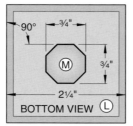

90°
¾"
¾"
2¼"
BOTTOM VIEW (L)

Note: (M) must be square with (L).

each edge of each strip at 45°, where shown on the Bottom View within **6–9**. Check the fit of the octagonal pieces in the mortise holes in the top of each leg. Trim more if necessary until the pieces slide in easily. Crosscut eight cap supports (M) to 3 ⅜" long each. Sand a ⅛" chamfer on each end, where shown on the drawing.

4 Place a dab of glue in the ¾" hole in each post cap. Then, use a mallet to drive a cap support into the hole. For the caps to fit squarely on the legs later, align the edges of the support square with those of the cap, where shown in **6–8**. You may have to rotate the supports slightly for a proper fit.

5 To form the bolt covers (N), rip and crosscut four pieces of ³⁄₈"-thick stock to 1⅛ x 4". Tilt the blade on your tablesaw 45° away from the fence, and cut a chamfer on both ends of the bolt-cover blanks, using a wooden extension on your miter gauge to support the piece when making the cuts. See **6–10** for reference. Remove the miter gauge, and use the tablesaw fence as a guide when cutting chamfers along the edges.

6 Cut a piece of ½" or ¾" stock to the same size as the bolt covers. Drill a pair of ³⁄₈" holes 2" on center through the stock, where dimensioned in **6–10**. Now, use this as a template to position your drill bit, and drill

6–9.
CUTTING THE POST CAP

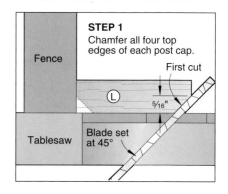

Fence

STEP 1
Chamfer all four top edges of each post cap.

First cut

(L)

⁵⁄₁₆"

Tablesaw

Blade set at 45°

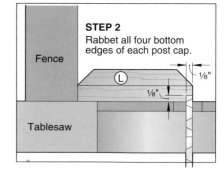

Fence

STEP 2
Rabbet all four bottom edges of each post cap.

(L)

⅛"

⅛"

Tablesaw

6–10.
BOLT COVER PATTERNS

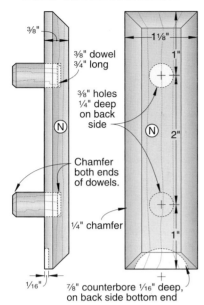

³⁄₈"

³⁄₈" dowel
³⁄₄" long

³⁄₈" holes
¹⁄₄" deep
on back
side

(N)

Chamfer
both ends
of dowels.

(N) 2"

1"

1"

¹⁄₄" chamfer

¹⁄₁₆"

⁷⁄₈" counterbore ¹⁄₁₆" deep,
on back side bottom end

1¹⁄₈"

a pair of ³⁄₈" holes ¹⁄₄" deep 2" on center on the inside face of each bolt cover.

7 Using the same positioning jig, drill a pair of ³⁄₈" holes ⁵⁄₈" deep in the legs, centering the holes over the top and bottom of the legs' bolt holes. See **6–7** (*page 127*) for reference.

8 Using a ⁷⁄₈" Forstner bit, drill a ¹⁄₁₆"-deep depression on the back side at one end of each cover, where shown in **6–10**. The depression acts as a finger recess when removing the covers from the bed later to access and loosen and tighten the bolts.

9 Crosscut eight pieces of ³⁄₈" dowel stock to ³⁄₄" long. Chamfer both ends, and glue them into the bolt covers, where shown in **6–10**.

Add the Safety Rails

Note: When turning one of the beds over and stacking it on top of the other bed to make a top bunk, you'll need to add a head rail at one end and a pair of side rails to the top bunk to keep children from falling out of bed. You'll also need to rotate the bedrails (I) to keep the cleat (J) along the bottom edge of the rail.

1 Cut the side rails (O) and headboard rail (P) to size. Mark a 2" radius on each corner, and cut and sand to shape.

2 Cut the supports (Q) to size. Rout a ¹⁄₈" round-over along the edges noted in **6–11**. Using the same drawing for reference, drill mounting holes and screw the supports to the head and side safety rails.

A Ladder for the Top Bunk

1 Cut the ladder sides (R) to shape, using **6–11** for reference.

2 Mark the dado and slot locations on both ladder rails. Cut the slots to shape. Note that the pieces must be mirror images of each other; be careful not to make two left-hand or two right-hand ladder sides.

3 Transfer the full-size ladder catch outline to ³⁄₄" stock, and cut the catches (T) to shape. Glue them to the top of the ladder sides (R), where shown in **6–12** (*page 130*).

4 Rout ¹⁄₈" and ¹⁄₄" round-overs along all edges (including the hand-hold slots), where shown in **6–12** (*page 130*).

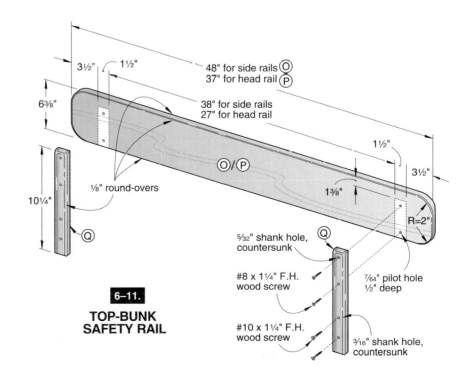

6–11.
TOP-BUNK SAFETY RAIL

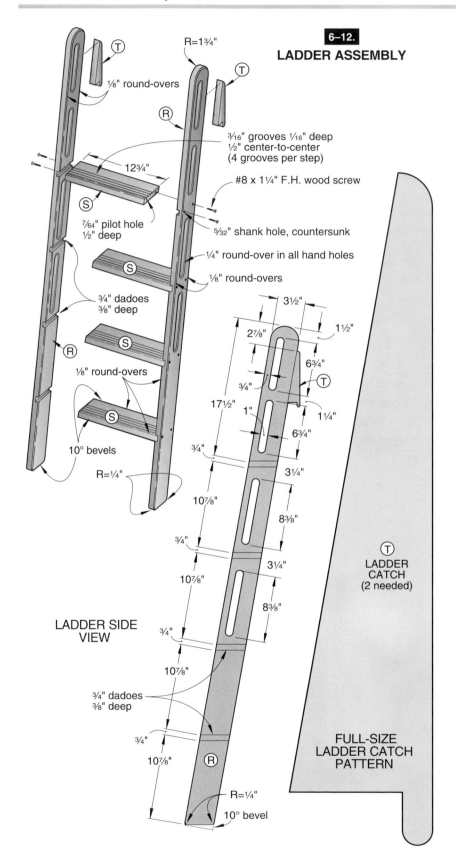

6–12.
LADDER ASSEMBLY

⊤

R=1¾"

⊤

Ⓡ

⅛" round-overs

³⁄₁₆" grooves ¹⁄₁₆" deep
½" center-to-center
(4 grooves per step)

#8 x 1¼" F.H. wood screw

12¾"

Ⓢ

⁷⁄₆₄" pilot hole
½" deep

⁵⁄₃₂" shank hole, countersunk

¼" round-over in all hand holes

Ⓢ

⅛" round-overs

¾" dadoes
⅜" deep

Ⓢ

Ⓡ

⅛" round-overs

Ⓢ

10° bevels

R=¼"

3½"

2⅞"

1½"

6¾"

⊤

¾"

1¼"

17½"

1"

6¾"

¾"

3¼"

10⅞"

8⅜"

¾"

3¼"

10⅞"

8⅜"

¾"

⊤
LADDER
CATCH
(2 needed)

LADDER SIDE
VIEW

10⅞"

¾" dadoes
⅜" deep

¾"

10⅞"

Ⓡ

R=¼"

10° bevel

FULL-SIZE
LADDER CATCH
PATTERN

5 Using your tablesaw fitted with a dado blade and a long wooden extension attached to your miter gauge, cut four dadoes at a 10° angle in each side piece, where marked. Mark screw-hole centerpoints on the outside face of the sides, centered over the dadoes.

6 Cut the steps (S) to size, bevel-ripping the front and rear edges at 10°. Using a ³⁄₁₆" veining bit, rout a set of grooves in each step, where shown in **6–12**. Glue and screw the steps in place. Sand a ⅛" round-over along all edges of the steps.

Finishing and Final Assembly

1 Finish-sand the beds, side and headboard safety rails, and ladder. Apply a stain if desired. (We left ours natural.) Apply the finish, lightly sanding between coats with 320-grit sandpaper.

2 Reassemble the beds in the bedroom, screwing the plywood bottoms (K) to the top of the cleats (J). If used as bunk beds, use the holes in the safety rail supports (Q) as guides to drill mating holes in the top bunk bed rail (I). Screw the side and head safety rails in place.

Nightstand

MATERIALS LIST FOR NIGHTSTAND

PART	FINISHED SIZE			Mtl.	Qty.
	T	W	L		
A front legs	1¾"	1¾"	28"	O	2
B back legs	1¾"	1¾"	28"	O	2
C upper side rails	¾"	1¾"	11½"	O	2
D middle side rails	¾"	1¾"	11½"	O	2
E lower side rails	¾"	1¾"	11½"	O	2
F upper back rail	¾"	1¾"	12½"	O	1
G lower back rail	¾"	1¾"	12½"	O	1
H front skirt	¾"	1¾"	12½"	O	1
I upper front rail	¾"	1⅜"	11½"	O	1
J lower front rail	¾"	1⅜"	11½"	O	1
K slats	⅜"	1½"	14¼"	O	6
L slat-groove fillers	⅜"	⅜"	1½"	O	16
M side panels	¼"	11½"	6"	OP	2
N back panel	¼"	12½"	6"	OP	1
O* drawer guides	½"	¾"	12⅜"	O	4
P* shelf	¾"	10"	13"	EO	1
Q drawer fronts	¾"	3⅝"	11⅜"	O	2
R drawer sides	½"	3⅝"	12"	O	4
S drawer backs	½"	3⅛"	10⅞"	O	2
T drawer bottoms	¼"	9½"	10⅞"	OP	2
U* top	1¹⁄₁₆"	15⅛"	18"	EO	1

*Parts initially cut oversize. See the instructions.

Materials Key: O = oak; OP = oak plywood;
EO = edge-joined oak.
Supplies: #8 x 1¼" flathead wood screws;
#8 x¾" flathead wood screws; #6 x 1¼" panhead
pocket-hole screws; #6 x ¾" flathead wood screws;
tabletop fasteners; #8 x ¾" panhead wood screws; 1½"
round face-grain oak pulls with mounting screws; finish.

NIGHTSTAND

You won't have to look far to find the perfect spot in your home for this multi-purpose table. We think of it and photographed it as a nightstand, but you could use it as a telephone stand, occasional table, plant stand, or entry hall table. Its timeless beauty is matched only by the pride you'll feel after building it.

CUTTING DIAGRAM FOR NIGHTSTAND

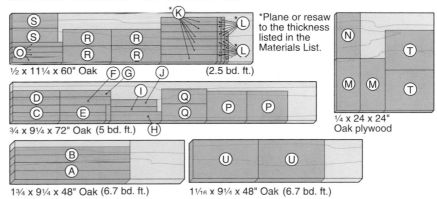

½ x 11¼ x 60" Oak   (2.5 bd. ft.)

*Plane or resaw to the thickness listed in the Materials List.

¾ x 9¼ x 72" Oak (5 bd. ft.)

¼ x 24 x 24" Oak plywood

1¾ x 9¼ x 48" Oak (6.7 bd. ft.)

1¹⁄₁₆ x 9¼ x 48" Oak (6.7 bd. ft.)

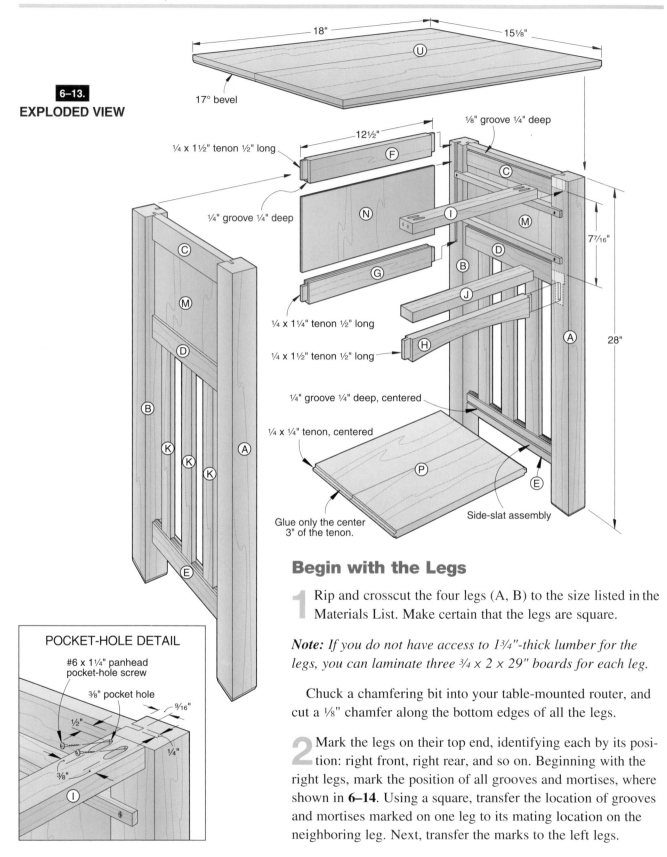

6–13.
EXPLODED VIEW

18"

15⅛"

U

17° bevel

⅛" groove ¼" deep

12½"

¼ x 1½" tenon ½" long

F

C

¼" groove ¼" deep

N

I

M

7⁷⁄₁₆"

G

D

B

J

¼ x 1¼" tenon ½" long

H

¼ x 1½" tenon ½" long

A

28"

¼" groove ¼" deep, centered

¼ x ¼" tenon, centered

P

Glue only the center
3" of the tenon.

Side-slat assembly

C

M

D

B

K

K

K

A

E

POCKET-HOLE DETAIL

#6 x 1¼" panhead
pocket-hole screw

⅜" pocket hole

9⁄16"

½"

¼"

⅜"

I

Begin with the Legs

1 Rip and crosscut the four legs (A, B) to the size listed in the Materials List. Make certain that the legs are square.

Note: If you do not have access to 1¾"-thick lumber for the legs, you can laminate three ¾ x 2 x 29" boards for each leg.

Chuck a chamfering bit into your table-mounted router, and cut a ⅛" chamfer along the bottom edges of all the legs.

2 Mark the legs on their top end, identifying each by its position: right front, right rear, and so on. Beginning with the right legs, mark the position of all grooves and mortises, where shown in **6–14**. Using a square, transfer the location of grooves and mortises marked on one leg to its mating location on the neighboring leg. Next, transfer the marks to the left legs.

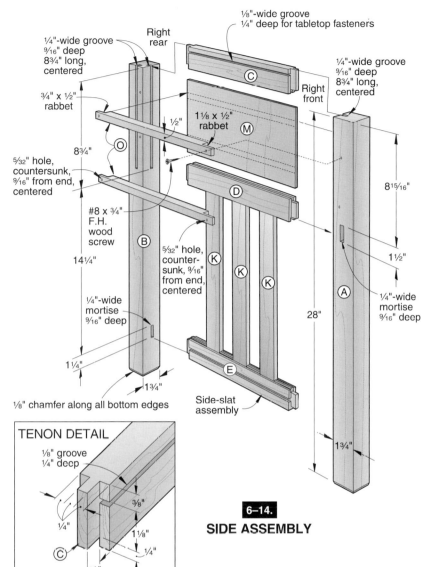

6–14.
SIDE ASSEMBLY

Note: The right and left pairs of legs are mirror images; they are not identical.

3 Chuck a ¼" straight bit into your table-mounted router, and adjust the fence so the straight bit is centered on the width of the leg. Clamp a stopblock to your router fence to make the 8¾"-long grooves, as shown in **6–15**, on *page 134*. Rout the grooves in several passes, raising the bit each time.

Note: Make multiple passes over the router bit, increasing the depth of cut incrementally between cuts to avoid overloading your router.

Next, set up a fence on your drill-press table, centering the width of the leg under a ¼" Forstner bit; then drill the mortises. Use a chisel to clean up the sides of the mortises and to square the ends of the grooves and mortises.

Make the Rails Next

1 Rip rails C, D, E, F, and G, and the front skirt (H) to 1¾" wide from ¾"-thick stock. Reset your rip fence for a 1⅜"-wide cut, and rip rails I and J from ¾"-thick stock. Next, clamp a stopblock to an extension on your tablesaw's miter gauge, and crosscut rails C, D, E, I, and J to 11½" long. Reset the stopblock to crosscut parts F, G, and H to 12½" long. Mark each part for quick identification, to prevent mistakes during later machining and assembly steps.

2 Drill the pocket holes in the upper front rail (I), where dimensioned on the Pocket Hole Detail in **6–13**. Then, set aside parts I and J for now.

3 Install a ½" dado blade in your tablesaw, and adjust the height of the cutter to machine ¼ × ½" tenons on both ends of the upper side rails (C), middle side rails (D), lower side rails (E), upper back rail (F), lower back rail (G), and front skirt (H). Attach a stopblock to your tablesaw's miter gauge extension, as shown in **6–16**, to ensure that all tenons are identical. Make test cuts first in scrap stock, test-fitting the tenon for a snug fit into the grooves and mortises in the legs.

4 Change to a ¼" dado blade, and cut a ¼"-wide groove ¼" deep the full length of one edge of parts C, D, F, and G, where shown on the Exploded

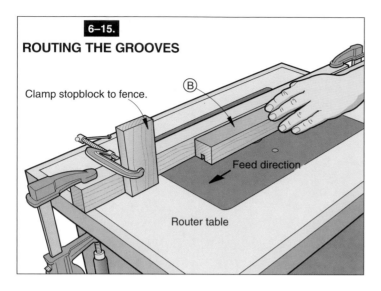

6–15.
ROUTING THE GROOVES

Clamp stopblock to fence.

Ⓑ

Feed direction

Router table

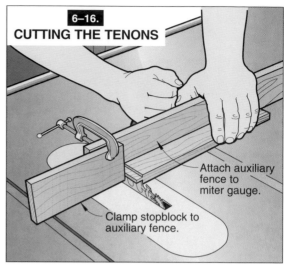

6–16.
CUTTING THE TENONS

Attach auxiliary fence to miter gauge.

Clamp stopblock to auxiliary fence.

View drawing in **6–13** and in **6–14**. Next, cut a ¼"-wide groove ¼" deep centered on the inner face of each lower side rail (E). Switch to a ⅜" dado blade, and cut a ⅜"-wide groove ¼" deep the full length of the bottom edge of both middle side rails (D) and in the top edge of the lower side rails (E), where dimensioned on the Middle Side Rail Tenon Detail and the Lower Side Rail Tenon Detail drawing in **6–17**.

5 Cut a ⅛"-wide groove ¼" deep and ⅜" from the top, along the inner face of the upper side rails (C) for the tabletop fasteners fit into.

Note: You should double-check the location of this groove against the actual dimensions of your tabletop fasteners.

6 Transfer the arch pattern for the front skirt (H) from **6–19** to your workpiece. Bandsaw just to the waste side of the cutline,

and then sand the arch smooth. (We used a drum sander mounted in a drill press.)

Make the Slats and Slat-Groove Fillers

1 Plane or resaw stock to ⅜" thick for the slats (K), and double-check its thickness against the grooves in the middle (D) and lower (E) side rails. Rip and crosscut the slats to the dimensions in the Materials List.

2 Rip a 28"-long piece of ⅜"-thick stock to 1½" wide. Next, set your tablesaw blade to 30°, and bevel-rip the edges of the workpiece, as shown on **6–17** and the Slat-Groove Filler detail in **6–18**. Rip the blank to ⅜" wide, and crosscut 16 slat-groove fillers (L) 1½" long.

Next, Glue Up the Side Assemblies

1 Dry-assemble (no glue) one of the side-slat assemblies, (D, E,

K, L). Make any adjustments necessary, and then finish-sand the parts. Next, glue and clamp the assembly, making sure it is flat, and then check for square by measuring the diagonals. (The assembly is square when the diagonal measurements are equal.) Use glue sparingly to avoid messy squeeze-out. Repeat the process for the other side-slat assembly. Let the glue dry, and then unclamp.

2 Cut the side panels (M) and back panel (N) to the sizes

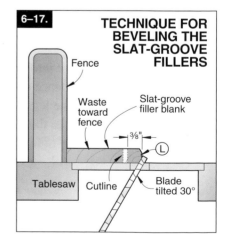

6–17.
TECHNIQUE FOR BEVELING THE SLAT-GROOVE FILLERS

Fence

Waste toward fence

Slat-groove filler blank

⅜"

Ⓛ

Tablesaw   Cutline

Blade tilted 30°

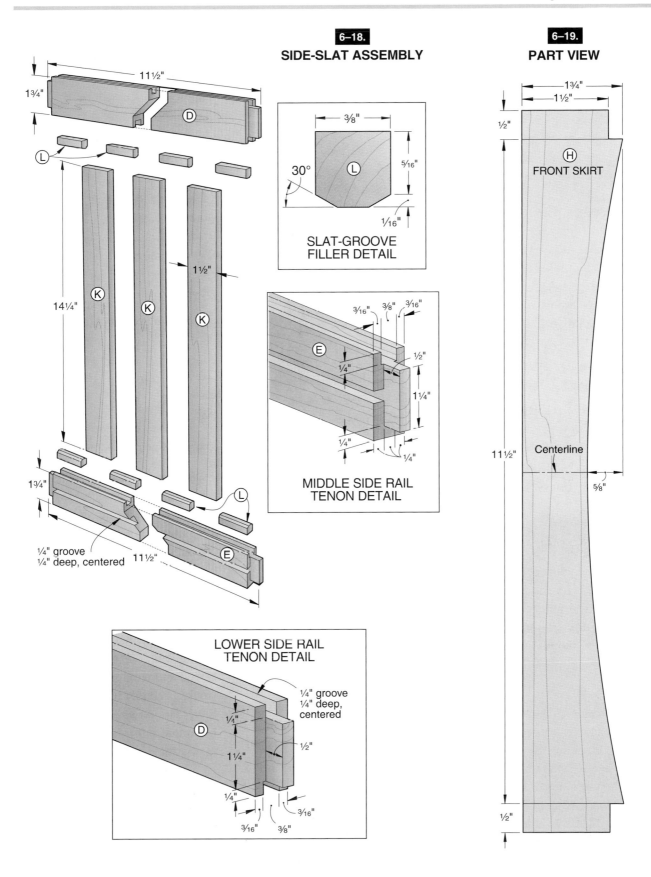

6–18.
SIDE-SLAT ASSEMBLY

11½"

1¾"

D

L

K

14¼"

1½"

K

K

**SLAT-GROOVE
FILLER DETAIL**

3/8"

30°

L

5/16"

1/16"

**MIDDLE SIDE RAIL
TENON DETAIL**

3/16"   3/8"   3/16"

E

1/2"

1/4"

1¼"

1/4"

1/4"

1¾"

L

E

¼" groove
¼" deep, centered

11½"

**LOWER SIDE RAIL
TENON DETAIL**

¼" groove
¼" deep,
centered

1/4"

D

1/2"

1¼"

1/4"

3/16"

3/16"   3/8"

6–19.
PART VIEW

1¾"

1½"

1/2"

H

FRONT SKIRT

11½"

Centerline

5/8"

1/2"

listed in the Materials List. Note that the grain direction runs vertically on these parts.

3 Dry-assemble the side panels (M) between the upper side rails (C), and the completed side-panel assemblies into the front legs (A) and back legs (B). Be certain that the grooves in the sides of the upper (C) and lower (E) rails face the inside of the nightstand. When you are satisfied with the fit, finish-sand all the pieces. Next, glue and clamp the assemblies, making sure they are flat and square.

Make the Drawer Guides and Shelf

1 Make the drawer guides (O) by starting with a ¾ × 3 × 12½" blank. Use a dado blade in your tablesaw to cut a 1⅛ × ½" rabbet into one end of the blank and a ¾ × ½" rabbet into the other end, where dimensioned in **6–14**, on *page 133*.

2 Change to your regular tablesaw blade, and rip four ½"-wide drawer guides from the blank. Drill ⁵⁄₁₆" countersunk holes, where dimensioned in **6–14**. Set the guides aside for now.

3 Edge-join 14" lengths of ¾"-thick stock to make an oversized blank for the shelf (P). Rip and crosscut the blank to the finished dimensions of the shelf as listed in the Materials List on *page 131*. Mount a dado blade in your tablesaw, and cut the tenons

on both ends of the shelf to the dimensions shown on the Exploded View drawing in **6–13**.

Assemble the Carcase

1 Dry-assemble the front rails (H, I, F), back rails (F, G), back panel (N), and shelf (P) between the two side assemblies. See the Shop Tip on *page 137* for a method of ensuring that the drawer opening is the right size.

2 When all parts fit properly, disassemble, finish-sand, and glue the carcase together.

Note: Center the shelf (P) and glue only the center 3" of the shelf tenons into the lower side rails (E) to allow for expansion and contraction of the shelf. Glue and clamp the lower front rail (J) to the front skirt (H). Then, drive pocket-hole screws to attach the upper front rail (I) to the legs.

Align the back edges of the upper (I) and lower (J) front rails flush with the back edge of the front legs. Let the glue dry, and then unclamp.

Make the Drawers Next

Note: The specified width of the drawer fronts and sides (Q, R) is based on a vertical opening size in the carcase (between the upper and lower front rails [I,J]) of 7⁷⁄₁₆", with ¹⁄₁₆" clearance between the two drawer fronts, and ¹⁄₁₆" clearance between the drawer fronts and parts I and J. The

drawer front length of 11⅜" is based on a horizontal carcase opening of 11½", with ¹⁄₁₆" clearance allowed at each end. If the measurements of your night-stand vary, you will have to adjust the size of the drawer components.

1 Rip a 24" length of ¾"-thick stock to 3⅝" wide for the drawer fronts (Q). Crosscut the drawer fronts to finished length. Rip two 28" lengths of ½"-thick stock to 3⅝" wide for drawer sides (R).

2 Mount a ½" dado blade in your tablesaw, and cut a ³⁄₁₆"-deep groove centered in the width of the drawer sides.

Note: Accurately centering the groove is an important step in getting drawers that fit properly.

Next, switch to your regular tablesaw blade, and crosscut the sides to their finished length of 12", and save the cut-off scraps for the next step. Drill counter-sunk ⁵⁄₁₆" holes into the drawer sides, where shown in **6–20**.

3 Make a drawer-guide spacing jig from the drawer side cutoffs and ¹⁄₁₆"-thick shims ripped and crosscut from ½"-thick stock, as shown in **6–21**. See the Shop Tip, on *page 138*, for important information on fine-tuning the jig.

4 Put the nightstand carcase on its side on your workbench. Then, position two drawer guides, using the spacing jig, as shown in

6–20.
DRAWER ASSEMBLY

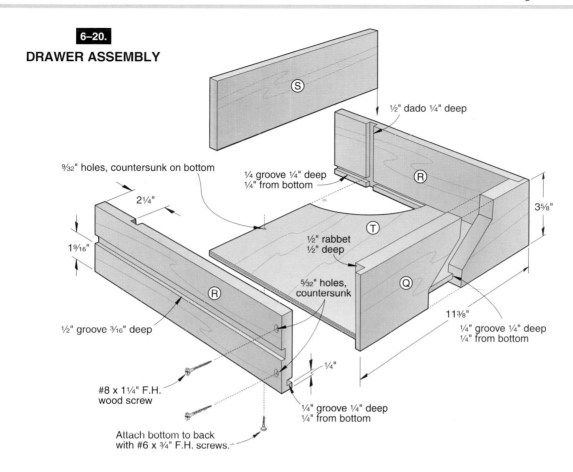

½" dado ¼" deep

9⁄32" holes, countersunk on bottom

¼ groove ¼" deep
¼" from bottom

2¼"

1⁹⁄16"

3⁵⁄8"

½" rabbet
½" deep

½" groove ³⁄16" deep

5⁄32" holes,
countersunk

11³⁄8"

¼" groove ¼" deep
¼" from bottom

#8 x 1¼" F.H.
wood screw

¼"

¼" groove ¼" deep
¼" from bottom

Attach bottom to back
with #6 x ¾" F.H. screws.

(S) (R) (T) (Q) (R)

Step 1 in **6–23**. Drill pilot holes into the front legs through the countersunk holes in the drawer guides, and drive the mounting screws. Remove the spacing jig, and use a square to position the drawer guide on the back leg, as shown in Step 2 in **6–23**. Drill pilot holes into the back legs,

and drive the mounting screws. Repeat the process for the other pair of drawer guides.

5 Mount a ¼" dado blade in your tablesaw, and set it for a ¼"-deep cut. Adjust your rip fence, and then cut the groove for the drawer bottom into the drawer sides and

front, where shown on the Drawer Assembly drawing in **6–20**.

6 Cut a ½" rabbet ½" deep in the drawer front ends, where dimensioned in **6–20**. Note: The depth of the rabbet should exactly match the stock thickness of the drawer sides (R).

6–21.
DRAWER-GUIDE SPACING JIG

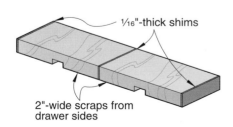

1⁄16"-thick shims

2"-wide scraps from
drawer sides

SHOP TIP

Make Sure the Drawer Will Fit

While assembling the carcase, clamp 7⁷⁄16"-long scraps to the legs to make sure the drawer opening will be the correct size as shown on right. Position the scraps during dry assembly, and leave in place during glue-up.

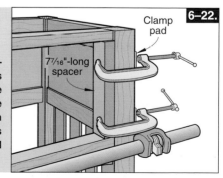

Clamp
pad

7⁷⁄16"-long
spacer

6–22.

6–23.
STEPS FOR POSITIONING THE GUIDES

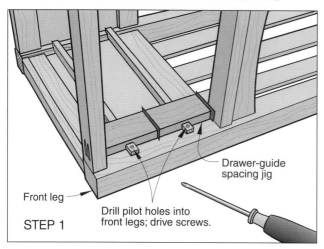

Front leg

Drawer-guide
spacing jig

Drill pilot holes into
front legs; drive screws.

STEP 1

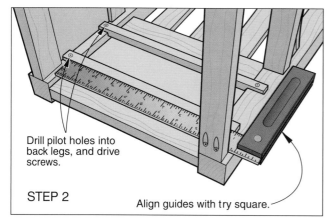

Drill pilot holes into
back legs, and drive
screws.

STEP 2

Align guides with try square.

7 Switch to a ½" dado blade, and cut the ¼"-deep dado for the drawer back into the drawer sides, where dimensioned in **6–20**. Rip and crosscut the drawer back (S) to size.

8 Glue and clamp the drawer front, sides, and back (Q, R, S) together. Using the countersunk holes in the drawer sides as guides, drill ⁷⁄₆₄" pilot holes ¾"

Fine-Tune the Drawer-Guide Jig

Adjust the fit of the drawer-guide jig before gluing it by test-fitting it into the drawer opening. If you don't get a perfect fit on the first try, cut shims that are slightly thicker or thinner until you are satisfied with the fit. This way, you keep all of the clearance gaps equal.

deep into the drawer front. Then, drive the screws to attach the sides to the front. Rip and crosscut the drawer bottom (T) to the dimensions listed in the Materials List, slide it into the groove in the drawer sides and front, and attach it to the drawer back with #6 × ¾" flathead wood screws.

9 Test-fit the drawers. You may need to sand the drawer guides slightly to get a perfect fit. Work carefully, noting whether you need to remove stock on the top, bottom, or face of the drawer guides.

Make the Top, Complete the Assembly, and Add the Finish

1 Crosscut 20" lengths of 1¹⁄₁₆"-thick stock to edge-join an oversized blank for the top (U). When the glue dries, rip and crosscut the top to 15⅛ × 18".

2 Adjust your tablesaw blade to 17° from vertical, set your rip fence, hold the top on edge, and cut the bevel on the bottom front edge and both ends of the top, where shown in **6–24**.

6–24.
TOP BEVEL DETAIL

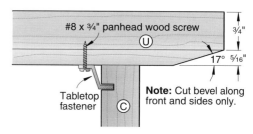

#8 × ¾" panhead wood screw

U

¾"

17° ⁵⁄₁₆"

Tabletop
fastener

C

Note: Cut bevel along
front and sides only.

3 Finish-sand all parts, and stain, if desired. Then apply a clear finish.

4 Place the top upside down on a blanket on your workbench. Position the carcase flush with the back edge and centered side-to-side. Mark the location of the tabletop fasteners, drill ⁷⁄₆₄" pilot holes ¾" deep for the screws, and attach the top. Drill holes centered in the drawer fronts, and mount the drawer knobs.

Accessories for the Home

HOMES OF THE ARTS AND CRAFTS PERIOD *featured plenty of extra detail to supplement the furniture in them. Walls often were lightly stenciled with natural or geometric motifs. Stained glass was prominent. And area rugs in earthy colors were a treat to the eye.*

The Arts and Crafts era coincided with the availability of residential electricity. Therefore table and floor lamps, as well as wall and ceiling fixtures, were designed in the style. Finely crafted lamps of wood, hammered copper, and other materials frequently exhibited the same details as the furniture and hardware. Beginning on the next page, you'll find the easy-to-follow instructions for building an Arts and Crafts table lamp. Its design was drawn from museum-quality originals. Following that, we present an easy-to-make floor lamp that you also can build as a coat tree. See it on page 144. Then, we've included the plans, starting on page 149, for a beautiful wooden wall sconce with all the recognizable features of the Arts and Crafts period.

On the remaining pages of this chapter you'll discover other accessories in the style. You'll like the shelf clock on page 156, and then we present plans for building nesting tables on page 160 that will draw raves from friends and neighbors.

TREASURE OF A TABLE LAMP

This wonderful-looking table lamp was designed to include elements of original Arts and Crafts lamps that now reside in museums. The lamp captures all the subtle features that give this style its enduring appeal. A low-wattage bulb in the lantern base casts a warm glow through the stained glass for a pleasing decorative touch.

***Note:** You'll need some 3/16", 3/8", and 5/8"-thick stock for this project. You can resaw or plane thicker stock to size.*

Begin with the Frames

1 Rip a total of 12 lineal feet of 3/4"-thick oak to 1" wide for the stiles (A) and rails (B). Plane or resaw to 5/8" thick. Attach an extension to your tablesaw's miter gauge. Clamp a stopblock to the extension, and crosscut the eight stiles to 11 7/8" long. Then, adjust the stopblock, and cut the eight rails to 5 1/8" long.

2 Change to a dado blade, and cut 1" half-lap joints on the inside face of the stiles and the outside face of the rails. See **7–2**

Table lamp

CUTTING DIAGRAM

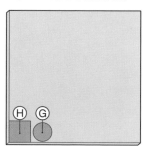

1/8 x 24 x 24" Hardboard

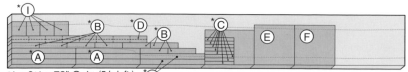

3/4 x 9 1/4 x 72" Oak (5 bd. ft.)
*Plane or resaw to the thicknesses listed in the Materials List.

MATERIALS LIST FOR TABLE LAMP

PART	FINISHED SIZE			Mtl.	Qty.
	T	W	L		
A stiles	5/8"	1"	11 7/8"	O	8
B rails	5/8"	1"	5 1/8"	O	8
C* grille stiles	3/8"	5/8"	5 1/4"	O	8
D* grille rails	3/16"	5/8"	3 1/8"	O	16
E* base	3/4"	7 3/8"	7 3/8"	O	1
F* top	3/4"	7 3/8"	7 3/8"	O	1
G cover plate	1/8"	3 7/16" diam.		H	1
H base insert	1/8"	3 7/8"	3 7/8	H	1
I feet	3/8"	2 5/8"	2 5/8	O	4

*Parts initially cut oversize. See the instructions.

Materials Key: O = oak; H = hardboard.
Supplies: Stained glass; #8 x 1 1/4" flathead wood screws; #18 x 5/8" brads; #6 x 1/2" flathead wood screws; stain, finish.
Lamp Parts. Two-circuit turn-knob socket; candelabra socket; lamp harp; cord set; 7 1/2-watt bulb; and miscellaneous lamp hardware (at hardware and electrical parts suppliers).

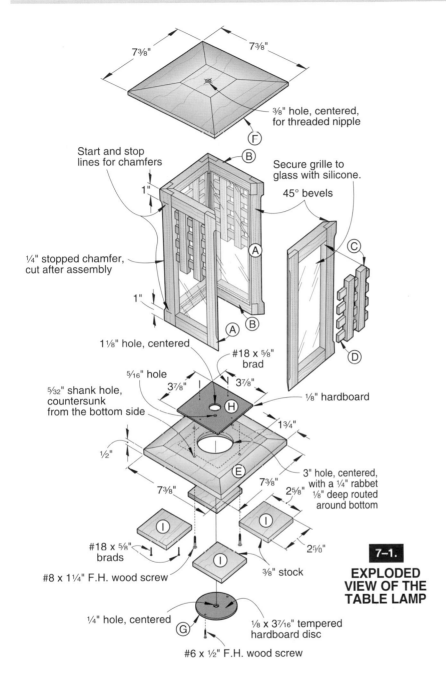

7⅜" 7⅜"

⅜" hole, centered,
for threaded nipple

Ⓕ

Ⓑ

Start and stop
lines for chamfers

Secure grille to
glass with silicone.

1"

45° bevels

¼" stopped chamfer,
cut after assembly

Ⓐ

Ⓒ

1"

Ⓐ Ⓑ

Ⓓ

1⅛" hole, centered

#18 x ⅝"
brad

⁵⁄₁₆" hole

⁵⁄₃₂" shank hole,
countersunk
from the bottom side

3⅞"   3⅞"

⅛" hardboard

Ⓗ

½"

1¾"

Ⓔ

3" hole, centered,
with a ¼" rabbet
⅛" deep routed
around bottom

7⅜"   7⅜"

2⅝"

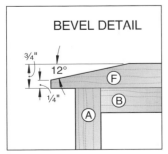

#18 x ⅝"
brads

Ⓘ

Ⓘ

2⁵⁄₀"

7–1.

**EXPLODED
VIEW OF THE
TABLE LAMP**

#8 x 1¼" F.H. wood screw

Ⓘ

⅜" stock

¼" hole, centered

Ⓖ

⅛ x 3⁷⁄₁₆" tempered
hardboard disc

#6 x ½" F.H. wood screw

BEVEL DETAIL

¾"

12°

Ⓕ

¼"

Ⓑ

Ⓐ

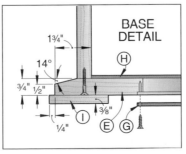

**BASE
DETAIL**

1¾"

14°

Ⓗ

¾" ½"

Ⓘ

⅜"

¼"

Ⓔ Ⓖ

7–2. **FRAME ASSEMBLY**

Bevel-cut frames at 45° after assembly.

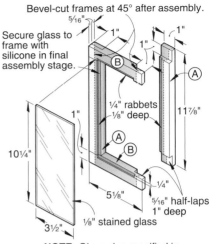

⁵⁄₁₆"

Secure glass to
frame with
silicone in final
assembly stage.

1"   1"

Ⓑ

1"

¼" rabbets
⅛" deep

11⅞"

Ⓐ

Ⓐ
Ⓑ

10¼"

¼"

⁵⁄₁₆" half-laps
1" deep

5⅛"

3½"

⅛" stained glass

NOTE: Glass size specified is
⅛" less than rabbeted opening.

for reference. Glue and clamp the
four frames, making certain that
they are flat and square. Unclamp
when the glue has dried, and
mark the outside face of each
frame with masking tape.

3 Put a ¼" piloted rabbeting
bit into your table-mounted
router. Adjust the depth of cut to
the actual thickness of the stained
glass you will be using. (Our
glass measured ⅛".) Rabbet the
recess for the glass panels, where
shown on **7–1**. Square the corners
with a chisel.

4 Bevel-cut all long edges of
the four frames. But before
you do, make test cuts on scrap
lumber to ensure tight joints.
Adjust your rip fence so the cut
will be right at the corner of the
frames, retaining their full 5⅛"
width. Now, glue up the four
frames, clamping with band clamps.
Use your try square to make sure
that the lantern assembly is square.

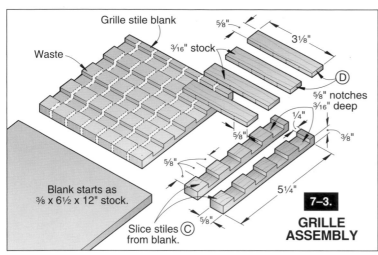

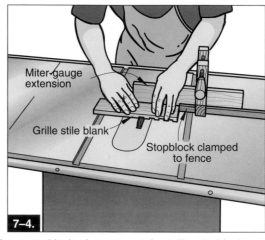

Grille stile blank

Waste

³⁄₁₆" stock

⁵⁄₈"

3⅛"

Ⓓ

⁵⁄₈" notches ³⁄₁₆" deep

¼"

⁵⁄₈"

³⁄₈"

⁵⁄₈"

5¼"

⁵⁄₈"

Blank starts as ³⁄₈ x 6½ x 12" stock.

Slice stiles Ⓒ from blank.

⁵⁄₈"

7–3.
GRILLE ASSEMBLY

Miter-gauge extension

Grille stile blank

Stopblock clamped to fence

7–4.

Use a stopblock when you cut the grille stile blanks.

5 Mark start and stop lines for the chamfers, where dimensioned in **7–1**. Put a piloted 45° chamfer bit into your table-mounted router, and adjust the height. You can guide the cuts freehand or attach a fence with stopblocks on your router table.

The Grilles are an Authentic Touch

1 Start with a piece of ¾"-thick oak, initially cutting it over-sized to approximately 6½" wide by 12" long. Plane the blank to ⅜" thick. Use a dado blade in your tablesaw to cut the ⅝" dadoes ³⁄₁₆" deep, where shown in **7–3**. To do this, attach an extension to your tablesaw's miter gauge. Next, clamp a stop-block to the extension, positioning it to make the edge of the first dado ¼" from the end, and make the cut, as shown in **7–4**. After you have cut all the dadoes, trim the ends of the blank to reduce its length to 5¼". Rip the grille blank to make eight stiles ⅝" wide.

Note: The edge of the bottom dado is ⅝" from the blank's end.

2 Rip a 30" length of ¾"-thick oak to ⅝" wide for the grille rails (D) making sure you double-check the actual width of these pieces against the size of the dadoes you cut in the grille stiles (C). If necessary, plane to get a tight fit. Now, resaw the stock in half, and then plane to the finished ³⁄₁₆" thickness.

3 Check the finished dimension of the grille rails against the frame opening of the lantern assembly, and then crosscut the grille rails to final length.

4 Glue up the grilles, using ⅝"-wide scraps to space the stiles. Use only a small dot of glue in each notch. Keep the grilles square.

Make the Base and Top

1 Rip and crosscut two pieces 7⅜" square from ¾"-thick oak. One will be the base (E), and

the other is the top (F). Draw diagonal lines from the corners of each piece to locate the centers. Drill a ⅜" hole in the top (F), and then set it aside for now.

2 Referring to **7–5**, put a circle cutter in your drill press, and cut a 3" hole in the base (E). For safety, use a slow speed (250 rpm or less).

7–5.
CIRCLE-CUTTING TECHNIQUES

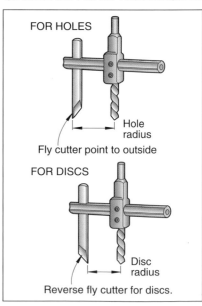

FOR HOLES

Hole radius

Fly cutter point to outside

FOR DISCS

Disc radius

Reverse fly cutter for discs.

3 Go to your table-mounted router, and install a piloted ¼" rabbeting bit. Cut a rabbet ⅛" deep on the bottom side of the base.

4 Fasten a 6" high auxiliary fence to your table-saw's rip fence, as shown on **7–6**. Lower the blade completely, and fit your tablesaw with a new wood or plastic insert. Move the rip fence over the edge of the insert to hold it in place, set the blade angle at 14°, turn on the saw, and raise the blade through the insert. Shut off the saw, move the rip fence into its final position, and adjust the blade height to about 1½". Make the bevel cuts on the top surface of the base (E) by keeping the rabbeted side of the hole against the fence.

5 For the top (F), completely lower the blade, change the blade angle to 12°, and then raise the running blade through the blade insert. You will have to adjust the rip fence and set the blade height to about 2½". Make the cuts in the top.

Assemble the Lantern to the Base

1 Mark the locations of the four screw centerpoints 1⅜" from the edges and along centerlines on the bottom of the base (E). Do not drill yet.

2 Clamp the lantern assembly to the base, as shown in **7–7**. Position the clamp bar diagonally so you have access to all four screw locations. Make registration marks on the inside of the lantern assembly and base so you can reassemble the parts in the same position later. Drill ⁷⁄₆₄" pilot holes for #8 × 1¼" screws through the base and into the lantern assembly. Be careful not to drill too deeply. Unclamp the base, enlarge the holes through the base to ⁵⁄₁₆", and countersink. Do not drive the screws yet.

Complete the Base

1 Use a circle cutter to make the 3⁷⁄₁₆" diameter cover plate (G) from ⅛"-thick tempered hardboard. Refer to **7–5** for the proper position of the fly cutter. Also see the Shop Tip on *page 144*.

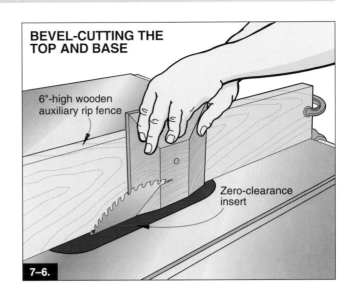

BEVEL-CUTTING THE TOP AND BASE

6"-high wooden auxiliary rip fence

Zero-clearance insert

7–6.

2 Now, cut the base insert (H), checking the dimensions against the inside of the lantern assembly. Draw diagonal marks to quickly locate the center, and then drill a 1⅛" hole.

3 Use a piece of ⅜"-thick stock to make the feet (I). Rip and crosscut four 2⅝" squares. Attach to the base (E) with glue and brads, allowing a ¼" projection on both outside edges of the feet. Be certain that the grain in the feet and the base runs in the same direction.

Final Touches

1 Glue the top to the lantern assembly, making certain it is centered and that the grain aligns

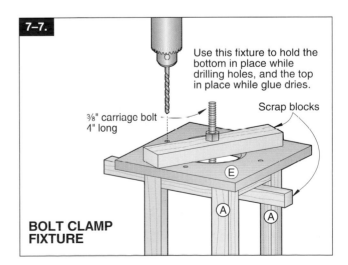

7–7.

Use this fixture to hold the bottom in place while drilling holes, and the top in place while glue dries.

⅜" carriage bolt 4" long

Scrap blocks

E

A   A

BOLT CLAMP FIXTURE

7–8.
WIRING DIAGRAM

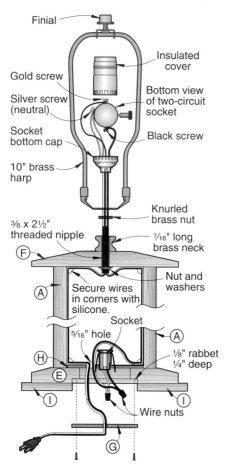

Finial

Insulated cover

Gold screw

Bottom view of two-circuit socket

Silver screw (neutral)

Socket bottom cap

Black screw

10" brass harp

Knurled brass nut

⅜ x 2½" threaded nipple

F

⁷⁄₁₆" long brass neck

A

Secure wires in corners with silicone.

Nut and washers

A

Socket

⁵⁄₁₆" hole

⅛" rabbet ¼" deep

H

E

I

I

Wire nuts

G

with the base. Refer to **7–7** for an easy way to hold the top in position while the glue dries.

2 Stain the parts before final assembly. (See Shop Tip *at right.*) Once the stain has dried, apply a clear finish.

3 Temporarily screw the lantern to the base assembly. Transfer the registration mark you made earlier on the base to the base insert (H), and then attach it with glue and brads. Remove the screws joining the base and lantern.

4 Have stained glass panels cut slightly undersized for the openings in the lantern. Now, secure the glass with a few dots of clear silicone adhesive around the perimeter of the glass inside the lantern. (See Shop Tip *below*.) Next, secure the grilles to the glass, holding them in place with masking tape until the silicone cures.

5 The lamp hardware we chose includes a two-circuit socket that allows you to independently switch the reading lamp and the light in the base. See the Materials List for the parts. Wire your lamp, referring to **7–8**.

SHOP TIP

Three Tips for Making the Lamp

1. When you cut disks with a circle cutter, adhere your stock to a backup scrap with double-faced tape. This will prevent the cutter from picking up and damaging the disk when the circle cutter exits the hardboard.

2. Wipe excess stain from the edges of the grille openings for consistent color. (We used a cloth over the end of a small square stick.)

3. Secure the stained glass with silicone adhesive. To reach inside the lantern assembly, put silicone adhesive on the end of a stick. Secure the first panel, and then prop the lantern diagonally to install a second piece of glass. Wait for the silicone to set up; and then do the two remaining glass panels.

FLOOR LAMP/ COAT TREE

These two projects exemplify the style principle basic to Arts and Crafts design: make it simple. It's a no-nonsense approach that guarantees popularity for years to come. So whether you build one or both of the two projects, they'll be popular (as well as functional) in your home for years.

Note: The two projects shown here contain posts that differ in length, hardware, and construction, depending on use. The base construction for both projects is the same. See the Materials List for the specialized hardware for each project.

Build the Lamp Post First

1 From 1¹⁄₁₆"-thick oak (commonly called five-quarter stock), cut two post halves to 2⅜" wide by 51" long each.

2 Cut or rout a ⅜" groove ³⁄₁₆" deep *centered* along the inside face of each post half. See the Lamp Post drawing in **7–9** (*page 146*) for reference.

3 Mark a line 3½" from the top end of each post half on the inside surface. Now, measure the thickness of the lamp-rod hex nut, and mark a second line this distance below the first marked line. See the Lamp Post drawing and accompanying Lamp-Post Nut Detail in **7–9**. Our hex nut measured ⅛" thick.

Floor lamp

Coat tree

4 Chuck a ⅛" bit into your drill press so only about ¾" of the bit protrudes from the chuck. On some smaller chucks, more might protrude. This will keep the bit from flexing. Now, drill overlapping holes to form a slot wide enough in both post halves for the nut to fit into once the post halves are laminated together. (We had to use a craft knife to clean up each slot.) Our nut measured ½" wide so our slots measured just over ¼" deep in each post half. See the Lamp-Post Nut Detail in **7–9** for reference. Now, thread the rod into the hex nut. Insert the rod/nut into the lamp post and hold the two post halves together. Make sure the two post halves come together tightly.

5 With the edges and grooved ends flush and the threaded lamp rod and hex nut in place in the groove, glue and clamp the two lamp-post halves together to form the lamp post (A). When applying the glue, hold it back from the groove about ½" to keep from getting glue in the groove.

6 After the glue dries, remove the threaded rod, leaving the nut in the post. Now, trim ⅛" off each laminated edge (the edges with glue joints) for a 2⅛" finished width.

7 Trim ½" off the top and bottom ends of the laminated post (A) for a 50"-long post.

MATERIALS LIST FOR FLOOR LAMP

PART	FINISHED SIZE			Mtl.	Qty.
	T	W	L		
A* post	2⅛"	2⅛"	50"	LO	1
B* feet	2⅛"	2¾"	18"	LO	2
C supports	1¹⁄₁₆"	4¼"	15"	O	4
D* finial	1¾"	1¾"	2⅛"	LO	1

*Initially cut parts oversized. Trim to finished size according to the instructions.

Materials Key: LO = laminated oak; O = oak.
Supplies: #8 x 2½" flathead wood screws; #8 x 3" flathead wood screws; stain; finish; brads; coat hooks. Floor lamp parts as shown in Lamp Section View in **7–9** from local lamp store or electrical supply.

8 Tilt your tablesaw blade 19° from center, and using a miter gauge with a long wood extension for support, angle-cut the top of the post to the shape shown on the Post and Finial Detail in **7–9**.

9 Fit your table-mounted router with a chamfer bit, and rout a ¼" chamfer along each corner of the post (A), starting 17" from the bottom end of the post. See **7–10** for reference. (We used a fence when routing the chamfer to prevent accidentally running the chamfer around the top chamfered end of the post.)

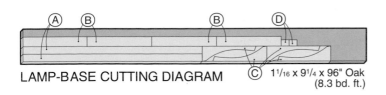

LAMP-BASE CUTTING DIAGRAM

Ⓒ 1¹⁄₁₆ x 9¼ x 96" Oak
(8.3 bd. ft.)

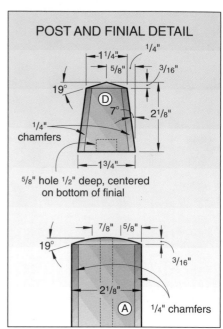

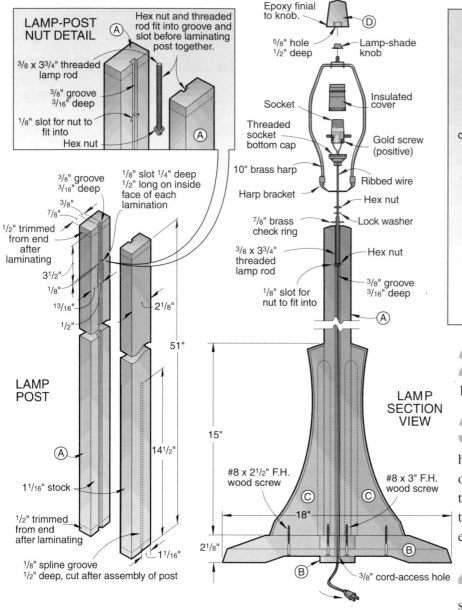

LAMP-POST NUT DETAIL Ⓐ

Hex nut and threaded rod fit into groove and slot before laminating post together.

3/8 x 3 3/4" threaded lamp rod

3/8" groove 3/16" deep

1/8" slot for nut to fit into

Hex nut

Ⓐ

3/8" groove 3/16" deep

1/8" slot 1/4" deep 1/2" long on inside face of each lamination

3/8"

7/8"

1/2" trimmed from end after laminating

3 1/2"

1/8"

13/16"

1/2"

2 1/8"

LAMP POST

Ⓐ

1 1/16" stock

1/2" trimmed from end after laminating

1/8" spline groove 1/2" deep, cut after assembly of post

1 1/16"

51"

14 1/2"

Epoxy finial to knob.

Ⓓ

5/8" hole 1/2" deep

Lamp-shade knob

Socket

Insulated cover

Threaded socket bottom cap

Gold screw (positive)

10" brass harp

Ribbed wire

Harp bracket

Hex nut

Lock washer

7/8" brass check ring

3/8 x 3 3/4" threaded lamp rod

Hex nut

3/8" groove 3/16" deep

1/8" slot for nut to fit into

Ⓐ

LAMP SECTION VIEW

15"

#8 x 2 1/2" F.H. wood screw

#8 x 3" F.H. wood screw

Ⓒ Ⓒ

18"

2 1/8"

Ⓑ

Ⓑ

3/8" cord-access hole

7–9.
LAMP POST AND LAMP SECTION VIEW

POST AND FINIAL DETAIL

1 1/4"

1/4"

5/8"

3/16"

19°

Ⓓ

7°

2 1/8"

1/4" chamfers

1 3/4"

5/8" hole 1/2" deep, centered on bottom of finial

7/8"

5/8"

19°

3/16"

2 1/8"

Ⓐ

1/4" chamfers

10 For adding and aligning the four supports (C) later, cut or rout a 1/8" groove 1/2" deep and 14" long centered along each face of the post at the bottom end. See **7–10** for reference. Use a stop for consistent 14"-long grooves.

Add the Feet for a Rock-Solid Base

1 To form the feet (B), start by cutting four pieces of 1 1/16"-thick stock to 2 7/8" wide by 19" long. Glue and clamp two pieces together face-to-face for each foot.

2 Remove the clamps and trim each foot to 2 3/4" wide by 18" long.

3 Using the dimensions on the pattern in **7–10**, mark the half-lap joint on the bottom side of one foot blank and on the top side of the other. Then, transfer cutlines to one side of each foot.

4 Fit your tablesaw with a dado blade, and cut the notches to size. Test-fit the pieces together.

5 Remove the dado set. Switch back to a regular blade. Tilt the blade 19° from center, and bevel-cut both ends of each leg.

6 Bandsaw the other angled cut on each end of each foot. Then, bandsaw the bottom of each foot to shape. Sand the bandsawn surfaces to remove the saw marks.

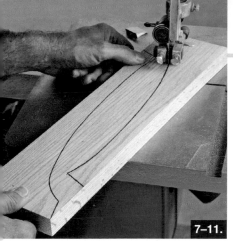

For minimal waste, we laid out the two supports side-by-side before we bandsawed them to shape.

7–11.

Using a handscrew clamp clamped to your disc-sander table for alignment, sand the angled ends of the supports.

7–12.

7 Fit the feet pieces together, but do not glue them yet. Rout ¼" chamfers along the top edges, where shown on **7–10**. Then glue and clamp the feet together.

Cut and Add the Four Lamp-Post Supports

1 Enlarge and transfer the half-size pattern *at right* to a piece of hardboard or thin plywood. Cut the template to shape, and use it to mark the outlines for four supports (C) on 1¹⁄₁₆" stock. As shown in **7–11**, bandsaw the supports to shape.

2 Using a drum sander, sand up to the marked line to make the curved edge of each support.

3 Using a disc sander, sand the angled ends of each support. (For consistent 19° angled ends, we clamped a handscrew clamp to our disc-sander table and used it as a guide, as shown in **7–12**.)

4 Rout a ³⁄₁₆" chamfer along the outside edge of each support, where shown on **7–10**.

5 Cut four ¹⁵⁄₁₆"-wide by 13⁷⁄₈"-long splines from ⅛" stock. Sand the top end of each spline to fit into the routed mating grooves in the post and supports.

7–10.

POST SUPPORT AND FOOT HALF-SIZE PATTERNS
(Enlarge patterns to 200 %)

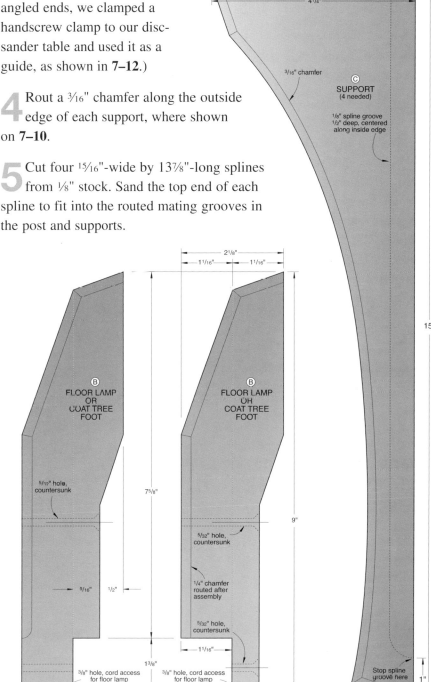

Add the Base to the Post

1 Working from the bottom side of the base assembly, drill countersunk mounting holes through the base for attaching it to the post and supports later.

2 Mark the mating centerpoint, and drill a 3/8"cord-access hole through the base.

3 Center the base on the bottom end of the post. Using the previously drilled shank holes in the base as guides, drill pilot holes into the bottom end of the post. Secure the two assemblies together with 3" flathead wood screws. Check for square. If the base cord-access hole doesn't align perfectly with that in the post, enlarge the hole.

4 Test-fit the supports (C) with the splines in place. Drill pilot holes, then, glue, spline, screw, and clamp the supports in place.

MATERIALS LIST FOR COAT TREE

PART	FINISHED SIZE				
	T	W	L	Mtl.	Qty.
A* post	2 1/8"	2 1/8"	67 3/4"	LO	1
B* feet	2 1/8"	2 3/4"	18"	LO	2
C supports	1 1/16"	4 1/4"	15"	O	4

*Initially cut parts oversized. Trim to finished size according to the instructions.

Materials Key: LO = laminated oak; O = oak.
Supplies: #8 x 2 1/2" flathead wood screws; #8 x 3" flathead wood screws; stain; finish; brass coat hooks.

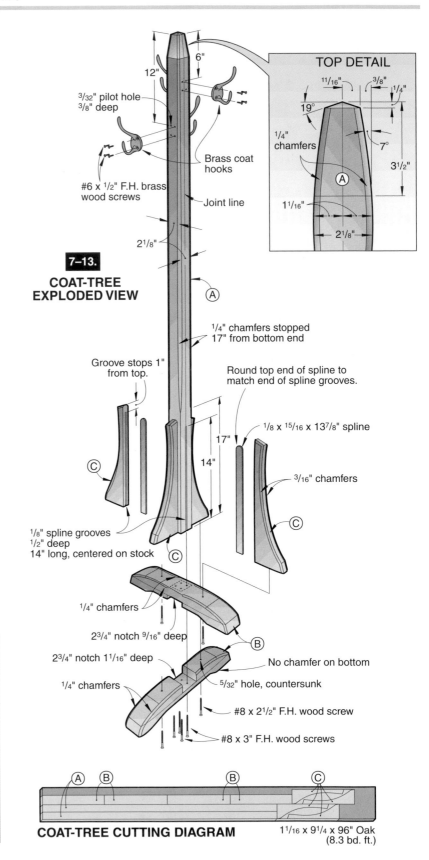

TOP DETAIL

3/32" pilot hole 3/8" deep

Brass coat hooks

#6 x 1/2" F.H. brass wood screws

Joint line

2 1/8"

7–13.
COAT-TREE EXPLODED VIEW

1/4" chamfers stopped 17" from bottom end

Groove stops 1" from top.

Round top end of spline to match end of spline grooves.

1/8 x 15/16 x 13 7/8" spline

17"

14"

3/16" chamfers

1/8" spline grooves 1/2" deep 14" long, centered on stock

1/4" chamfers

2 3/4" notch 9/16" deep

2 3/4" notch 1 1/16" deep

No chamfer on bottom

1/4" chamfers

5/32" hole, countersunk

#8 x 2 1/2" F.H. wood screw

#8 x 3" F.H. wood screws

COAT-TREE CUTTING DIAGRAM

1 1/16 x 9 1/4 x 96" Oak
(8.3 bd. ft.)

Top It Off with a Finial

1 Laminate, then plane 1¹⁄₁₆" stock to form a finial blank 1¾" square by 6" long. The extra length is necessary in the following steps for safety in machining.

Note: Use the same procedure described here to machine the top end of the coat tree. See the Top Detail in 7–10, on page 147, for reference.

2 Tilt your tablesaw blade 19° from center. Using a miter gauge with a wood extension for support, angle-cut all four edges of one end of the blank. See the detail in **7–10** for reference.

3 Lay out the 7° cutlines on the finial blank, and bandsaw the four tapers to shape. Sand the bandsawn surfaces.

4 Rout a ¼" chamfer on the final, where shown on the detail. Then crosscut the finial (D) to length.

5 Supporting the finial with a handscrew clamp, drill a ⅝" hole ½" deep in the bottom center of the finial. See the Lamp Section View in **7–9** for reference. Epoxy the lamp-shade knob into the hole.

Add the Stain, Finish, and Electrical Parts

1 Finish-sand the lamp-post assembly and finial. Stain and finish the parts.

Wall sconce

2 Install the electrical parts in the configuration shown on the Lamp Section View in **7–9**. (If you're not familiar with electrical wiring, check with a lamp or electrical supply shop.)

Now Make the Coat Tree

The construction procedure for the coat tree is nearly identical to that of the lamp except for the following changes: First, the coat tree uses a post 67¾" long, and the post is not hollow. Next, machine the top end of the coat tree using the same procedure as you did for the lamp's finial. Drill pilot holes and add the four brass coat hooks to the post, where shown on **7–13**.

WALL SCONCE

The warm, golden glow of an incandescent lightbulb shining through a sheet-mica diffuser is a hallmark of Arts and Crafts lighting. Add this ambience to your home with one or more of these oak and copper wall-mounted sconces.

Start with the Sconce's Lantern

Note: To accommodate the different thicknesses of stock required for this project, select a ¾ × 4¼ × 96" board. Cut a 12" length, and plane it to ½" thick for the G parts. Cut a 52" length, and plane it to ⅜" thick for parts A, D, E, F, I. Plane the remaining 32" piece to ¼" thick for parts B, C, H, J, K, L. The Materials List shows parts for one sconce.

CUTTING DIAGRAM

Note: All boards are cut and planed from one ¾ x 4¼ x 96" piece of white oak.

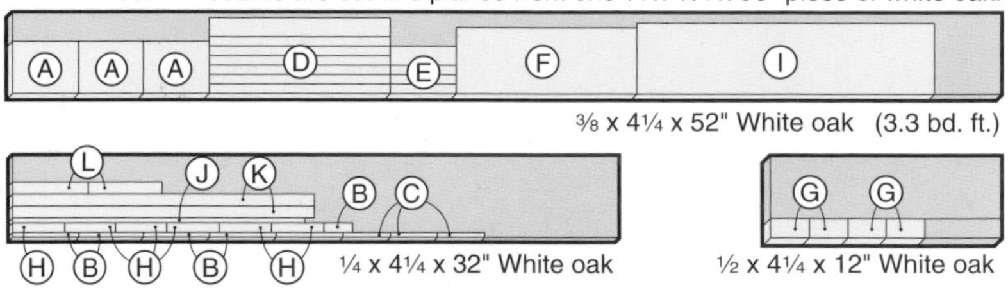
A
A
A
D
E
F
I
⅜ x 4¼ x 52" White oak (3.3 bd. ft.)
L
J
K
B
C
H
B
H
B
H
¼ x 4¼ x 32" White oak
G
G
½ x 4¼ x 12" White oak

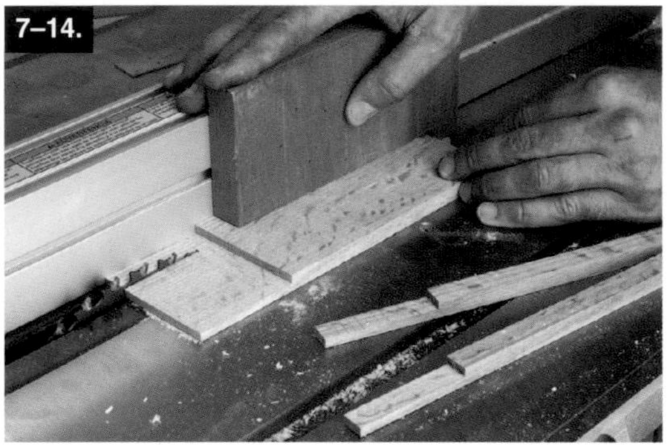
7–14.

Ripping the stiles from a single rabbeted blank ensures uniform lap joints.

MATERIALS LIST FOR THE SCONCES

PART	FINISHED SIZE T	W	L	Mtl.	Qty.
A* lantern panels	⅜"	2¾"	3½"	O	3
B horizontal mullions	¼"	¼"	3½"	O	5
C vertical mullions	¼"	¼"	2½"	O	3
D** stiles	⅜"	½"	9½"	O	6
E** rails	⅜"	½"	3½"	O	3
F lantern back	⅜"	3½"	9½"	O	1
G ring segments	½"	1"	2"	O	4
H** stops	¼"	½"	2¾"	O	6
I* escutcheon panel	⅜"	3¾"	15½"	O	1
J escutcheon mullion	¼"	¼"	15½"	O	1
K** side banding	¼"	⅝"	16"	O	2
L** end banding	¼"	⅝"	4"	O	2

*Initial size shown. Parts are smaller after machining.
**Parts initially cut oversize.

Material Key: O = oak.
Supplies: #6 x ¾" flathead brass wood screws; #4 x ½" roundhead brass wood screws; 25-watt frosted tubular lightbulb.
Parts for One Sconce: .030 sheet mica; .008 copper sheet; ½ x 1" copper pipe; ½" copper elbow; ¼ x ⅛" IP lamp reducing bushing; ⅛ x 1½" IP lamp nipple; ⅛" IP lamp nut; porcelain lampholder; crimp-on eyelet; metal-filled epoxy; #18 fixture wire (10" each: black, white, green). You'll find sheet copper and mica at hobby or craft stores, other materials at hardware or electrical supply stores.

1 From the ⅜" stock, cut the lantern panels (A) to the size listed in the Materials List. Install a ¼" dado blade in your tablesaw. Cut the grooves and dadoes in the backs of the pieces, as shown in Step 1 in **7–15**.

2 Now, rip and crosscut the lantern panels, as shown in Steps 2 and 3 of **7–15**. Discard the waste square, and glue and clamp the remaining pieces of the panel together, as shown in Step 4.

3 From the ¼" stock, cut the horizontal and vertical mullions (B) and (C) to size. Using your ¼" dado blade, cut the centered notches in the mullions for the half-lap joints, as shown in **7–15**. Set two of the horizontal mullions (B) aside for use later on the escutcheon panel (I). Glue the mullions into the lantern panels.

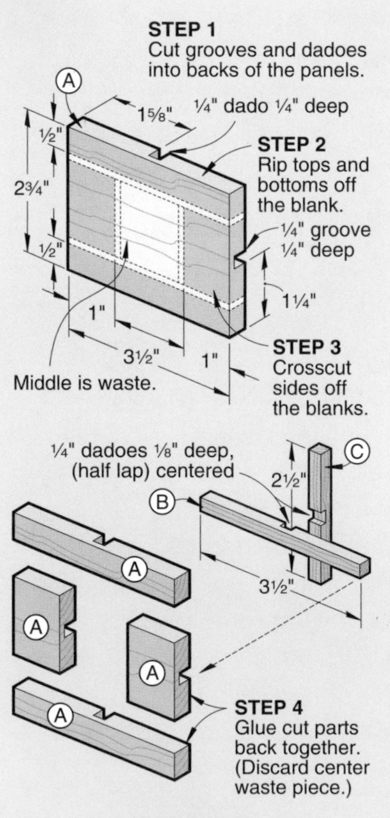
STEP 1
Cut grooves and dadoes into backs of the panels.
A
1⅝"
¼" dado ¼" deep
½"
2¾"
½"
STEP 2
Rip tops and bottoms off the blank.
¼" groove ¼" deep
1¼"
1"
3½"
1"
Middle is waste.
STEP 3
Crosscut sides off the blanks.
¼" dadoes ⅛" deep, (half lap) centered
2½"
C
B
A
3½"
A
A
A
STEP 4
Glue cut parts back together. (Discard center waste piece.)

7–15.
LANTERN PANEL DETAIL

4 From the ⅜" stock, cut a 4 x 9½" blank for the stiles (D) and a 2¼ x 3½" blank for the rails (E). Install a dado blade in your tablesaw, and cut the 2½" and ½" rabbets in the ends of the stiles blank, and the ½" rabbets in the ends of the rails blank and the lantern panels (A). The rabbets cut in these parts become the half-lap joints shown in **7–16**. Rip the stile blank into ½"-wide strips to form the stiles (D), as shown in **7–14**. Repeat this operation with the rail blank to form the rails (E).

5 Glue and clamp together the lantern panel assembly (A/B/C), the stiles (D), and the rails (E) to form the lantern lights.

6 From the ⅜" stock, cut the back (F) to the size listed. Drill the countersunk shank holes and the 7⁄16" hole, as shown on **7–17**.

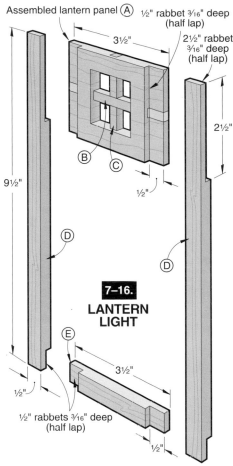

Assembled lantern panel Ⓐ

½" rabbet ³⁄₁₆" deep (half lap)

3½"

2½" rabbet ³⁄₁₆" deep (half lap)

2½"

9½"

Ⓑ
Ⓒ

½"

Ⓓ

Ⓓ

7–16.
LANTERN LIGHT

Ⓔ

3½"

½"

½" rabbets ³⁄₁₆" deep (half lap)

½"

7 Tilt your tablesaw blade to 45°. With the fence positioned so the blade tilts away from it, bevel-rip the lantern lights and the lantern back (F), as shown on the Exploded View drawing in **7–18**, on *page 152*.

Wrap Up the Lantern

1 Rip a 1"-wide strip from the ½"-thick stock for the mounting ring segments (G). Miter-cut them to the length listed. Glue the ring together, as shown in **7–18**.

2 Adhere the mounting ring to the outside face of the lantern back (F) with double-faced tape,

where shown on **7–17**. Using the previously drilled holes in the lantern back (F) as guides, drill screw pilot holes in the mounting ring. For accurate reassembly later, make index marks on the ring and back. Remove the ring and set it aside.

3 Position the three lantern lights and the back, outside faces up, on a flat surface so the points of the beveled edges are touching and the top and bottom edges are aligned. Fasten the parts together, top, bottom, and center, with strips of masking tape. Turn the taped-together parts over, and spread glue on the beveled edges. Roll up the assembly, and secure the closing miter with more tape. Wipe off any glue that squeezes out, and set the assembly aside.

4 Rip a ½ × 18" strip from the ¼" stock for the mica stop

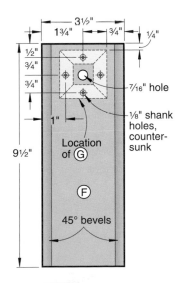

3½"

1¾"   ¾"   ¼"

½"
¾"
¾"

⁷⁄₁₆" hole

⅛" shank holes, counter-sunk

1"

Location of Ⓖ

9½"

Ⓕ

45° bevels

7–17.   **BACK**

(H). Cut a ⅛" rabbet the thickness of the mica panel on one edge, and cut the stops to length. Miter both ends of the front stops, and one end of the side stops, as shown on the Exploded View drawing in **7–18**. Glue and clamp the top three stops in place. Set the others aside.

Craft a Matching Escutcheon

1 From the ⅜" stock, cut the escutcheon panel blank (I) to the size listed. Now, in a process similar to that you used to form the lantern side and front panels, follow the four steps shown in the Escutcheon Panel Detail in **7–19**, shown on *page 153*, to form this part. When glued back together, the panel has two dadoes and a groove to accept mullions (B, J) and a 1½ × 1½" cutout at each end.

2 Cut the escutcheon mullion (J) from the ¼" stock to the size listed. Form the two notches near each end, where shown in **7–19**. Retrieve the set-aside horizontal mullions (B), and glue them and the escutcheon mullion in place.

3 Drill the countersunk screw shank holes and the ⁷⁄₁₆" hole, where shown on **7–20**. The countersinks are on the back of the escutcheon panel.

4 Chuck a keyhole bit in your table-mounted router, and adjust it to cut ¼" deep. Position

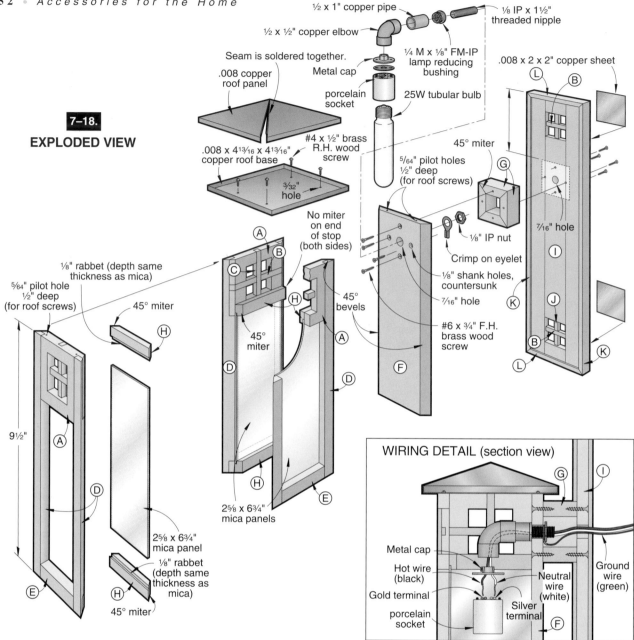

7–18.
EXPLODED VIEW

½ x 1" copper pipe

⅛ IP x 1½" threaded nipple

½ x ½" copper elbow

Seam is soldered together.

.008 copper roof panel

Metal cap

¼ M x ⅛" FM-IP lamp reducing bushing

porcelain socket

25W tubular bulb

.008 x 2 x 2" copper sheet

.008 x 4¹³⁄₁₆ x 4¹³⁄₁₆" copper roof base

#4 x ½" brass R.H. wood screw

⁵⁄₆₄" pilot holes ½" deep (for roof screws)

45° miter

³⁄₃₂" hole

⅛" IP nut

7⁄₁₆" hole

No miter on end of stop (both sides)

Crimp on eyelet

⅛" shank holes, countersunk

7⁄₁₆" hole

#6 x ¾" F.H. brass wood screw

⅛" rabbet (depth same thickness as mica)

⁵⁄₆₄" pilot hole ½" deep (for roof screws)

45° miter

45° bevels

45° miter

9½"

2⅝ x 6¾" mica panels

2⅝ x 6¾" mica panel

⅛" rabbet (depth same thickness as mica)

45° miter

WIRING DETAIL (section view)

Metal cap

Hot wire (black)

Gold terminal

porcelain socket

Neutral wire (white)

Silver terminal

Ground wire (green)

---

the fence to center the bit on the width of the escutcheon panel. Clamp stopblocks to the fence to position the keyhole slots where shown. Switch on the router, and with the top of the panel against the right stopblock, lower it onto the running bit, and then move it to the left until it contacts the other stopblock. Turn off the router, and wait for the bit to stop

before sliding the panel back and lifting it from the bit. You need a separate stopblock setup to rout each keyhole slot.

5 Adhere the mounting ring to the front face of the escutcheon panel (I) with double-faced tape, where shown on **7–20**. Using the previously drilled holes in the panel as guides, drill screw

pilot holes in the mounting ring. Make sure the index mark previously made on the ring is in the proper orientation. Remove the ring and set it aside.

6 From your ¼" stock, rip strips ½" longer than listed for the side banding (K) and end banding (L). Miter-cut the parts to length, and glue and clamp them

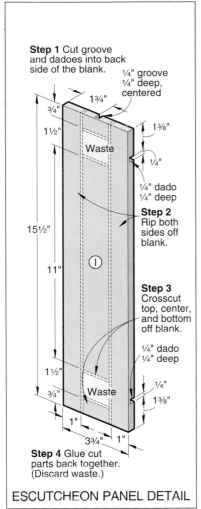

Step 1 Cut groove and dadoes into back side of the blank.

¼" groove ¼" deep, centered

1¾"

¾"

1½"

1⅜"

Waste

¼"

¼" dado ¼" deep

Step 2 Rip both sides off blank.

15½"

11"

I

Step 3 Crosscut top, center, and bottom off blank.

¼" dado ¼" deep

1½"

¾"

Waste

¼"

1⅜"

1"

3¾"

1"

Step 4 Glue cut parts back together. (Discard waste.)

ESCUTCHEON PANEL DETAIL

to the escutcheon panel, leaving a ⅛" overhang at both front and back, as shown on the Escutcheon drawing in **7–19**.

Wire the Wall Sconces

1 Cut a 1"-long piece of copper pipe, and epoxy it into a ½" copper elbow, then epoxy a ¼ x ⅛" IP reducing bushing into the open end of the pipe, as shown in **7–18** and the accompanying Wiring Detail drawing. Remove the metal cap from a lampholder's porcelain socket, and epoxy it into the open end of the elbow, as shown. We used metal-filled epoxy because it is heat resistant and adheres well

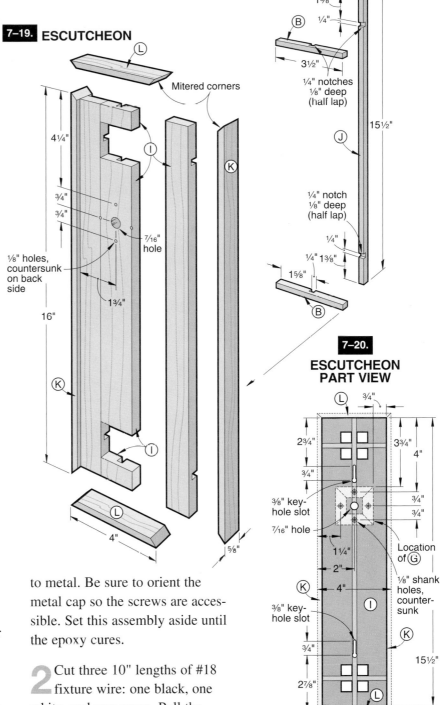

7–19. **ESCUTCHEON**

L

Mitered corners

4¼"

I

¾"

¾"

⅛" holes, countersunk on back side

7/16" hole

1¾"

16"

K

K

I

L

4"

5/8"

B

1⅜"

¼"

3½"

¼" notches ⅛" deep (half lap)

15½"

J

¼" notch ⅛" deep (half lap)

¼"

¼" 1⅜"

1⅝"

B

7–20.

ESCUTCHEON PART VIEW

L

¾"

2¾"

3¾"

4"

¾"

¾"

¾"

3/8" key-hole slot

7/16" hole

Location of G

1¼"

2"

K

4"

⅛" shank holes, counter-sunk

I

3/8" key-hole slot

K

¾"

15½"

2⅞"

L

to metal. Be sure to orient the metal cap so the screws are accessible. Set this assembly aside until the epoxy cures.

2 Cut three 10" lengths of #18 fixture wire: one black, one white, and one green. Pull the black and white wires through the assembly. Connect the black wire to the gold (hot) terminal and the white wire to the silver (neutral) terminal on the porcelain lamp socket. Reattach the socket to its metal cap.

3 Slip the threaded pipe nipple over the wires, and screw it into the bushing. Crimp the eyelet onto the green wire. To check the fit of the lampholder assembly, insert the pipe nipple through the

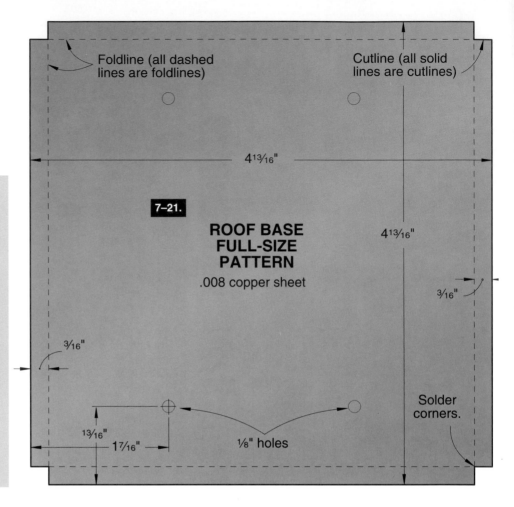

Foldline (all dashed lines are foldlines)

Cutline (all solid lines are cutlines)

7-21.

ROOF BASE FULL-SIZE PATTERN
.008 copper sheet

4¹³⁄₁₆"

4¹³⁄₁₆"

³⁄₁₆"

³⁄₁₆"

Solder corners.

1⁷⁄₁₆"

¹³⁄₁₆"

⅛" holes

hole in the lantern back, slip on the ground wire eyelet, and fasten the whole assembly with a ⅛" IP nut, as shown on the Wiring Detail in **7–18** (*page 152*). Remove the lampholder assembly and set it aside.

A Little Metal Work Makes a Roof

1 Photocopy the full-size roof and roof base patterns from *above* and *opposite page*, and adhere them to .008" copper sheet. Cut along the pattern lines with metal snips. Use an awl or utility knife to lightly score the foldlines. Drill the holes in the roof base. Remove the patterns.

2 Cut a 45° bevel on a hardwood block that is as wide as the bend you need to make. Place the roof on your workbench, and press the bevel point down on the scored line. Bend the copper sheet up away from the bench surface, as shown in **7–23**. Make the interior bends first, then the perimeter ones. Repeat with the roof base. To give the roof an oxidized patina, see the Shop Tip *above*.

3 Solder the lap joint on the roof, then the corner joints of the roof and roof base. Bend the roof lap to the inside, and solder all the joints from the inside.

4 Center the roof base on top of the lantern. Using the previously drilled holes in the base as guides, drill the screw pilot holes in the top of the lantern. Set the roof and roof base aside.

Finish and Assemble the Parts

1 Finish-sand all parts and assemblies to 220 grit. Because of the number of intricate sconce parts that need to be finished, we used spray varnish, applying two coats of satin, sanding lightly with 220-grit sandpaper between coats.

2 Cut two 2 x 2" copper sheet squares, and epoxy them from

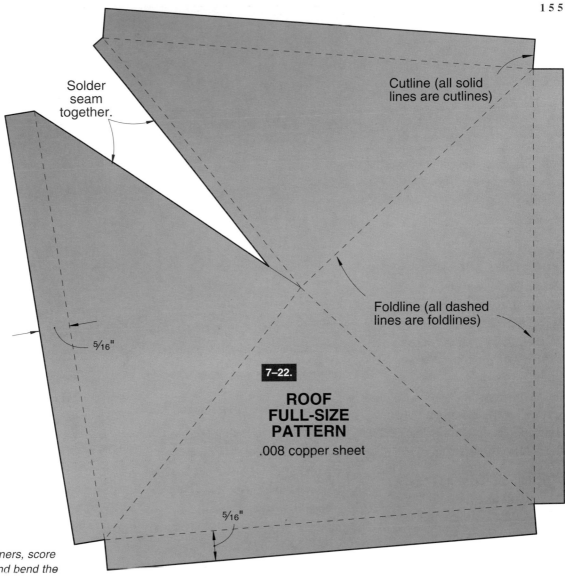

Solder
seam
together.

Cutline (all solid
lines are cutlines)

Foldline (all dashed
lines are foldlines)

⁵⁄₁₆"

⁵⁄₁₆"

7–22.

**ROOF
FULL-SIZE
PATTERN**

.008 copper sheet

*To get crisp corners, score
the fold lines, and bend the
copper sheet against the
edge of a beveled block.*

7–23.

the rear over the "windows" in
the escutcheon. Then set it aside
until the epoxy cures.

3 Fasten the mounting ring to
the lantern back with brass
wood screws, as shown in **7–18**
(*page 152*). You can access the
screw holes through the front
lantern panel. Make sure you
align the index marks. Reinstall
the lampholder assembly in the
lantern as before.

4 Cut three 2⅝ x 6¾" mica
panels on your tablesaw.
Slide them into the lantern,
engaging the top stops. Glue and

clamp the bottom stops in place,
as shown on the Exploded View
drawing in **7–18**.

5 Feed the wires through the
hole in the escutcheon.
Screw the escutcheon to the
mounting ring, as shown. Screw
the roof base onto the top of the
lantern, and fit the roof over the
base. The roof-to-base connection
is a friction-fit joint. It can be
adjusted for tightness by bending
the flanges on the base.

Mount the Sconce on Your Wall

1 Mark the vertical centerline and the location of the top of the sconce escutcheon on the wall. Have an electrician install a standard switch box so the top fixture screw hole is on the centerline, and 3" below the top mark.

2 Tap the top fixture screw hole in the switch box for a #8 × 1" roundhead machine screw, and install the screw. With an appropriate hollow wall anchor, install a #8 × 1¼" roundhead wood screw on the centerline and 9¼" below the machine screw. Let the screws protrude enough to engage the keyhole slots in the back of the sconce escutcheon.

3 Shut off the power to the circuit that feeds this box. Connect the fixture wires to the box wires with wire nuts. Making sure the wires tuck into the box, press the sconce against the wall, engaging the screw heads in the keyhole slots. Slide the sconce downward until the screws contact the tops of the slots.

4 Screw in the lightbulb, turn on the power, flick the switch, and enjoy the soft, golden glow.

Note: This fixture is designed to accommodate a 25-watt frosted tubular bulb.

Clock

CLOCK

Looking at the simple lines, graceful proportions, and figured grain of this clock's quartersawn oak, it's easy to see why pieces in this style are so admired. To help you achieve the same results, we've provided easy-to-follow, step-by-step instructions.

Start with the Front and Back Parts

1 From ¾"-thick stock, cut the stiles (A) to the size listed in the Materials List. Cut a ¼" groove ¼" deep, centered on an edge of each stile, where shown on **7–24**.

2 From ½"-thick stock, cut the face (B) to size. On the back of the face, cut a ¼" rabbet ¼" deep along the side edges, where

shown. You'll drill the hole in the face to receive the clock movement later.

3 Cut the face-trim pieces (C) and the bottom rail (D) to size from ¾"-thick stock. Then, using a dado blade, form the ¼ × ¼" tenons centered on the rail ends, where shown. Make two copies of the full-size arch pattern on *page 159* (**7–30**). Apply one pattern to a face of the rail with spray adhesive, and set the other pattern aside. Bandsaw to the pattern line to form the arch, and sand smooth.

4 From ¼"-thick stock, rip a ¼ × 24" blank for forming the fillers (E, F) and grille parts (G, H, I); then cut the parts to size. Set the grille parts aside.

5 From ½"-thick stock, cut the back (J) to size. Cut a ¼" rabbet ¼" deep along the sides on the inside face, where shown in **7–24**. Then, adhere the second copy of the arch pattern to the back at its bottom, and bandsaw and sand the arch.

CUTTING DIAGRAM FOR CLOCK

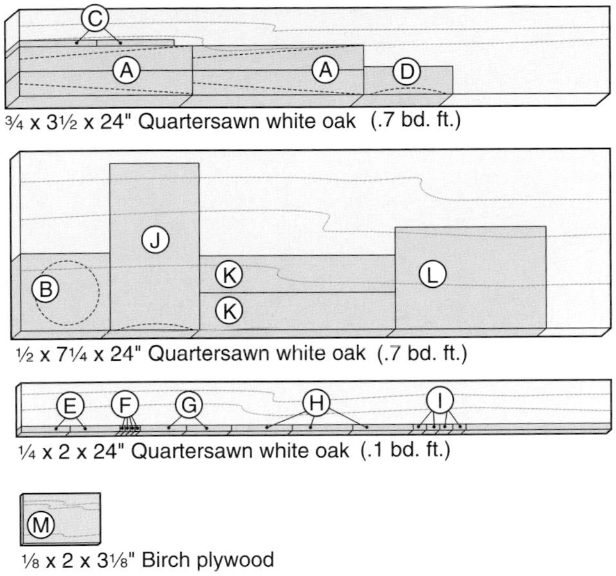
C
A
A
D
3/4 x 3 1/2 x 24" Quartersawn white oak (.7 bd. ft.)
J
B
K
K
L
1/2 x 7 1/4 x 24" Quartersawn white oak (.7 bd. ft.)
E
F
G
H
I
1/4 x 2 x 24" Quartersawn white oak (.1 bd. ft.)
M
1/8 x 2 x 3 1/8" Birch plywood

MATERIALS LIST FOR CLOCK

PART	FINISHED SIZE T	W	L	Mtl.	Qty.
A stiles	3/4"	1"	7"	QO	4
B face	1/2"	3 1/8"	3 5/8"	QO	1
C face trim	3/4"	1/4"	3 1/8"	QO	2
D bottom rail	3/4"	1 1/8"	3 5/8"	QO	1
E* long fillers	1/4"	1/4"	2 1/4"	QO	2
F* short fillers	1/4"	1/4"	1/4"	QO	4
G* grille sides	1/4"	1/4"	2"	QO	2
H* grille rails	1/4"	1/4"	2 5/8"	QO	3
I* grille uprights	1/4"	1/4"	5/8"	QO	4
J back	1/2"	6 3/4"	3 5/8"	QO	1
K* sides	1/2"	1 1/2"	7 1/16"	QO	2
L top	1/2"	4 1/8"	6 1/8"	QO	1
M backer	1/8"	2"	3 1/8"	BP	1

*Parts initially cut oversize. See the instructions.

Materials Key: QO = quartersawn white oak; BP = birch plywood.
Supplies: 1/4" hardboard; epoxy; N battery. Clock: 2 3/8"-diameter press-in clock movement (1); 2 x 3 1/8" mica (1). See What is Mica? on *page 159* for a discussion of mica.
Blades and Bits: Dado blade; 2 3/8" Forstner bit or circle cutter; 1/2" round-over bit.

7–24.
EXPLODED VIEW

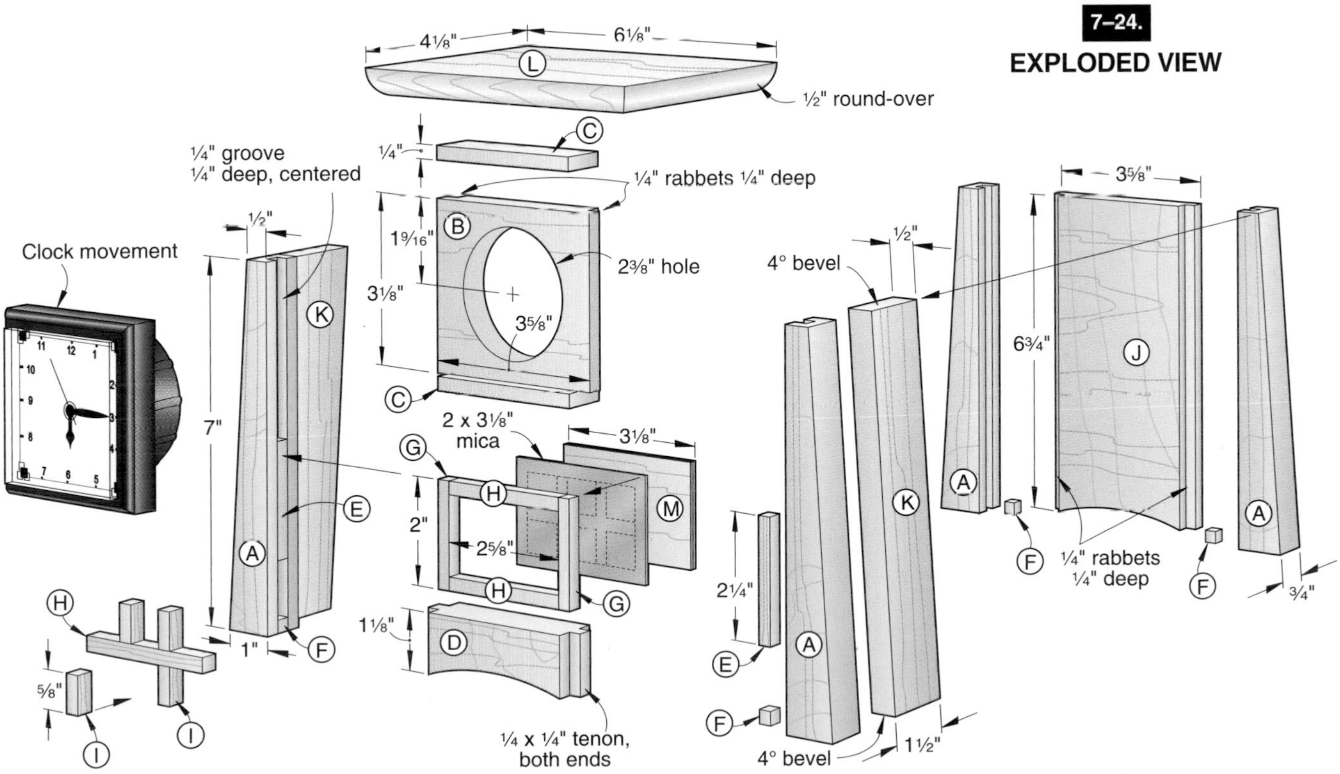
4 1/8"
6 1/8"
L
1/2" round-over
1/4"
C
1/4" groove 1/4" deep, centered
1/4" rabbets 1/4" deep
1/2"
B
1 9/16"
Clock movement
2 3/8" hole
3 1/8"
K
3 5/8"
C
7"
2 x 3 1/8" mica
3 1/8"
G
H
M
E
2"
2 5/8"
A
H
G
H
1 1/8"
D
1"
F
5/8"
I
I
1/4 x 1/4" tenon, both ends
3 5/8"
1/2"
4° bevel
6 3/4"
J
A
K
A
F
1/4" rabbets 1/4" deep
F
3/4"
2 1/4"
E
A
F
4° bevel
1 1/2"

7–25.

With the face (B) clamped (no glue) between the stiles (A), glue and clamp the face trim (C) to the face's top and bottom edges.

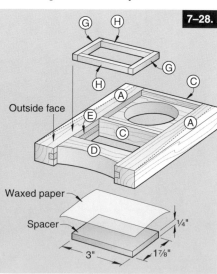

7–26.

Glue and clamp a long filler in each stile's groove, sliding it behind the bottom face-trim piece and tight against the face. Remove any squeeze-out.

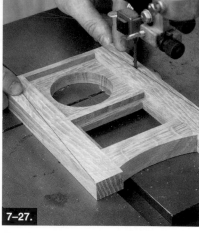

7–27.

Band-saw the stiles to the marked lines to form the tapered sides. Start the cut at the bottom of the stile, and finish at the top. Sand smooth.

Assemble and Glue the Parts

1 To assemble the front of the clock case, first place two stiles (A) and the face (B) on your work surface, outside face up. Without gluing, clamp the face between the stiles with its top edge positioned ¼" below the top of the stiles. Now, glue the face-trim pieces (C) to the face, as shown in **7–25**.

2 Check that the top face-trim piece is flush with the top of the stiles. Then, glue and clamp a long filler (E) in each stile, as shown in **7–26**. This will leave 1⅜" of open groove at the bottom of each stile to receive the 1⅛"-wide bottom rail (D) and the ¼" short filler (F). Separate the stiles from the face/trim assembly.

3 Apply glue to the rabbeted ends of the face and to the bottom rail's tenons (D). Now, assemble the face, bottom rail, and stiles, with the bottom rail tight against the long fillers. Clamp the assembly.

4 Place a dab of glue into the stiles' grooves just below the bottom rail. Then, install and clamp a short filler (F) in each groove.

5 To assemble the back of the clock case, first apply glue to the rabbeted sides of the back (J), and clamp it between the remaining stiles with their top edges flush. Then, glue and clamp the remaining short fillers (F) into the stiles.

6 From ¼" hardboard, cut a 1⅞ × 3" spacer for positioning the grille side and rail pieces (G, H) in the clock's front opening, ¼" back from the front edge. See the Shop Tip *at left*. With the front assembly outside face up on your work surface, position the spacer in the grille opening. Then, glue the grille side pieces to the long fillers (E) in the stiles, and glue the rail pieces to the lower face trim (C) and the bottom rail (D). Press the pieces firmly down against the spacer.

SHOP TIP

Prevent Glue from Sticking to Unwanted Surfaces

Glue squeeze-out can cause parts to become joined where unintended. To prevent this, place a piece of waxed paper between the surfaces that you don't want joined, where possible. For example, when gluing the grille sides (G) and the rails (H) in the clock's opening, put waxed paper on top of the spacer. The glue will not stick to the paper, so you'll find it easy to remove the spacer and scrape off any residual glue.

7–28.

Outside face

Waxed paper

Spacer

3"   1⅞"   ¼"

7–29.

Install the remaining grille rail and uprights in position, pressing the epoxied edges against the mica. Check for proper alignment.

7 Using a 2⅜" Forstner bit, or a circle cutter set to cut a 2⅜" hole, drill a centered hole through the face (B) to receive the clock movement.

8 Mark the taper on each of the stiles (A), where dimensioned. Then, bandsaw the tapers, cutting just outside the marked lines, as shown in **7–27**. Then, sand to the lines.

What is Mica?

Mica is used for the clock's grille. "Mica" is a general term for a group of more than 30 slightly different silicate minerals. Commonly known for their translucent properties, micas are commercially used in decorative applications, such as lampshades, ceiling panels, and the grille back in our shelf clock.

Mica typically is mined in chunks that get split and further processed into films, flakes, and powders for various uses. Fabricated mica sheets, like those used in this clock, get formed by combining mica flakes with binding resins of contrasting colors.

Add the Sides and Top

1 From ½"-thick stock, cut two 1½ × 8" blanks for the sides (K). Tilt your tablesaw blade to 4° from vertical. Now, bevel-cut the blanks to their finished length of 7¹/₁₆" with a 4° bevel on each end, where shown.

2 Glue and clamp the sides to the front assembly, keeping the top and bottom ends and the angled sides flush. With the glue dry, glue and clamp the back assembly to the sides. When dry, remove the clamps, and sand the sides and the top and bottom edges of the case smooth.

3 From ½"-thick stock, cut the top (L) to size. Rout a ½" round-over along the bottom edges, where shown. Sand the top, including a light sanding of the top edges. Now, center the top, front to back and side to side, on the case, and glue and clamp it in place.

Complete the Clock

1 Finish-sand the clock case and remaining grille parts (H, I) to 220 grit, and remove the dust. Apply a stain of your choice to the clock case. Also, stain all but

one edge (for gluing) of the remaining grille parts. Then, apply a clear finish, sanding to 400 grit between coats, and removing the dust.

2 Cut the backer (M) to size, and cut a piece of mica (or stained glass, as an option) to the same size. (We cut our mica using a bandsaw and a zero-clearance insert.) Adhere the mica to the backer with epoxy.

3 Through the bottom of the clock case, apply a small amount of epoxy to the back of the grille sides (G) and rails (H). Insert the mica/backer through the bottom, and press it into the opening against the epoxied parts. Apply masking tape to hold the mica/backer in position while the epoxy cures.

4 Apply epoxy to the unstained edges of the remaining grille rail and uprights, and install these pieces, as shown in **7–29**. Finally, install an N-size battery in the clock, set the time, and press the clock into the hole in the face.

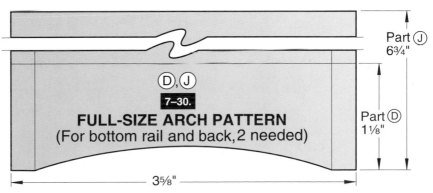

Ⓓ, Ⓙ

7–30.

FULL-SIZE ARCH PATTERN
(For bottom rail and back, 2 needed)

Part Ⓙ
6¾"

Part Ⓓ
1⅛"

3⅝"

Nesting tables

NESTING TABLES

Y ou can't beat nesting tables for versatility. We've designed these three beauties not only for visual appeal but to go together with minimum fuss and maximum workshop enjoyment.

Note: Although the three tables are different sizes, the methods for making the parts for each one are identical. We suggest machining the parts for all three tables at the same time. That way, you'll only have to make each setup once.

Make a Dozen Legs

1 Laminate stock for the legs (A), and cut them to the sizes shown for each table in the Materials List. To do this, laminate two 1¾"-wide pieces of ¾"-thick white oak about 1" longer than the finished length of each leg. Joint one edge of each lamination, and rip the opposite edge for a piece 1" wide. Joint the sawn edge to finished width, and trim the leg to length.

2 Mark each leg's location, such as "right rear," "left front," etc., on its top. Orient the lamination lines, as shown in **7–31**, on *page 162.*

3 Lay out the mortises on the legs, referring to **7–31** and the Mortise Detail in **7–38** (*page 165*). Stand the legs for each table in assembly order to verify the mortise layouts are accurate.

4 Form the leg mortises. To do this, refer to Steps 2 to 4 in **7–32**, on *page 162.* For accuracy, drill the holes with a drill press, setting a fence to center the bit on the leg. Clean out the mortises with a chisel.

CUTTING DIAGRAM FOR NESTING TABLES

Large Table *Plane or resaw to the thicknesses listed in the Materials List.

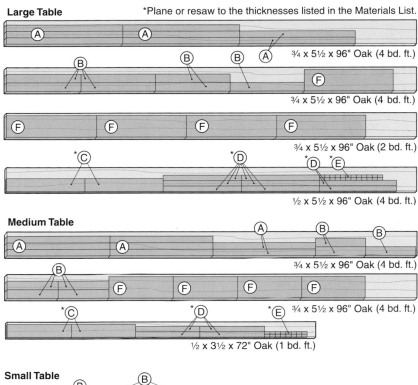

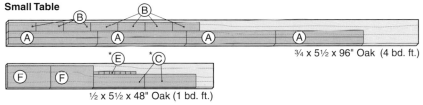

MATERIALS LIST FOR NESTING TABLES

PART	FINISHED SIZE			Mtl.	Qty.
	T	W	L		
LARGE TABLE					
A* legs	1½"	1½"	27¼"	LO	4
B rails	¾"	2"	17⅜"	O	7
C wide slats	¼"	3"	18¼"	O	2
D narrow slats	¼"	1¼"	18¼"	O	8
E fillers	¼"	⅝"	1¼"	O	24
F top	¾"	20"	20"	EO	1
MEDIUM TABLE					
A* legs	1½"	1½"	24"	LO	4
B rails	¾"	2"	11⅞"	O	7
C wide slats	¼"	3"	15"	O	2
D narrow slats	¼"	1¼"	15"	O	4
E fillers	¼"	⅝"	1⅛"	O	16
F top	¾"	14½"	14½"	EO	1
SMALL TABLE					
A* legs	1½"	1½"	20¾"	LO	4
B rails	¾"	2"	6⅜"	O	7
C wide slats	¼"	3"	11¾"	O	2
D narrow slat	not used in this table				
E fillers	¼"	⅝"	1¹¹⁄₁₆"	O	8
F top	¾"	9"	9"	EO	1

Parts initially cut oversize. See the instructions.

Materials Key: LO = laminated white oak; O = white oak; EO = edge-joined white oak.
Supplies: Tabletop fasteners; #8 x ¾" flathead wood screws.

5 Rout or sand ⅛" chamfers at the bottom of each leg, where shown.

Make the Rails

1 Cut the rails (B) to size for each table. At the same time, cut two or three scrapwood test rails to test tenon size (small-table size would be fine).

2 Cut ⅜ x 1¼" tenons ¹⁵⁄₁₆" long on the rail ends, where shown on the Tenon Detail in **7–38** (*page 165*). Later you'll miter-cut the tenons to give them the shape shown in the drawing.

To cut the tenons, install a ¾" dado blade on your tablesaw. Position the tablesaw's rip fence ³⁄₁₆" from the dado blade, as shown in **7–33**. Attach an auxiliary fence to the saw's miter gauge, extending it to the rip fence, as shown on the drawing. Set the cutting depth to ³⁄₁₆", and cut both faces at one end of a test rail, holding the end against the rip fence. Make another pass with the end pulled back far enough to cut the end of the tenon. Insert a corner of the tenon into a mortise to check its fit. Adjust the cutting

depth as necessary. When correct, cut both faces at both ends of all 21 rails for all three tables.

Next, set the cutting depth at ¼". Stand the test rail on one edge, and cut the tenon. Ensure that this distance from the rail edge to the tenon will place the rail's top edge flush with the leg top. Adjust if needed. Then cut one edge of each rail end.

Finally, set the cutting depth at ½". Saw the other edge of the test rail's tenon. Test-fit the pieces and adjust as before, and then cut the remaining rail edges. After

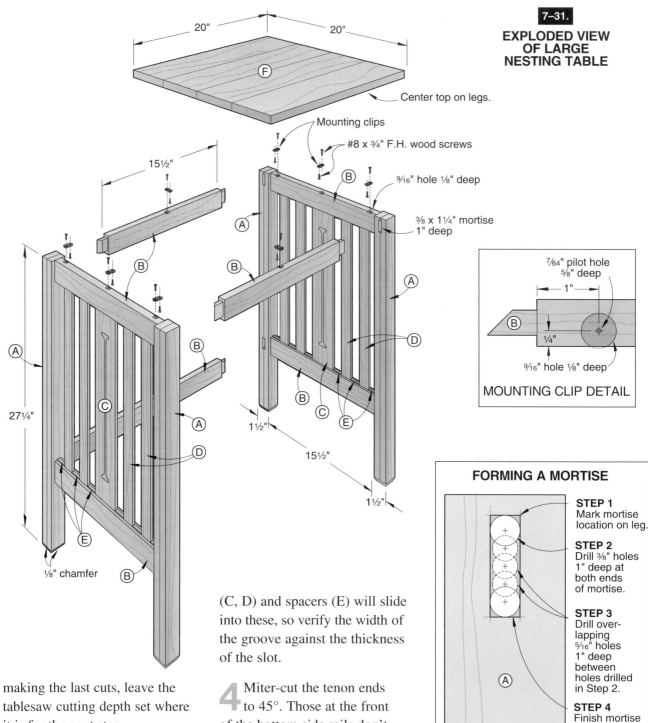

7–31.

EXPLODED VIEW OF LARGE NESTING TABLE

20" 20"

F

Center top on legs.

Mounting clips

#8 x ¾" F.H. wood screws

B

9/16" hole ⅛" deep

⅜ x 1¼" mortise 1" deep

15½"

A

B

B

A

A

B

D

27¼"

C

A

B

C

E

D

E

1½"

B

15½"

1½"

⅛" chamfer

B

MOUNTING CLIP DETAIL

7/64" pilot hole ⅝" deep

1"

B

¼"

9/16" hole ⅛" deep

FORMING A MORTISE

STEP 1
Mark mortise location on leg.

STEP 2
Drill ⅜" holes 1" deep at both ends of mortise.

STEP 3
Drill overlapping 5/16" holes 1" deep between holes drilled in Step 2.

A

STEP 4
Finish mortise with a chisel, cutting sides and ends square.

7–32.

(C, D) and spacers (E) will slide into these, so verify the width of the groove against the thickness of the slot.

making the last cuts, leave the tablesaw cutting depth set where it is for the next step.

3 Change to a ¼" dado blade, and saw a centered groove ½" deep on four of the seven rails for each table. The slats

4 Miter-cut the tenon ends to 45°. Those at the front of the bottom side rails don't require mitered ends. But cutting all of them makes the side rails interchangeable, heading off a complication come assembly time.

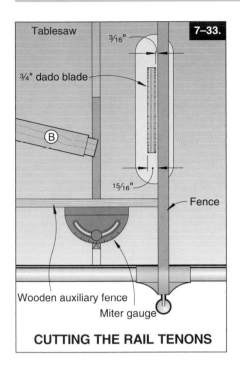

CUTTING THE RAIL TENONS

Saw the Slats and Spacers

1 Cut the wide slats (C), narrow slats (D), and spacers (E) to size from ¼"-thick stock. Note that the small table doesn't call for any narrow slats.

2 Make 12 photocopies of **7–35** on *page 164*. Adhere two copies to each part C, placing the top of each pattern at one end of the part. Spray adhesive (follow the label instructions for temporary bonding) or rubber cement will hold them in place.

3 Drill ⅜" start holes in each wide slat (C), where shown.

4 Rout the straight center portion of the cut-out design. To do this, install a ¼" straight bit in your table-mounted router. Position a fence to center the bit on the wide slat. Clamp another

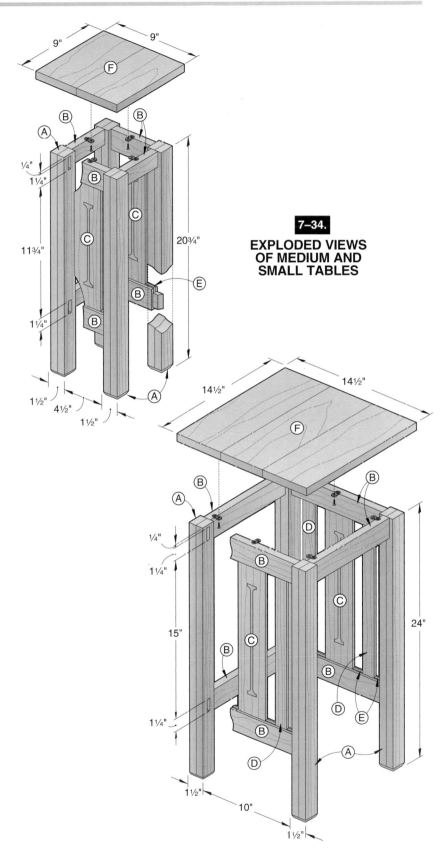

7–34.
EXPLODED VIEWS OF MEDIUM AND SMALL TABLES

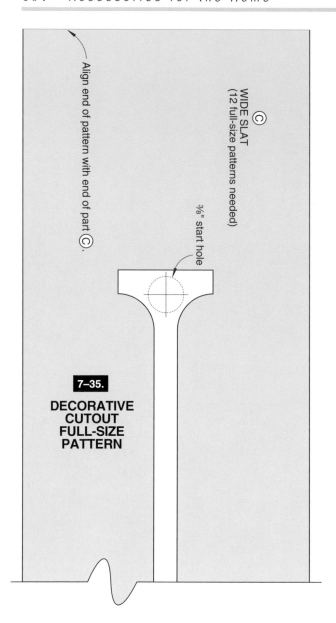

Align end of pattern with end of part Ⓒ.

WIDE SLAT
(12 full-size patterns needed)

Ⓒ

⅜" start hole

7–35.

**DECORATIVE
CUTOUT
FULL-SIZE
PATTERN**

7–36.

*Parallel fences help you rout an arrow-straight slot
between two holes for the cut-out design in the wide slat.*

7–37.

*Scroll-saw the ends of the decorative cutout. A #4 blade
(.035 × .015", with 18 teeth per inch) is a good choice.*

fence along the other edge of the part, as shown in
7–36. Then, with the cutting depth set to about ⅜",
place the hole at the left end of the part over the bit,
start the router, and cut the decorative slot between
the two holes.

5 Scroll-saw the ends of the decorative cutout, as
shown in **7–37.** Sand the routed and sawn edges,
as needed; then remove the patterns.

6 Finish-sand the legs, rails, slats, and spacers.
(We sanded to 220 grit.)

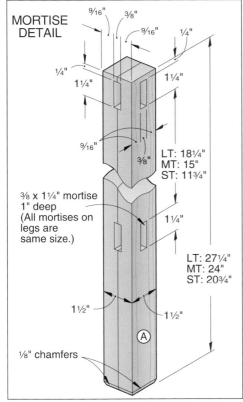

MORTISE DETAIL

9/16" 3/8"
9/16" 1/4"
1/4"
1/4"
1 1/4" 1 1/4"
9/16"
3/8"
LT: 18 1/4"
MT: 15"
ST: 11 3/4"
3/8 x 1 1/4" mortise 1" deep
(All mortises on legs are same size.)
1 1/4"
LT: 27 1/4"
MT: 24"
ST: 20 3/4"
1 1/2" 1 1/2"
1/8" chamfers
A

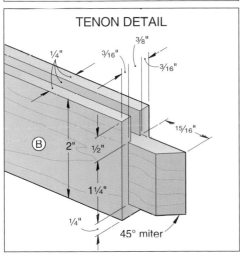

TENON DETAIL

1/4" 3/16" 3/8"
3/16"
B 2" 1/2"
15/16"
1 1/4"
1/4"
45° miter

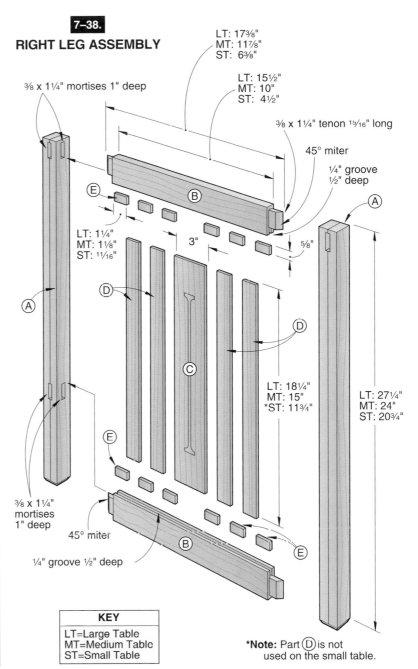

7–38.
RIGHT LEG ASSEMBLY

LT: 17 3/8"
MT: 11 7/8"
ST: 6 3/8"

LT: 15 1/2"
MT: 10"
ST: 4 1/2"

3/8 x 1 1/4" mortises 1" deep

3/8 x 1 1/4" tenon 15/16" long

45° miter

1/4" groove 1/2" deep

E
B
A

LT: 1 1/4"
MT: 1 1/8"
ST: 11/16"
3"
A
D
5/8"

D
C

LT: 18 1/4"
MT: 15"
*ST: 11 3/4"

LT: 27 1/4"
MT: 24"
ST: 20 3/4"

E
3/8 x 1 1/4" mortises 1" deep
45° miter
B
1/4" groove 1/2" deep
E

KEY
LT=Large Table
MT=Medium Table
ST=Small Table

***Note:** Part Ⓓ is not used on the small table.

Next, Assemble a Bunch of Bases

1 Dry-assemble (without gluing) the legs, rails, and slats for the right leg assembly, referring to the Right Leg Assembly drawing in **7–38**. You can leave out the spacers (E) for this test-fitting. Check for joint fit and squareness, and ensure that the top of the rail lies flush with the leg tops. Unclamp the parts, and disassemble.

2 Glue together the rails and slats for the assembly. To do so, start by placing the center slat exactly in the middle of one rail. Put a dab of glue in the groove on each side of the slat, and slip a spacer into the groove against each edge of the slat. Center the

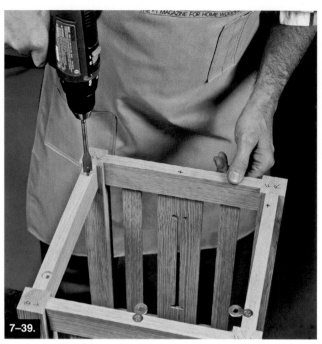

7–39.

Bore recesses for the tabletop connectors with a 9/16" spade bit. The bit's point simultaneously drills a screw pilot hole.

other rail on the other end of the slat, and glue in the spacers. Slide in the first narrow slat, and fix it in place with spacers. Continue until all slats and spacers are in place.

3 After the glue dries, glue the front and back legs to the assembled rails and slats.

4 Put together the left leg assembly in the same way. Build the left and right leg assemblies for the other tables.

The leg assemblies for the other tables differ from the drawing only in the number of narrow slats (D). The medium table has two narrow slats per assembly; the small table, none.

5 Connect the leg assemblies for each table base with the remaining rails, referring to **7–31**, on *page 162*. To ensure wobble-free tables, assemble them on a known flat surface, such as your tablesaw's table.

Make the Top

1 For each table, edge-glue stock to make a blank slightly larger than the tops, and cut the tops (F) to sizes in the Materials List.

2 Install figure-eight-type tabletop connectors on each frame assembly, where indicated on the Exploded View drawing in **7–31** and **7–34**. Locate the center of the 9/16" hole for each connector 1/4" from the inside edge on top of the rail. Drill the holes with a portable drill, as shown in **7–39**.

3 Lay the top face down on the workbench, and center the inverted base assembly on it. Mark centers for the attaching screws. Drill pilot holes, taking care not to go through the top. Attach the top with screws.

4 Finish-sand the top. Finish the set as desired. (We stained the tables and then applied satin polyurethane.)

CHAPTER 8

An Arts and Crafts Makeover

 *ITH ALL THE ARTS AND CRAFTS STYLE projects we put together for this book, we decided that a room was needed to showcase many of them. So, we put on our work gloves and assaulted a 1960s-era gathering place, as shown in 8–1. In this chapter we'll show you how we achieved the makeover, converting a dated family room into a space any woodworker would be proud to create. On the following pages you'll discover how to build and install all of the woodwork that surrounds the fireplace and lines the walls.*

Although our room has a distinctive Arts and Crafts flair because of such elements as the wall stenciling, framed pictures, stained glass, and furnishings, the design of the built-in woodwork complements most traditional interiors. Of course, you're not limited to an Arts and Crafts treatment. You could change the stain color, wood species (we used quartersawn solid oak and riftsawn oak plywood throughout), or hardware to suit your interior. For example, the same woodwork in walnut would lend a study area a rich, library-like feel. Or, switch to cherry, substitute wooden knobs on the bookcase doors, and delete the plate rail and its brackets, and the room will have a distinctly Shaker flair.

And certainly you could pick and choose from among the ideas presented in this room. You may just want to build the bookcases described on page 178, or skip those and add the paneling only as described in the pages that follow.

The original space, complete with sheet paneling and shag carpeting, had a distinctly '60s look.

TRANSFORMING A FAMILY ROOM STEP-BY-STEP

Although the complete renovation of a family room may seem like a daunting task, you can achieve impressive results through a series of simple steps. Here, in order, is how this family room took shape. The items listed below are cross-referenced by number in **8–4**, on *pages 170 and 171*. You'll find complete how-to instructions for the wall-paneling and bookcases on the following pages. You'll find the wall sconces on *page 149* of Chapter 7.

1 Wall preparation. Rather than tear out the dated sheet paneling on the walls, we covered it with a heavy wall covering that provides a joint- and groove-free surface.

2 Oak paneling installation. We installed shop-made paneling of solid oak and oak plywood as described beginning on *page 170*.

3 Heat duct enclosure. To hide the heat ducts above the fireplace, we built an enclosure of ¾" plywood and 1 x 2 cleats screwed to the wall and ceiling. We extended the ducts and added elbows so now the heat vents out the sides of the new enclosure.

4 Wall paint. The walls were sponge painted, and then stenciled.

The renovated room, with some of the furniture in this book, presents an Arts-and-Crafts style.

5 **Hardwood floor.** An engineered hardwood floor was glued to the concrete slab.

6 **Upper mantel.** Two 1½ x 4½" beams laminated using ¾" plywood support an upper mantel of ¾" oak plywood. 1 x 1½" upper mantel support posts attached to the side walls support the outer front edge of this mantel.

7 **Built-in bookcases.** Before building and installing the bookcases (see *page 178*), we screwed bookcase support blocking to the wall and fireplace brick with masonry anchors. We then finish-nailed the baseboards to the blocking and upper-mantel support posts.

8 **Lower mantel.** The lower mantel with brackets was fitted between the bookcases. We nailed a ¾" oak-plywood ceiling, with recessed-light holes, to the laminated beams. We constructed a center panel of ¾" oak and ¼" oak plywood that hides low-voltage transformers (**8–3**). ¾ x 1½" panel stops with four magnetic catches hold the panel in place.

9 **Fireplace.** We applied cultured stone directly against the lower brick surface with construction adhesive. A hearth of 12 x 12" ceramic tiles was added. Then, we applied cultured stone to the upper vertical brick surface. Brass trim strips were riveted to the existing fireplace-insert doors, and the frames and doors were painted black.

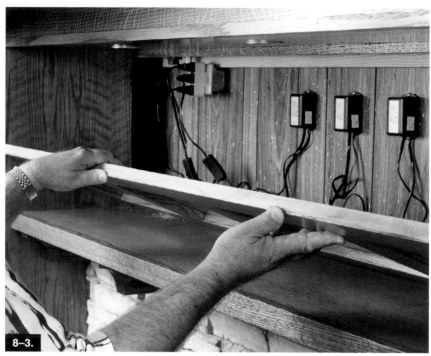

8–3.

A center panel in the lower mantel hides low-voltage transformer lighting.

10 **Stained-glass windows.** The existing window panes were replaced with stained-glass panels.

11 **Wall sconces.** To build and install these beautiful Arts and Crafts-style light fixtures, see *page 149*.

Oak Wall Paneling

Fine furniture and elegant accessories shine brightest in a proper setting, so give them the rich wood surroundings they deserve.

That drab, fake-wood paneling looked outdated about a month after somebody nailed it to your family room walls. Never fear, it won't happen this time. When you wrap a room with hardwood plywood panels, separated by solid-wood mullion and topped by a handsome plate rail, you not only add quality materials, you invest in a classic, time-honored style.

As a key part of our family room makeover, we covered a tedious expanse of 1960s-style paneling in this lower-level family room with an elegant Arts and Crafts treatment, featuring quartersawn oak.

Plan the Panels

You'll find the woodworking for this project fairly straightforward. But the planning stage could pose a bit of a challenge. Will you need to add or move electrical outlets and switches? How will you handle the heat registers? If you have windows to trim around, does that dictate the mullion spacing?

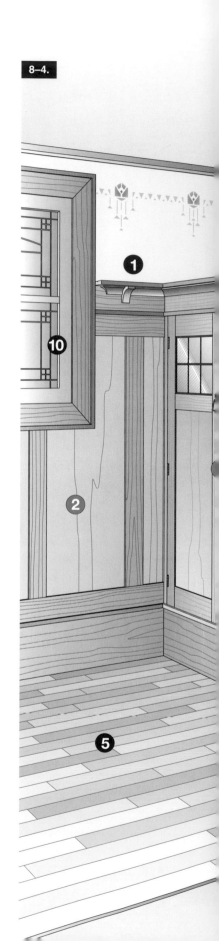

8–4.

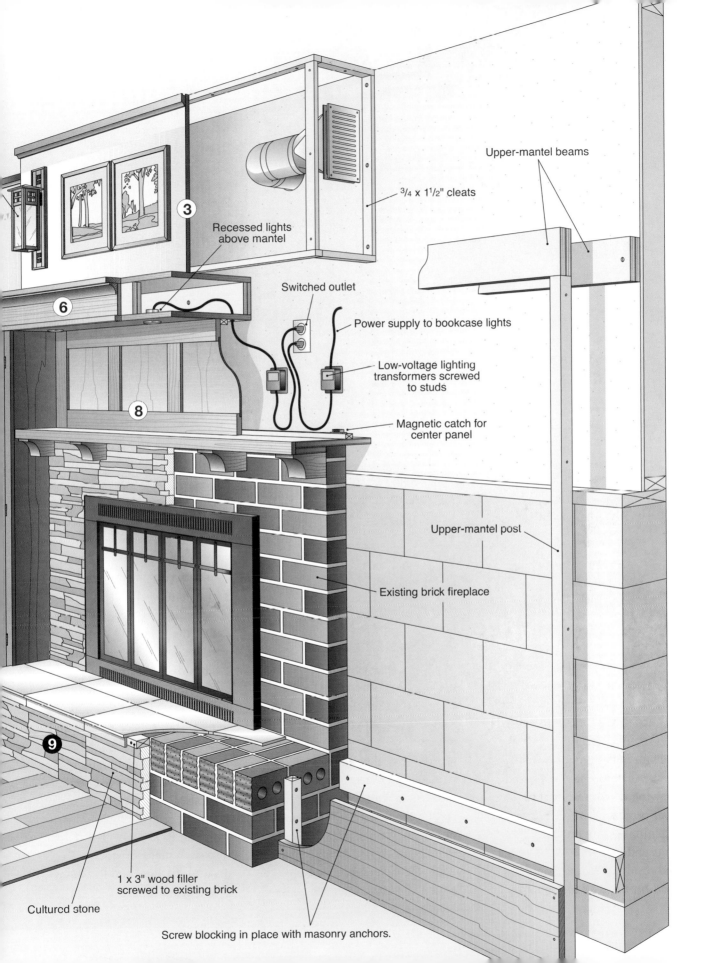

3

6

8

9

Recessed lights
above mantel

Switched outlet

Power supply to bookcase lights

Low-voltage lighting
transformers screwed
to studs

Magnetic catch for
center panel

³/₄ x 1¹/₂" cleats

Upper-mantel beams

Upper-mantel post

Existing brick fireplace

1 x 3" wood filler
screwed to existing brick

Cultured stone

Screw blocking in place with masonry anchors.

8–5.

Wall paneling sets the stage for the rest of the room.

to center one mullion on the wall and one under each window for a nice, symmetrical look. Don't drive yourself crazy trying to find the one width that will work perfectly all around the room. If you need to make an end panel wider than the rest by an inch or so, go ahead—no one will notice the difference. As for the height, plan for the plate rail to perch about 6' above the floor. You might choose to vary the distance slightly to suit personal taste— or personal height.

Start Shaping the Pieces

Measure the thickness of your plywood before you begin shaping the rabbets on the mullion. Sometimes, ¼" plywood is less than ¼" thick. The panels must fit snugly in the rabbets for the project to look its best.

If your wall has windows with interior trim that won't match your new paneling, replace the trim with a flat frame of oak. We cut the trim pieces 4" wide. Rather than working on the wall, we used a biscuit joiner to assemble each frame in the shop, carried it to a window, and nailed it in place. Doing it that way helps ensure square corners and tight miter joints.

We made the plate rail brackets from 8/4 lumber, or you could laminate pieces of 4/4 stock. Cut a template to match the shape shown in **8–7.** Trace that shape onto each piece of stock, saw close to the line, and finish up with a drum sander.

You can apply the following technique in any family room or den, whether it's in the basement or upstairs. Concrete block walls will require furring strips and drywall before you start to panel.

In any case, make a scale drawing of each wall involved in your project. It will focus your attention on any potential problems and help you visualize the end result. The dimensions we used for the wall elements are shown in **8–6.** You might use different measurements for the panels, for example, but use the drawing to plan your construction details.

Just like cabinet doors, these panels need proper proportions to look good. To avoid waste, you could plan to cut a 4 × 8' sheet of ¼" plywood lengthwise into three equal strips, each 15⅞" wide. However, we ended up with 17" widths when we chose

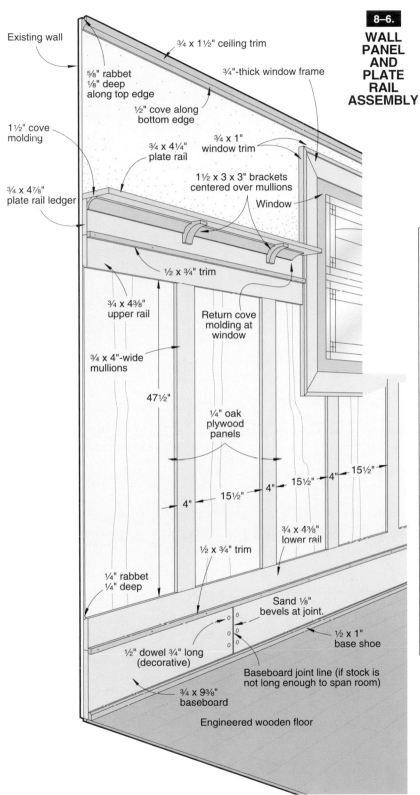

8–6.

WALL PANEL AND PLATE RAIL ASSEMBLY

Existing wall

¾ x 1½" ceiling trim

⅝" rabbet ⅛" deep along top edge

¾"-thick window frame

½" cove along bottom edge

1½" cove molding

¾ x 4¼" plate rail

¾ x 1" window trim

1½ x 3 x 3" brackets centered over mullions

Window

¾ x 4⅞" plate rail ledger

½ x ¾" trim

¾ x 4⅜" upper rail

Return cove molding at window

¾ x 4"-wide mullions

47½"

¼" oak plywood panels

4"   15½"   4"   15½"   4"   15½"

¾ x 4⅜" lower rail

½ x ¾" trim

¼" rabbet ¼" deep

Sand ⅛" bevels at joint.

½ x 1" base shoe

½" dowel ¾" long (decorative)

Baseboard joint line (if stock is not long enough to span room)

¾ x 9⅜" baseboard

Engineered wooden floor

A pneumatic brad nailer really speeds up a big project like this one. When you're all done, stain and varnish everything before filling the brad holes with putty that matches the stained wood. Then apply a second coat of varnish.

See **8–6** to **8–8** for the dimensions of the mullion, baseboard, rails, ledger, and plate rail.

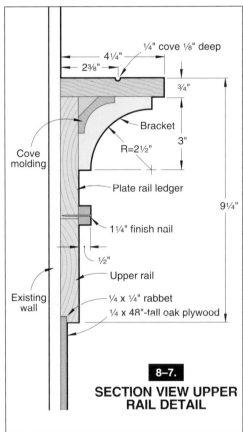

4¼"

2⅜"

¼" cove ⅛" deep

¾"

Bracket

R=2½"

3"

Cove molding

Plate rail ledger

1¼" finish nail

9¼"

½"

Upper rail

Existing wall

¼ x ¼" rabbet

¼ x 48"-tall oak plywood

8–7.

SECTION VIEW UPPER RAIL DETAIL

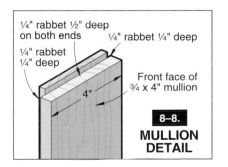

¼" rabbet ½" deep on both ends

¼" rabbet ¼" deep

¼" rabbet ¼" deep

Front face of ¾ x 4" mullion

4"

8–8.

MULLION DETAIL

Six Steps to Installation

1 Base. In most situations, you can put your new panels right over the existing wall, as we did. Above the area to be paneled, we covered the old paneling with a heavy-duty wallpaper specially made for hiding imperfections.

Begin building at the bottom with a big, solid-looking baseboard. We used ¾" boards 9⅜"-wide, cut a slight chamfer on the edge of any boards that butt together, and used a biscuit joiner to keep those joints lined up. We used a level to keep the boards straight despite an uneven floor. Slight gaps disappeared when we laid a wood floor on top of the existing concrete.

A ¾" board 4⅜" wide sits on top of the baseboard and serves as the lower rail for the panel frames. Nail those boards into the wall studs. Later, after our new flooring was in place, we nailed on a piece of base shoe.

2 Paneling. Temporarily set the mullion in place, as shown in **8–9**. Mark their locations on the wall. We used a strip of masking tape at the top end so the marks would stand out. Drive a screw into the wall just above the rabbeted tongue. The screw head keeps the board in place. Then make matching alignment marks on the tape and the board. Once they're all up and the layout looks good, cut the panels to fit.

Stock up on construction adhesive because those tubes

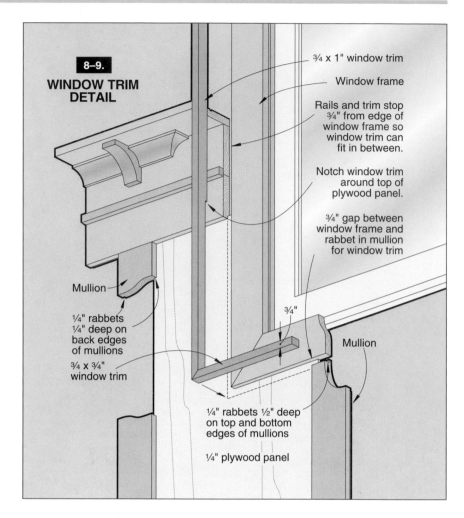

8–9.
WINDOW TRIM DETAIL

¾ x 1" window trim

Window frame

Rails and trim stop ¾" from edge of window frame so window trim can fit in between.

Notch window trim around top of plywood panel.

¾" gap between window frame and rabbet in mullion for window trim

Mullion

¼" rabbets ¼" deep on back edges of mullions

¾ x ¾" window trim

¾"

Mullion

¼" rabbets ½" deep on top and bottom edges of mullions

¼" plywood panel

will empty quickly from this point on. Starting at one end of a wall, fasten the first mullion into place, keeping it square with the baseboard. Apply a wavy bead of adhesive down its back and two nails through the tongue of the upper rabbet.

Apply a wide, wavy bead of adhesive to a panel, slip it into the rabbet of the baseboard, as shown in **8–10**, and then slide it into the side rabbet of the mullion (**8–11**) and press it against the wall. When you come to the new window frame, cut panels to fit snugly against it.

Leave a ¾" gap between the window frame and the face of each mullion, as seen in **8–12**. This gap allows for the piece of trim that comes next.

3 Window trim. Cover the seam between the window frame and wall panel with a ¾ x 1" strip. As shown in **8–13**, you'll cut a notch on the side strips that's ¼" deep and runs from the lower end of the trim strip to the top edge of the paneling. The strip along the bottom of the window is ¾ x ¾". (Refer to **8–9**.)

8–10.

Apply adhesive to the panel.

8–11.

Slide the panel into place.

Nail these trim pieces to the frame with brads. Our pneumatic nailer sent several brads curving out through the face of the wood. If you have the same trouble, you can switch to a hammer.

4 Upper rail and ledger. Mirroring the baseboard design, an upper rail and a plate rail ledger run across the top of the paneling. The rabbet along the bottom edge of the upper rail mates

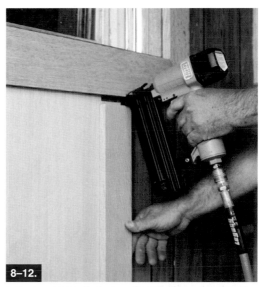

8–12.

Leave a space between the window space and mullion.

8–13.

Then fit the window trim pieces into place.

8–14.

Fit the plate rail ledger board in place on top of the upper rail.

with the panels and the rabbeted end of each mullion.

The plate rail ledger sits atop the upper rail, as shown in **8–14**. Fasten both of those boards to the wall studs with finish nails.

A ½ × ¾" trim strip covers the seam between the ledger and upper rail, and another strip of the same dimensions covers the seam between the baseboard and lower rail. Use a homemade gauge (**8–16**) to help you install each trim piece perfectly straight. Glue two scraps together to form a gauge that hangs on the top edge of the ledger and locates the top edge of the trim. Make another such gauge for the narrower lower rail.

5 Brackets. Drill pocket-screw holes in the top of each bracket, and center a bracket above each full-length mullion, using a square to mark the loca-

tion on the ledger. Align the top surface of each bracket with the top edge of the ledger to support the plate rail shelf.

Hold a small square against

SHOP TIP

Create a Pegged Look

For a classy finishing touch, we went for a "pegged" look at each joint along the baseboard. Drill three ½" holes ⅜" deep along each side of the joint, 1" from the joint and evenly spaced across the width of the board. Cut ⁵⁄₁₆"-long plugs from a ½" oak dowel, dab on a bit of yellow glue, and place them in the holes. Set each plug flush by holding a block of wood on top of it and tapping the block with a hammer. You also can use this technique for built-in cabinets and hardwood flooring, as long as it suits the style of the room.

8–15.

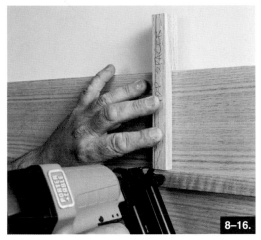

8–16. *This simple jig helps you keep the trim strip straight.*

8–17. *Pocket-hole joinery speeds the bracket installation.*

8–18.

Use a brad nailer for the molding.

the bracket to keep it lined up while you nail through the lower end. Then drive a self-tapping pocket screw through the hole, as shown in **8–17**. If you don't have a pocket screw jig, you can toenail the bracket in place from the top.

6 Plate rail shelf. Nail the plate rail shelf to the ledger and the support brackets. The final bit of trim consists of 1½" oak cove molding, available at home centers. Cut pieces to fit exactly between the brackets, and nail them in place, as shown in **8–18**.

When we came to the windows, we cut the end piece of molding to make a "return." See **8–19** for cutting details. Glue the return to the molding as shown. It sits 2" from the end of the shelf in the Top View in **8–19**.

8–19.

Miterbox fence

Cut #1

Cut #3

Cut #2

1½" cove molding

Return piece

Cove molding

TOP VIEW

END VIEW

MATERIALS LIST FOR BUILT-IN BOOKCASE

PART	FINISHED SIZE			Mtl.	Qty.
	T	W	L		
CASE					
A sides	¾"	11⅞"	57"	OP	2
B top & bottom	¾"	11⅞"	44"	OP	2
C fixed shelf	¾"	10¾"	44"	OP	1
D fixed-shelf edge banding	¾"	1"	44"	O	1
E back	¼"	45½"	57"	OP	1
F vertical face frames	¾"	1¾"	55½"	O	2
G lower trim	¾"	1⅜"	45½"	O	1
H upper trim	¾"	1¼"	*	O	1
I adjustable shelves	1"	11¼"	43¹³⁄₁₆"	LO	2
DOOR					
J door stiles	1"	3"	55¼"	LO	4
K upper & lower rails	1"	3⅞"	14⅞"	LO	4
L center door rails	1"	3"	14⅞	LO	2
M door panels	½"	15¼"	34"	LP	2
N vertical panel stop	¼"	¼"	34⅛"	O	4
O horizontal panel stops	¼"	¼"	15⅜"	O	4
P vertical glass stops	¼"	⅜"	11⅜"	O	4
Q horizontal glass stops	¼"	⅜"	15⅜"	O	4

*Upper trim runs full length of room across both bookcases, and is installed after the bookcase is in place.

Materials Key: O = oak; LO = laminated oak; LP = laminated plywood; OP = oak plywood.
Supplies: #10 biscuits; 48" brass-finish shelf standards; shelf clips with nails; ¾" brad nails; 1" brad nails; stain; clear finish.
Hardware: Mission-style hinges (6 needed per bookcase); low-profile double magnetic catches (2); Mission-style vertical door pull (2); low-profile halogen lights (3) with transformers.

BUILT-IN BOOKCASE

Take a look around your home. Chances are, you'll spot any number of ideal locations for a built-in bookcase like this one. These rock-solid storage and display cases fill the void. They look great flanking a fireplace or entertainment center, tucked into a nook, or lining the walls of your home's study area. They're easy to make, and add lasting value to your home.

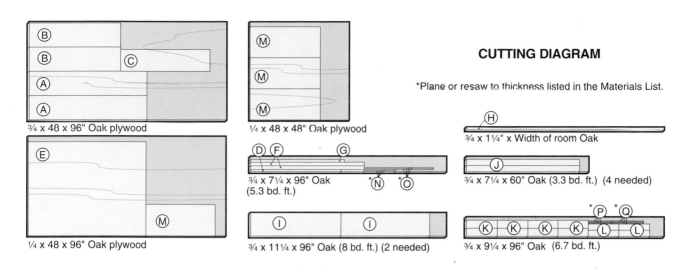

³⁄₄ x 48 x 96" Oak plywood

¼ x 48 x 48" Oak plywood

¼ x 48 x 96" Oak plywood

CUTTING DIAGRAM

*Plane or resaw to thickness listed in the Materials List.

³⁄₄ x 7¼ x 96" Oak
(5.3 bd. ft.)

³⁄₄ x 11¼ x 96" Oak (8 bd. ft.) (2 needed)

³⁄₄ x 1¼" x Width of room Oak

³⁄₄ x 7¼ x 60" Oak (3.3 bd. ft.) (4 needed)

³⁄₄ x 9¼ x 96" Oak (6.7 bd. ft.)

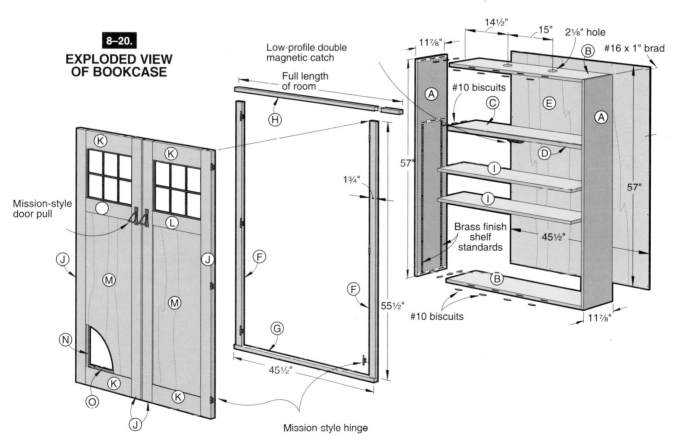

8–20.
**EXPLODED VIEW
OF BOOKCASE**

Low-profile double
magnetic catch

Full length
of room

Mission-style
door pull

Mission-style hinge

Brass finish
shelf
standards

#10 biscuits

#10 biscuits

2⅛" hole

#16 x 1" brad

Note: We'll show you how to build the bookcase
that fits into the space available in our handcrafted
family room. You'll need to adjust some or most of
the dimensions to fit your location. We used quarter-

sawn oak and straight-grained oak plywood
for an authentic Arts and Crafts look, but you can
substitute other woods to match your home's interior.

8–21.

SIDE VIEW

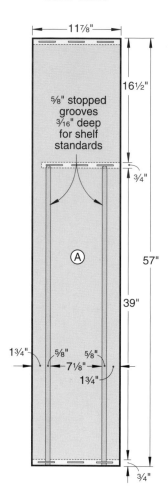

- 11⁷⁄₈"
- 16½"
- ⅝" stopped grooves ³⁄₁₆" deep for shelf standards
- ¾"
- Ⓐ
- 57"
- 39"
- 1¾"
- ⅝" ⅝"
- 7⅛"
- 1¾"
- ¾"

First, Build the Cabinet Case

1 Cut the cabinet sides (A), top and bottom (B), fixed shelf (C), and fixed-shelf edge banding (D). See the Materials List for the dimensions we used.

Note: Before taking the next steps, check the 2 × 4 framed opening in your wall. If the opening is plumb, level, and square, the outside dimensions of the case should be ⅛" smaller in width and length than the opening. It's a good idea to cut the back (E) to size and check if it will fit into the opening before proceeding.

2 Mark the positions of the grooves for the shelf standards, where shown on **8–21**. Use a straightedge, router, and ⅝" straight bit set ³⁄₁₆" deep to rout the grooves. Be sure to stop the groove so the fixed shelf covers its rounded end.

3 Use a drill press and holesaw to cut the 2⅛" holes for the lights, where shown on **8–20**.

4 Adjust your biscuit joiner's fence so the machine cuts a centered slot in the edge of ¾"-thick stock. Set its cutting depth for the #10 biscuits used throughout this project.

If you don't own a biscuit joiner, you can use rabbets and stopped dadoes, going with a slightly longer fixed shelf, top, and bottom.

5 Cut the biscuit slots for joining the ends of the sides (A) and tops and bottoms (B), as shown in **8–22**.

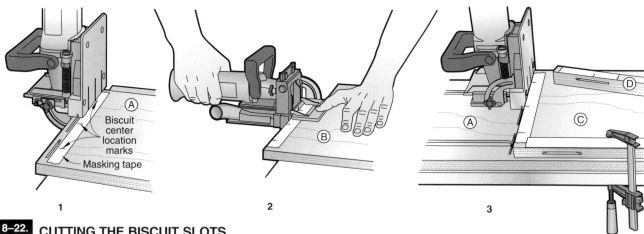

8–22. CUTTING THE BISCUIT SLOTS

6 Cut biscuit slots for joining the fixed-shelf edge banding (D) to the fixed shelf (C). Next, cut the slots for joining the fixed shelf to the sides, as shown in the third drawing in **8–22**. To do this, use the fixed shelf as a reference and straightedge for aligning and positioning the slots in the sides (A).

7 Glue and clamp the edge banding to the fixed shelf. Then, glue and clamp together the sides (A), top and bottom (B), and fixed shelf (C/D), checking for square.

8 Cut the back (E) according to the Materials List, making sure it is square. Lay the A/B/C/D assembly on its front face and attach the back with 1" brads. (If you prefer air guns, use 1" narrow-crown staples. Air-driven brads will not hold the back sufficiently.)

9 Lay the assembled case on its back. Cut the vertical face frames (F) and lower trim (G) to size. Biscuit, glue, and clamp these in place. Cut the biscuit slots for the upper trim (H).

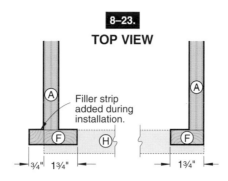

8–23.

TOP VIEW

Filler strip added during installation.

¾"   1¾"   1¾"

As shown in **8–23,** we made one of the vertical face frames ¾" wider than the other so we could scribe it to fit the wall (more on that later).

10 Cut the adjustable shelves (I) to size. Set aside for now.

Make the Doors

Note: Before cutting your door stiles and rails in the next step, check the size of the face-frame opening. Allow for these clearances: 3/32" between the doors and the face frame along the hinged edges, 1/8" at the tops and bottoms of the doors, and 1/16" between the doors.

1 From 5/4 stock cut the door stiles (J), upper and lower door rails (K), and center door rails (L) to size. Because 5/4 quartersawn oak is hard to find, we laminated 4/4 boards and planed the laminations to 1" thick.

2 Mark the locations where the rails and stiles meet. Cut two slots for #10 biscuits at each joint.

3 Assemble the doors with glue, biscuits, and clamps. Keep the door flat by working on a flat work surface, and check the glue-up for square by measuring diagonally. To precisely space the center door rails, use spacers, as shown in **8–24**.

4 With a router and bearing-piloted rabbeting bit, cut a ¼" rabbet, ¾" deep around the inside openings of the door. Make the cut in three successively deeper passes, as shown in **8–25.** For chip-free results, move the router counterclockwise (known as a "climb cut"). Square the corners with a chisel.

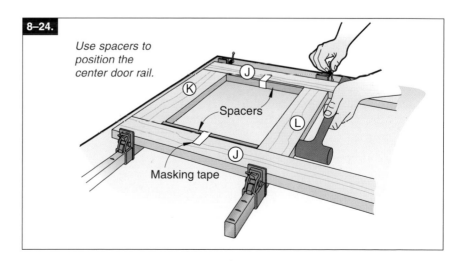

8–24.

Use spacers to position the center door rail.

Spacers

Masking tape

8–25.

Rout the rabbeted panel and glass openings in the doors in three passes for accurate, chip-free results.

Install the Cabinet into Your Wall

1 Attach the 2 × blocking needed to hold the cabinet securely in position. (See how we supported the cabinet in the cutaway view of the room makeover on *pages 170* and *171*.)

2 Slide the cabinet into its opening, as shown in **8–26**. Temporarily position the doors in the openings with spacers to set the clearances. Check the squareness of the case against the doors and shim around the edges of the case to make it fit the doors. The case should sit plumb and level.

5 Laminate the door panels (M) from two pieces of ¼" plywood. (We laminated these because of the difficulty of finding ½" plywood with two good faces.) Place the panels in their openings.

6 Cut the vertical panel stops (N) and horizontal panel stops (O) to fit the panel opening. Miter their ends and secure in position with ¾" brads.

7 Cut and fit the vertical glass stops (P) and horizontal glass stops (Q). You will attach them later.

8 Apply stain and clear finish to the entire project. (We used a gel stain topped with two coats of fast drying satin polyurethane.)

8–26.

The opening for the bookcase should include blocking that supports the bottom along its front and back edges.

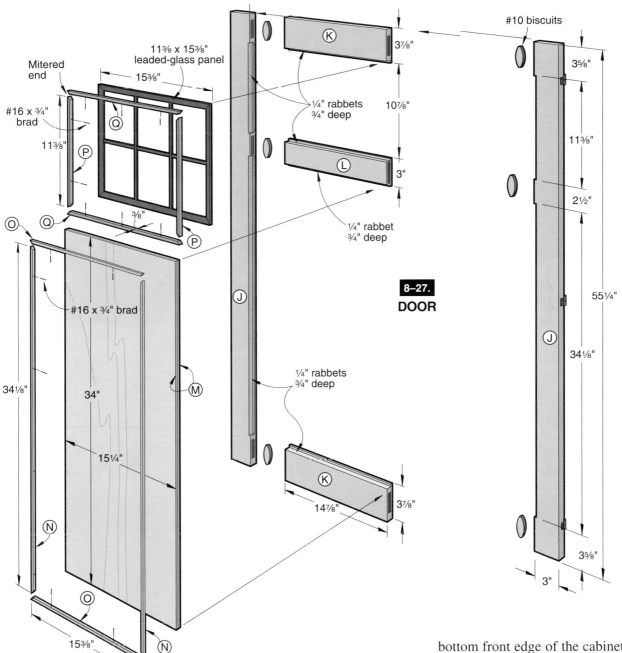

Mitered end

11⅜ x 15⅜"
leaded-glass panel

15⅜"

#16 x ¾"
brad

11⅜"

Ⓠ

Ⓟ

Ⓞ

Ⓠ

⅜"

Ⓟ

#16 x ¾" brad

Ⓜ

34⅛"

34"

15¼"

Ⓝ

Ⓞ

Ⓝ

15⅜"

Ⓚ

3⅞"

¼" rabbets
¾" deep

10⅞"

Ⓛ

3"

¼" rabbet
¾" deep

Ⓙ

¼" rabbets
¾" deep

Ⓚ

14⅞"

3⅞"

8–27.
DOOR

#10 biscuits

3⅝"

11⅜"

2½"

55¼"

Ⓙ

34⅛"

3⅝"

3"

3 Scribe the vertical face frames to fit adjoining walls. In the case of our cabinet, we had to place a ¾"-wide filler strip between the wall and face frame, as shown in **8–29**, and scribe it to fit the wall.

4 Place the bookcase back into its opening. Secure it by driving nails through the cabinet sides or face frames and into surrounding blocking or other sturdy supports. We secured our bookcase with nails driven into the base board directly below the

bottom front edge of the cabinet, as well as into the framing directly above the top front edge of the cabinet.

5 Install the light fixtures. We used low-voltage fixtures with long-life halogen bulbs. Plug the transformers into switched power outlets.

8–28.

Use a scrap of wood and sharp pencil to transfer the hinge position to a piece of masking tape on the vertical face fame.

SHOP TIP

Fit the Frame

Here's a quick and easy way to fit cabinet face frames to walls. All you need are two ½"-thick scraps of wood and a pencil. First, use one scrap spacer to distance the cabinet face frame a maximum of ½" from the wall at any point along the face frame. Then, use the other ½" spacer and a pencil to scribe the wall contour onto the face frame or a filler strip edge-glued to the face frame. (In this instance we used a filler strip to fill the void between the edge of the face frame and the wall panel.) Simply plane or cut along the scribed line for a perfect fit to the wall.

8–29.

6 Glue, biscuit, and nail the upper trim (H) in place along the cabinet's top.

Attach the Doors

1 Mark the locations of the top and bottom hinges onto the door, where shown on **8–27**. Center the middle hinge between the top and bottom hinges. Attach the non-mortise hinges with the supplied screws.

2 Position the doors in the cabinet opening, and place ⅛"-thick spacers underneath them. Transfer the locations of the hinges onto the vertical face frame, as shown in **8–28**. Attach the other halves of the hinges to the face frame at the marked locations.

3 Lift the doors off the installed hinges. Attach the door pulls and magnetic catch, where shown on the Exploded View drawing in **8–20**, on *page 179*.

A Few Final Touches, and You're Done!

1 Cut the brass-finish shelf standards to length with a hacksaw, and nail them into the ½" grooves in the cabinet sides. Use a needle-nose pliers to hold the tiny shelf-standard nails as you drive them with a hammer.

2 Place the shelf clips where desired, and install the adjustable shelves.

3 Secure the 11⅜ × 5⅜" glass panels with the stops (P,Q) and ¾" brads. We used a leaded-glass panel to accentuate the Arts and Crafts look of the bookcase, but a single pane of glass would work fine. Hang the doors and that's it.

METRIC EQUIVALENTS CHART
Inches to Millimeters and Centimeters

MM=MILLIMETERS   CM=CENTIMETERS

INCHES	MM	CM	INCHES	CM	INCHES	CM
⅛	3	0.3	9	22.9	30	76.2
¼	6	0.6	10	25.4	31	78.7
⅜	10	1.0	11	27.9	32	81.3
½	13	1.3	12	30.5	33	83.8
⅝	16	1.6	13	33.0	34	86.4
¾	19	1.9	14	35.6	35	88.9
⅞	22	2.2	15	38.1	36	91.4
1	25	2.5	16	40.6	37	94.0
1¼	32	3.2	17	43.2	38	96.5
1½	38	3.8	18	45.7	39	99.1
1¾	44	4.4	19	48.3	40	101.6
2	51	5.1	20	50.8	41	104.1
2½	64	6.4	21	53.3	42	106.7
3	76	7.6	22	55.9	43	109.2
3½	89	8.9	23	58.4	44	111.8
4	102	10.2	24	61.0	45	114.3
4½	114	11.4	25	63.5	46	116.8
5	127	12.7	26	66.0	47	119.4
6	152	15.2	27	68.6	48	121.9
7	178	17.8	28	71.1	49	124.5
8	203	20.3	29	73.7	50	127

INDEX

CREDITS

Special thanks to the following people or companies for their contributions:

David Ashe, for project design in Chapter 6

King Au, for photographs in Chapters 6 and 7

Baldwin Photography, for photographs in Chapters 2, 3, 4, and 7

Marty Baldwin, for photographs in Chapters 4, 7, and 8

Jim Boelling, for project design in Chapter 7

Kevin Boyle, for project designs in Chapters 4 and 7 and text in Chapter 7

Craig Carpenter, for photographs in Chapter 6

Bob Colpetzer, for project designs in Chapter 5

James R. Downing, for project designs in Chapters 2, 5, 6, and 7, text in Chapters 4 and 8, and layout in Chapter 8

Kim Downing, for drawings in Chapters 4, 5, 7, and 8

Owen Duvall, for text in Chapter 7

Michael Gatzke, for drawings in Chapter 6

Kerry Gibson, for text in Chapter 2

Jeff Hayes, for project design in Chapter 4

Chuck Hedlund, for project designs in Chapters 4, 5, and 6 and text in Chapters 4 and 8

John Hetherington, for photographs in Chapters 2, 5, and 7

Hetherington Photography, for photographs in Chapters 4, 5, and 6

William Hopkins, for photographs in Chapters 3, 4, 5, 7, and 8

Brian Jensen, for drawings in Chapters 1 and 2

Lorna Johnson, for drawings in Chapters 4, 5, 7, and 8

Marlen Kemmet, for text in Chapters 2, 4, 5, 6, and 7

Bill Krier, for text in Chapters 3, 4, and 8 and layout in Chapter 8

Roxanne LeMoine, for drawings in Chapters 2, 4, 6, and 7

Scott Little, for photographs in Chapter 4

Carson Ode, for drawings in Chapters 6 and 7

Jim Pollock, for text in Chapters 2 and 8

Ted Scherrer, for project designs in Chapter 4

Studio Au, for photographs in Chapter 6

Jan Svec, for text in Chapters 3, 4, and 7 and project designs in Chapters 6 and 7

Peter J. Stephano, for text in Chapter 3

Joe Warwick, for project design in Chapter 7

better · quicker · smarter

WOOD Magazine

Only WOOD Magazine delivers the woodworking know-how you need, including ...

- Over 50 new shop-tested projects a year
- Time-saving tips and techniques
- Ingenious jigs and fixtures
- Full-size pull-out patterns
- America's best tool reviews
- Space-saving shop ideas

To get your best deal on WOOD, call 1-800-374-9663

or visit us online at www.woodonline.com

This seal is your assurance that we build every project, verify every fact, and test every reviewed tool in our workshop to guarantee your success and complete satisfaction.